Ghost Riders

Ghost Riders

When US and German Soldiers
Fought Together to Save
the World's Most Beautiful Horses
in the Last Days of World War II

Mark Felton

DA CAPO PRESS

Da Capo Press
Hachette Book Group
1290 Avenue of the Americas, New York, NY 10104
www.dacapopress.com
@DaCapoPress, @DaCapoPR

Originally published in 2018 by Icon Books Ltd in the UK

First U.S. Edition: October 2018

Published by Da Capo Press, an imprint of Perseus Books, LLC,
a subsidiary of Hachette Book Group, Inc.
The Da Capo Press name and logo is a trademark of the Hachette Book Group.

The Hachette Speakers Bureau provides a wide range of authors for speaking events.
To find out more, go to www.hachettespeakersbureau.com or call (866) 376-6591.

The publisher is not responsible for websites (or their content) that are not owned by the publisher.

Print book interior design by Marie Doherty.

Library of Congress Cataloging-in-Publication Data has been applied for.
ISBNs: 978-0-306-82559-0 (hardcover); 978-0-306-82560-6 (ebook)

To Fang Fang
with love

Contents

A NOTE ON THE TEXT

Most of the dialogue sequences in this book come from the veterans themselves, from written sources, diaries or spoken interviews. I have at times changed the tense to make it more immediate. Occasionally, where only basic descriptions of what happened exist, I have recreated small sections of dialogue, attempting to remain true to the characters and their manners of speech.

Prologue

September 10, 1944. The banshee wails of air raid sirens were the first intimation that trouble was coming, their mournful rising and falling sending people scattering to public shelters, subway stations and basements. At the Spanish Riding School, the world's most famous horse training academy inside Vienna's Hofburg Palace, the well-practiced operation of moving the priceless white stallions under cover swung smoothly into action.

The director of the school, the tall, aristocratic-looking 46-year-old Alois Podhajsky burst from his office and immediately began organizing the grooms and riders, who were unlocking stalls and leading out the horses towards a shelter beneath another part of the school. Podhajsky had been born in Mostar,* then part of the Hapsburg Empire, and had risen to the rank of colonel in the Austrian Army. Soon after the Nazi takeover of Austria Podhajsky had been appointed director of the Spanish Riding School and become a colonel in the German Army. He was widely known and admired in the worldwide dressage community and had won a bronze medal at the 1936 Berlin Olympics. Now, the institution that he had devoted his life to, and which had endured for nearly 400 years in the heart of Vienna, was in danger of being snuffed out in an afternoon.

Colonel Podhajsky was surprised, and saddened, to see that his stallions were becoming used to the raids—each time the sirens began their awful lament, the horses would move to the doors of their stalls and stand there patiently waiting to be let out, their large and

---

* Today in Bosnia and Herzegovina.

1

expressive dark eyes peering through their stall bars.[1] The American
bomber streams were targeting Vienna more and more frequently as
the strategic bombing campaign across Europe aimed to pulverize the
Nazi military-industrial complex. The bombing was inaccurate, with
ordnance often landing in the city's historic heart, with its palaces,
museums, cathedral and zoo all coming under attack.

The Lipizzaner stallions' hooves clattered on the flagstones
as they were led from their ornate stables, equipped with marble
drinking troughs and smart black stall doors, into a concrete shelter
that had been specially designed for these circumstances, their
compact, muscular bodies moving without panic, tails held high and
heads inquisitive and alert.

Soon, two new and disturbing sounds could be heard, as the sirens
wailed mournfully on. The first was the firing of anti-aircraft guns
across the city, the sky above filling with dirty brown and black puffs
as the shells exploded among the high-flying bomber streams. Then
a thumping sound grew progressively louder, much louder than the
roaring of the guns: bombs were being released from the bellies of
the 344 American B-17 Flying Fortresses and B-24 Liberators that
filled the sky.

Podhajsky and the others stared up at the gray concrete roof of
their shelter and then down at their equine charges, whose small
ears rotated in alarm at the violent sounds, their nostrils flaring
as they shuffled their feet, snorted and stamped. The detonations
were getting closer, the ground reverberating as the large bombs
impacted on their targets. The horses did not panic, thrash about or
try to stampede. Podhajsky was pained to see that these fine beasts,
representing five centuries of careful breeding and training, cowered
just like the humans as the explosions grew louder and louder,
lowering their heads to the ground in fear and confusion. On and on
came the detonations, the sonic waves making the ground shake and
little pieces of debris fall from the ceiling, almost invisible against the
Lipizzaners' gray-white hair. The humans held the horses' heads and

bowed down like their charges, some praying, others cursing as the American bombers passed over the Hofburg Palace. Bombs started to land all around the Spanish Riding School, detonating with huge concussive blasts in the Michaelerplatz and Stallburggasse,[2] shrapnel lacerating the white Baroque façades of the tall buildings, stripping off roof tiles or caving in houses and shops with direct hits.

Inside the white Winter Riding School arena, constructed on the orders of Emperor Charles VI in 1729, the windows that backed the three levels of public seating areas vibrated madly at each detonation before suddenly imploding, shattered glass raining down like ice on to the sanded riding area. The huge and priceless crystal chandeliers that had hung from the 59-foot-tall ceiling were spared, having been packed up on Podhajsky's orders. Above the royal box the huge portrait of the emperor, to which generations of riders had raised their birch-branch riding crops in salute, was also gone, leaving just a discolored patch of paintwork where it had hung. Where once Strauss had wafted from speakers, and white and gray stallions had performed with bicorn-hatted riders astride them, now the drone of aircraft engines, the wail of sirens and the thump of further detonations intruded on this unique survival of a bygone age.

When Colonel Podhajsky emerged from the air raid shelter he stood and stared at the broken glass that littered the arena. He shook his head but knew that they had been lucky. It had been the closest raid yet, but the Spanish Riding School had been spared heavy damage. The stallions, as traumatized as the grooms, were led back to their stalls while firemen tackled blazes in nearby streets and medics rushed the wounded to hospital. Podhajsky knew that this could not go on. It was his responsibility to preserve the world's oldest riding school for Austria. But how?

Colonel Podhajsky had watched as the Nazi state had progressively interfered with the Spanish Riding School. The brood mares that provided the stallions for the school had already been taken from their special stud farm at Piber Castle in Upper Austria

3

and transferred to German Army control. In 1942, these irreplaceable animals that carried, and with each foaling renewed, the bloodlines of the Lipizzaner had been sent to Hostau in Czechoslovakia, beyond Podhajsky's influence. That left the stallions. But the Nazis, who had taken over Austria in 1938, had so far refused all his entreaties to have the precious animals evacuated to the country before the school was seriously hit. To the local Nazi leaders, evacuation of the Spanish Riding School, one of the preeminent symbols of Austria, would be defeatism.[3] The citizens of Vienna had crowded the Winter Riding School for performances or to watch the morning exercises until May. It had provided them with some relief and diversion from the stresses of total war. But Alois Podhajsky would not stop until he had made the Nazis see sense. There was nothing that he could do about the grand buildings and stables, but it was the Lipizzaner stallions that were the heart of the school, its raison d'être. The school was alive and without the stallions the buildings were but museums to a finer and more refined age. The school had to be moved, the horses' intensive training continued elsewhere and the legacy of half a millennium given a chance to live.

Podhajsky's temporary solution to the danger of aerial bombing had been to house the sixty-five stallions in wooden stables at Lainzer Tiergarten, a 6,000-acre wooded wildlife preserve and former Imperial hunting ground in the southwest corner of Vienna. In this way there was no disturbance to their intricate training program. It wasn't ideal, but the business of training the horses for the arena had to continue. Then the bombing intensified, and even the Lainzer was no longer safe, near misses landing close to the stables.

Colonel Podhajsky had continued to press the authorities for the orderly transfer of the stallions to the countryside. But he also began to make secret preparations to ensure that if the worst happened, the school could leave under its own power. Podhajsky was forced to take some of the stallions and put them in harness like common drays to pull wagons loaded with treasures and equipment. "They forgot the delicate dancing steps of the piaffe, the lively leaps of the capriole and the courbette, and the statuesque immobility of the levade,"[4] wrote Podhajsky with sorrow. But he was determined that when the time arrived and the authorities finally caved in to his demands, the Spanish Riding School would not be helpless.

In December 1944, Podhajsky was thrown a lifeline. The castle of Anton, Count von Arco auf Valley, outside Linz in Upper Austria had been mooted as a possible refuge for the stallions and riders from Vienna. The count was a notorious fellow, having assassinated Kurt Eisner, the first premier of Bavaria in February 1919. Pardoned in 1927 and released from prison, the count was currently residing in a concentration camp, having been taken into "protective custody" by the Gestapo after remarking that he would be happy to assassinate again, which the Nazis interpreted as a threat to Hitler.[5]

His elegant wife, Countess Gabriele, showed Podhajsky over the castle, which was crammed to capacity with refugees from the east. Podhajsky was pleased to see that the stabling was more than adequate.

Though a home had been found for the stallions, the authorities were still loath to permit their evacuation, even as the Red Army bore down upon Vienna from the east. "The Spanish Riding School was a symbol for Vienna," wrote a frustrated Podhajsky, "and it was feared that its departure would bring home to the already uneasy population the hopelessness of the situation."[6] But Podhajsky managed, through a series of clever ruses, to move out forty-five of the stallions by February 1945, leaving just fifteen in Vienna.[7] And then, following a massive air raid, the high command finally caved in and issued the necessary evacuation orders authorizing the transfer of the Spanish Riding School to Arco Castle.

Though the army had given the order, the ultimate responsibility lay with the top Nazi in Vienna. Without his consent, the horses, staff and remaining treasures were going nowhere. Podhajsky would have to plead his case one more time.

✴

Thirty-eight-year-old Gauleiter Baldur von Schirach was on the face of it an unlikely Nazi. His father, though a member of a noble German family, had been born an American citizen, the son of a major in the Union Army who had been part of the honor guard at President Abraham Lincoln's funeral. The major had married a member of the powerful Norris family of Philadelphia. Von Schirach's mother was also American, and from another wealthy Philadelphia family, the Tillons. The Gauleiter of Vienna was therefore descended from two signers of the Declaration of Independence, but had married the daughter of Heinrich Hoffmann, Hitler's personal photographer, and had served as Hitler Youth leader before going to the front in France to fight as a junior army officer, where he was decorated for gallantry. Hitler had appointed von Schirach Gauleiter of Vienna in 1940 and he had faithfully carried out the Führer's anti-Semitic policies, deporting 65,000 Viennese Jews to camps in the east, actions that he summed up as a "contribution to European culture."[8]

Alois Podhajsky met von Schirach face to face on March 5, 1945 at his villa at Pötzleinsdorf. The director of the Spanish Riding School was ushered into von Schirach's huge and ornate office. The most powerful man in Austria was seated behind a large antique desk and rose to greet the colonel, who saluted him formally. Von Schirach was of average height, with dark hair parted and slicked back from his face. Podhajsky was surprised to note that von Schirach was wearing an army uniform instead of the usual ornate brown and gold uniform of a high Party leader, seemingly to indicate his affinity with the troops and the precarious military position of Vienna as the Soviets closed on the city.

"Is everything under control with the Lipizzaners?" asked von Schirach, seating himself once again behind his desk after standing to greet Podhajsky.

"Herr Gauleiter, the situation demands the immediate evacuation of the horses," said Podhajsky without preamble. "The constant air attacks and the nearness of the front have rendered the School's position untenable."

Von Schirach said nothing for some time; the only sounds in the room the loud ticking of a large carriage clock atop the fireplace's mantel and the crackling of logs burning steadily beneath. The Gauleiter sighed.

"I must not lose my nerve and must consider what an adverse effect the removal of the Spanish Riding School must have on the people of Vienna," said von Schirach, almost to himself. "They would take it as an indication of the hopeless position of the city and be still more despondent." Von Schirach paused, inviting no reply from Podhajsky, who stood before the desk, his face a mask of frustration.

"But it is not just for these reasons, Colonel, for already in a day or two military measures can be brought in that will bring definite relief, so I ought not to upset even more the very sorely tried citizens."[9] Podhajsky had no idea to what "military measures" von Schirach referred, but he doubted whether the Gauleiter really believed such measures would make much difference at this stage of the war. Podhajsky pointed out to von Schirach that the Gauleiter himself had written to the army high command before the New Year complaining that it was madness to keep the horses at the Hofburg, and suggesting that they should remain at the Lainzer. Because of the constant air raids, even the Lainzer had become untenable. Therefore, the horses and staff must leave Vienna. Podhajsky could not understand, given von Schirach's evident interest in the Spanish Riding School, why he wanted to continue to expose the horses to air raids.[10] Another deathly silence fell between the two men. Von Schirach stood and walked over to one of the long windows that looked out on pleasant formal gardens that were white with snow, his hands clasped behind his back. Then he turned and looked sharply at Podhajsky.

"Looked at like that, you are right, but all the same it is not easy for me to agree to the evacuation, for I have always considered the

Spanish Riding School to be Vienna, and with the departure of the Lipizzaners a piece of Vienna goes from us." Podhajsky could see the conflict written across von Schirach's face, but he could also see that the Gauleiter had come to a decision.

"But I love them *too* much to leave them in danger any longer. So go to Upper Austria!"[11] Podhajsky was ecstatic—they would leave the following day. But though Podhajsky believed that he had saved the stallions, of the mares he had heard nothing for some time. As he hastened from von Schirach's office back to the Hofburg, Podhajsky wondered again what had happened to the hundreds of brood mares that the army had transferred to Czechoslovakia, and which Podhajsky had spent years trying to protect. For if the Spanish Riding School were truly to survive the war, both of its parts must be saved and eventually reunited. As Podhajsky looked out of the window of his car as he was driven through the snow back towards Vienna, the warm glow of his victory over von Schirach had already cooled and the horrible feeling that events were beyond his control had begun to reassert itself as a heavy, panicky sensation that unsettled his stomach and made his head ache.

CHAPTER 1

"Always Ready"

*"If it should be necessary for us to fight the
Russians, the sooner we do it, the better."*

General George S. Patton

O ppenheim, Germany, March 24, 1945. General George Patton, a riding crop grasped in one gloved hand, strode purposefully across a pontoon bridge spanning a wide river, a retinue of staff officers jogging to keep up with the US Third Army commander. Military traffic passed slowly over the bridge, causing it to creak and groan under the weight of Sherman tanks, half-tracks, trucks and jeeps. Everything was headed in one direction—east.

Both banks of the river were deeply scarred from heavy shellfire and fighting, houses reduced to burnt-out smoking shells or collapsed into piles of rubble and timber. The GIs passing over the bridge on foot, their weapons slung over their shoulders, were surprised and excited to see "Old Blood and Guts" Patton in the flesh, helmet festooned with three stars, pearl-handled revolver at his waist and tan riding breeches tucked into high brown boots.

Halfway across, Patton suddenly stopped and went to the rail. He looked down at the fast-flowing brown water before unbuttoning his fly and urinating into the river.[1] His shocked staff paused and then followed his lead. Grinning fiercely, Patton buttoned up and continued to the far bank, where he stooped and grabbed up two handfuls of mud. He announced in a loud voice: "Thus William the Conqueror!"[2]—a reference to the Duke of Normandy's famous declaration to his followers at the Battle of Hastings in 1066 when he snatched up two handfuls of earth and shouted, "See, I have taken England with both hands!"

It was an important moment not just for Patton but for the entire Allied cause. Later in the afternoon Patton sent a message to the Supreme Allied Commander, General Dwight D. Eisenhower. It consisted of one line: "Today, I pissed in the Rhine!"[3]

The Allies' most aggressive commander and one of its best armies were into Germany, and there was little to stop them. In less than a month the Third Army cut a glorious swathe through central Germany. They took over 400,000 prisoners and seemed poised to charge on to Berlin. But then General Eisenhower ordered Patton to turn south. "Old Blood and Guts" was beside himself—what the hell was south that mattered more than the lair of the Nazi beast, Berlin? Eisenhower told him that the Nazis planned to make a final stand amid the lofty crags of the Alps. Allied forces would head south into Bavaria, Austria and the Czech borderlands to prevent this nightmare scenario from becoming a reality. The "Alpine Redoubt" must be destroyed.

Patton, promoted to a four-star general, protested but was powerless to change Eisenhower's mind. Berlin would be left to the Soviet Union. Patton was appalled—he hated communism with a passion, and he felt personally robbed of a great victory. But he followed his orders. The mighty Third Army turned 90 degrees and headed south. Its 2nd Cavalry Group threw out its reconnaissance squadrons to protect Patton's flank as he advanced, dipping into western Czechoslovakia to secure small towns and villages. The Germans continued to resist fiercely in some places, but were also casting nervous looks over their shoulders at the Eastern Front, which by now stood just outside the Czech capital Prague and the Danube River. The distance between the American and Soviet lines was narrowing with each passing day. If the German armies protecting northeast Czechoslovakia collapsed, the Soviets would have Prague as well as Berlin, and all of the country up to the American lines. General Patton didn't much like this scenario for he secretly harbored another ambition—to piss in the River Danube as well as in the Rhine.

*

"Give me ten years and you won't recognize Germany," Adolf Hitler had declared shortly after he became chancellor in January 1933. This prophecy had come to fruition as far as 27-year-old Captain Ferdinand P. Sperl was concerned as he sat in the front passenger seat of a US Army jeep in Nuremberg.

The medieval city of Nuremberg, once one of the most famous historic centers in Europe, was now a smoking ruin, its once beautiful half-timbered Hansel and Gretel heart, the Old Town, reduced to piles of rubble, burnt wooden beams and the ghostly shells of buildings. As the spiritual home of Nazism, Nuremberg, infamous for its prewar torchlit rallies, had received special attention from British and American bombers and had been blown to pieces—all except the great Nazi Party rally grounds, which ironically survived perfectly intact. The city immortalized on celluloid in Leni Riefenstahl's *Triumph of the Will* was now just a brown smudge on the map of Germany, 95 percent of its historic quarter gone, a story that had been repeated the length and breadth of the "Thousand Year Reich."

Any further progress by Sperl's jeep was impossible—the road ahead was covered with several feet of rubble and charred wood.

"We'll never get through this lot," said Sperl to his driver. "Let's find another route." The private driving the jeep executed a rough three-point turn in the street, tires crunching over broken glass, the following jeeps and trucks doing likewise, as the little convoy slowly worked its way north through Nuremberg, headed for the American front lines on the Czechoslovak frontier.

Although Captain Sperl wore the olive-drab uniform of the US Army, he wasn't an American by birth but a "Ritchie Boy." The US Army realized that it needed language specialists for service overseas, and who better than natives of the countries that the US Army would fight through? To this end, over 15,000 young men either volunteered or were drafted into the Counter Intelligence Corps (CIC) and received intelligence and interrogation training at Camp Ritchie, Maryland. Among them were over 2,000 German and Austrian Jews who had fled the Nazis.

Sperl was a typical Ritchie Boy. Born into a family of hoteliers in Berne, Switzerland in 1918, he had come to America in 1939 as an exchange student at Cornell University.[4] He'd joined the army in 1941 and his language skills had led to his selection for intelligence work. Sperl had received further specialist training in England from the British Army's Combined Services Detailed Interrogation Centre (CSDIC), the intelligence outfit concerned with gathering information from captured enemy personnel. Sperl had landed in Normandy in the summer of 1944 with Interrogation Prisoners of War (IPW) 10, the US Army's version of the British unit. Each US division's G-2 intelligence section included a Military Intelligence Interpreter Team, an IPW team and an Aerial Photo Intelligence Team.[5]

IPW 10 was on a special mission that had been sanctioned directly by the Supreme Allied Commander, General Eisenhower. They had orders to move up to the Czech border where the 2nd Cavalry Group had established its headquarters. For several weeks now IPW 10 had been trailing American combat formations as they advanced steadily across southern Germany. Captain Sperl and his men, who were all German-speakers, were on the lookout for prisoners-of-war who might be candidates for detailed interrogation, but primarily they were interested in finding high-ranking Nazis in disguise. Reports had been circulating for some time that many senior Nazi officials and SS officers were passing themselves off as ordinary German soldiers in an effort to escape the Allied net that was rapidly closing around the remaining German-held areas. Particular targets were the SS who had commanded and operated the concentration camps, Abwehr and SD intelligence agents, Gestapo officers, SS field police,

Nazi Party officials and German military field intelligence units, not to mention the big "personalities"—the men closest to Hitler. Secret documents and files were sought that might prove of use to the Allies after the war.

Whenever Sperl and his unit came upon an American outfit that had taken prisoners they would question any who looked like good prospects or who behaved suspiciously. Any prisoners that they were especially interested in were sent back to the Seventh Army Interrogation Center established in Augsburg in Bavaria for detailed and often aggressive questioning. It was a nightmare job considering the number of prisoners the Allies were taking—in the Third Army's sector alone upwards of a thousand German servicemen *a day* were putting up their hands, providing many opportunities for the more unsavory Nazi leaders, functionaries and scientists to escape the Third Reich's rapidly sinking ship.

Captain Sperl and his unit had headed northeast towards Nuremberg, stopping for gas at a GI depot along the way where they had learned some momentous news. The American and Soviet armies had met somewhere along the Elbe River, meaning that Germany was now cut in two. More scuttlebutt told that communist partisans near Lake Como had shot Benito Mussolini, the strutting Italian dictator, along with his mistress, and that the Red Army was on the outskirts of Berlin.[6] To Sperl and his men, this news meant that the war couldn't last but a few more weeks at the most.

What they saw of Nuremberg confirmed in their minds that Germany had truly lost the war. And it was not just Nuremberg. Practically every city and large town that Sperl's unit had passed through had been heavily damaged by aerial attack, and almost every major bridge was down, either destroyed by Allied aircraft to stop the Germans escaping or demolished by the Germans to prevent the Allies from advancing. The roads between the devastated towns were filled with desperate refugees all trudging forlornly in one direction— west. Their only concern was to place as much distance between themselves and the brutal Red Army that was steamrollering in from the east and leaving a trail of human misery in its wake. But still the war went on. Sperl pointed his jeep in the direction of Czechoslovakia and started forward. Last reports were that the forward elements of 2nd Cavalry Group had been embroiled in a stiff fight for some town by the name of Asch.

*

A little American M-24 Chaffee tank crawled slowly down a narrow medieval street in the small town of Asch, just across the Czech border from American-occupied Bavaria. The tank's tracks crunched over shards of broken glass from windows blown out by artillery fire, with the dismounted soldiers of a platoon of Troop C, 42nd Cavalry Reconnaissance Squadron, 2nd Cavalry Group hugging the house fronts behind. Wooden shutters had been torn off many of the windows and lay in the streets, or hung at crazy angles on the faces of the stone and wood buildings. Black smoke billowed here and there from doorways and windows while some roofs showed the evidence of artillery strikes, with tiles missing and the gnarled stumps of broken wooden roof beams visible. No civilians were to be seen on the streets—they huddled in terror in their basements as the roar of the armored vehicles made the houses vibrate. Here and there Nazi propaganda posters remained pasted to walls, exhorting the populace to heroic resistance against the hated invader.

The GIs moved mostly silently, half bent over, communicating only by hand signals, their carbines and machine guns ready for instant action. Only their footfalls and the occasional curse as one of their number stumbled on smashed wood or masonry broke the men's steely silence. Their uniforms were dirty and stained, grenades dangling like green pineapples from their equipment straps, their young faces serious with concentration and grimy from the smoke and dust. Hardened veterans almost to a man, the GIs were taking no chances. Many had fought all the way from Normandy the summer before. No one wanted to be the last man to get shot in the European campaign.

Farther back along the road was a German motorcycle combination lying on its side, its rear tire shredded and almost torn from the wheel rim, a widening pool of gasoline flooding the road from its ruptured fuel tank. Its three occupants had been shot to pieces by the devastating fire of a four-barreled anti-aircraft gun mounted on the rear of an American half-track that the troops had grimly nicknamed "The Meat Chopper." Two of the Germans lay sprawled face-down in the road, dead, their bodies hideously mutilated by the thumb-sized machine-gun rounds—one almost decapitated—while an American medic, a red cross in a white circle painted vividly on four sides of his helmet, was patching up the third German, who lay groaning and half-conscious in a pool of his own sticky blood.[7] Different town, the same sights and sounds. The GIs had a word they used for almost every situation they encountered—"FUBAR." It meant "fucked up beyond all recognition." It was about the only word the troopers uttered now as they shuffled on with their mission. France, Germany and now Czechoslovakia. Different countries but always the same outcome: "FUBAR."

The 42nd Armored Reconnaissance Squadron (Mechanized), numbering 755 men, along with its sister unit called 2nd Squadron, formed the 2nd Cavalry Group. They were the eyes and ears of XII Corps, one of two corps that formed Patton's US Third Army, and they were always in the vanguard of each new assault. After landing in Normandy on July 19, 1944, the 2nd Cavalry Group's two squadrons had fought through France, in the bloody snows of the Ardennes, then crossed the Rhine into Germany, punching across Bavaria to the western border of Czechoslovakia.[8] Their job was to push ahead of the slower infantry divisions, seeking out the Germans and sometimes fighting them single-handed until help arrived. It had meant nine months of unremitting slaughter and stress for the young men of the 2nd Cavalry Group, and the route from Normandy to Asch was liberally dotted with the cold graves of their comrades and friends.[9] The 2nd Cavalry Group's assault on Asch was the first attempt by the Americans to capture a town of any significance in German-occupied Czechoslovakia.

The 2nd Cavalry's lineage was ancient by American standards and stretched back to two regiments of light dragoons that had been formed in the first decade of the 19th century. Every GI in the 2nd was proud of his regiment's lineage and battle honors, and like their forbears they had added only glory to an already glorious story.

The early dragoon regiments had seen plenty of action during the War of 1812, fighting against Britain. Amalgamated into a single regiment in 1814, when the war ended the following year it was disbanded. President Andrew Jackson re-activated the unit as the Second Regiment of Dragoons in May 1836, and for much of the 19th century it was present at the seemingly incessant Indian Wars that ravaged the western US as the nation sought to force the Native Americans on to reservations and appropriate their tribal lands for exploitation and settlement. The 2nd Cavalry first saw action against the Seminoles in Florida in the 1830s, lost men at the horrific Fetterman Massacre on the Great Plains in 1866, and was at the battles of Powder River and the Rosebud in 1876, shortly before George Armstrong Custer and the 7th Cavalry were obliterated at the Little Bighorn. In 1898 the 2nd were shoulder-to-shoulder with Teddy Roosevelt's Rough Riders up San Juan Hill in Cuba, and were fielded by General "Black Jack" Pershing during the Aisne-Marne Offensive in France in 1918, which also marked the regiment's last occasion in combat as horsed cavalry.

Their motto was, appropriately enough "*Toujours Prêt*" meaning "Always Ready," and as General Patton's vanguard reconnaissance unit for the Third Army in Europe they had earned the proud nickname "The Ghosts of Patton's Army" for their uncanny ability to get behind German lines time and again.

Since the mechanization of the US Army in the late 1930s, old horsed cavalry units like the 2nd had either morphed into the new armored divisions of the modern field army, or were re-roled as mechanized scouts. The 2nd had become a "Cavalry Group" in December 1943, one of a series of lightly equipped cavalry reconnaissance units that fulfilled for the modern battlefield a role equivalent to the horsed troopers of yesteryear—riding ahead of the line of advance to seek out the enemy, and often pinning him in place with aggressive offensive action until the armored and infantry boys arrived to finish him off.[10] The group was highly mechanized to an extent not seen in most armies at the time, reflecting America's massive industrial might, guaranteeing that the cavalry group was almost constantly in the van during the advance across Europe, with all the danger that that entailed. That danger hadn't diminished as Patton's forces entered Czechoslovakia, as the 42nd Squadron soon discovered.

"Contact left," yelled Major Robert Andrews, the squadron's S-3 or Operations Officer, who was personally leading the assault on Asch standing on the rear deck of the leading Chaffee tank manning its large .50 caliber Browning machine gun. Three German soldiers, rifles slung casually over their right shoulders, had unexpectedly emerged from an alleyway between two solidly built ancient houses. They appeared surprised to be confronted by the tank, which was advancing cautiously.[11]

Walking beside Major Andrews' tank was the young second-in-command of the 42nd's Troop C, First Lieutenant Bob McCaleb. When Andrews shouted his warning, McCaleb, his Colt .45 pistol drawn, motioned towards the three German soldiers who had wandered into the road, shouting "*Kommen sie hier!*"[12] Recovering from their shock, the Germans, instead of throwing up their hands in surrender, darted towards an alleyway between two tall brick buildings, unslinging their Mauser rifles as they ran. But they were not quick enough. Major Andrews swung the .50 cal. and loosed off a long thumping burst, the big rounds knocking two of the Germans down. The third just managed to make it into the alleyway before the tank gunner fired a 75mm high explosive shell that literally blew the two wounded Germans to pieces, scattering body parts all over the road in a gory dénouement.[13]

The GIs were not shocked by the mess spread across the road or hanging from a nearby lamppost—most had become desensitized to such horrific sights after months on the front line. Though most were barely out of their teens, they already had the weary look of veterans.

Although the 42nd had seen very hard fighting over the past months, recently everyone had started to notice a change in the enemy. More and more regular German soldiers were giving themselves up without much of a fight. They often presented a pitiable sight, with their uniforms worn and shabby and their bodies lean from food shortages. Many of Hitler's regular army soldiers, excluding the SS, were now frightened half-trained teenagers or middle-aged men, the scrapings of the Wehrmacht's manpower barrel, drafted into increasingly patched-together units to stave off a seemingly inevitable defeat.[14]

But though the Americans heavily outnumbered German forces along the Czech frontier, the fighting spirit of some enemy formations was startlingly undiminished. Though offensive action was now virtually impossible owing to a lack of tanks and a critical shortage of gasoline, some German units were able to man strongpoints and roadblocks, and could yet spring many a nasty surprise on the Americans as they invaded western Czechoslovakia. Towns and villages proved to be particularly difficult locations to take, with American armor funneled into narrow, mediaeval streets and squares overlooked by tall houses and churches.

The tank that Major Andrews rode on started to grind jerkily forward, the accompanying GIs hugging the buildings on either side of the road, many crouching even lower than before in an attempt to make themselves the smallest possible target as they nervously passed windows and doorways, ready to engage any lingering enemy soldiers. Suddenly, machine-gun rounds tore over their heads, stitching a neat row of holes in the wall above them, the weapon's unmistakable ripping report identifying it as a "buzz saw," as the GIs had nicknamed the German MG42 because of its stupendous rate of fire.

The bullets thudded into the upper stories of the surrounding buildings or ricocheted into the road, kicking up spurts of dust from the cobbles as the GIs hit the dirt or pressed themselves into narrow doorways. Andrews snatched up the field glasses that he was wearing around his neck and put them to his eyes. He could see puffs of smoke coming from a loading bay some distance away on the left.[15] He made ready to direct fire on to this new target when there was a sudden blinding flash and the road filled with smoke and flying debris.

Andrews was blown off the top of the tank, landing hard on the road surface where he lay stunned and winded as debris showered down all around him. Several other American soldiers were down, some wounded, others stunned by the concussive blast. Andrews rolled onto his back. All was confusion. Thick smoke and a pall of dust made it hard to see, and the explosion had temporarily muffled his hearing. He could see that Captain Harris, the commanding officer of Troop C, was down, both grimy hands clamped to one of his legs, red blood oozing from between his fingers as his lips pulled back from his teeth in a silent snarl of agony.

Lieutenant McCaleb was crouched in a nearby doorway and was shouting something, his combat jacket and trousers neatly sliced as if by claws, but the skin beneath miraculously untouched.[16] Andrews couldn't hear what McCaleb was yelling. He groaned and sat up, automatically checking his body for wounds. His clothes were also torn, but apart from a few cuts and scratches and having the wind knocked out of him, he appeared to be unwounded. The Company F Chaffee tank rolled on ahead of him, apparently out of control, smoke pouring from a neat hole drilled through its turret. Andrews knew then what had happened. One word was on his lips—"Panzerfaust."

Andrews' Chaffee had fallen victim to precisely the thing that American tankers most feared. It had been ambushed in a narrow, built-up street and hit by a weapon that the Americans were encountering in fearsome numbers all along the front, a last-ditch answer to the Allies overwhelming superiority in tanks and armored cars: the world's first rocket-propelled grenade. This cheap, throwaway tubular weapon with its bulbous shaped-charged warhead was being issued like candy to German foot soldiers and Volkssturm home guards. The weapon was shoulder-fired using a rifle bullet as a primer and could penetrate the armor of all Allied tanks, including the Sherman and the brilliant Soviet T-34. A little, lightly armored reconnaissance tank like a Chaffee stood no chance, particularly if the weapon was launched from just a hundred feet or less.

Andrews watched dazed as the mortally wounded Chaffee suddenly picked up speed, its engine whining as it blundered out of control up the road before slamming into the corner of a house, partially collapsing the building's façade. No sooner had the tank impacted the wall than there was a whoosh and a tremendous bang as another Panzerfaust round drilled through the turret. No one baled out of the burning tank, and Andrews knew instinctively that the five men inside were all dead.[17]

Andrews, his hearing gradually returning, picked up his helmet and yelled across at Bob McCaleb. "Get your men moving, Lieutenant!" McCaleb was to assume command of Troop C now that Harris was out of commission. Troop B hurried forward to take point while McCaleb got his men together and his casualties evacuated.[18]

Within seconds the dismounted troopers were hurrying forward ready to tackle the German position with carbine and grenade. Andrews moved with them, his body sore from being thrown from the tank. The war was supposed to be practically over, but it was clear that the defenders of Asch hadn't yet got the news. Andrews ducked as a sniper round pinged off a wall above his head. Breaking into Czechoslovakia was proving to be as costly and dangerous as any of the fights the 42nd had encountered since landing in Normandy nine bloody months before. He pulled his pistol from its leather holster, cocked it and stumbled forward, keeping low as he joined his men beside the road at a half-run.

*

When Captain Sperl and IPW 10 arrived at the 2nd Cavalry Group's headquarters on April 25, 1945, they discovered that the unit had requisitioned an old farmhouse outside the battle-scarred Bavarian town of Vohenstrauss, located just ten minutes by motor vehicle from the Czech frontier where the forward platoons had dug in following the battle for Asch.

Sperl ducked through the medieval building's low door and into a dining room that the 2nd Cavalry had hastily converted into a command center. A large oak dining table was covered with military maps, while a signaler sat at a small camp table in one corner monitoring a large green-painted army radio transmitter that occasionally buzzed with static and disjointed voices as units made reports. Clerks and staff officers bustled about, while the aroma of strong fresh coffee wafted from the kitchen down the hall. Sperl removed his helmet and sought out Colonel Charles Hancock "Hank" Reed, the illustrious commanding officer of the 2nd Cavalry Group.

Hank Reed, 44, was of average height and well built with dark brown hair neatly parted in the middle. He stood up from his desk to shake Sperl's hand and enquired about his journey in his courtly Southern accent. An orderly handed Sperl a tin mug full of steaming hot coffee.

Reed was a cavalryman of the old school who had started out in the horsed cavalry and been switched reluctantly to the impersonal steel beasts of modern mechanized warfare. Born on a farm near Richmond, Virginia, Reed was the son of a wealthy local merchant. He had grown up always with horses, riding before he could properly walk. Graduating from West Point in 1922, Reed had proved to be a great horseman, though an average academic student. His equestrian skills had seen him make the Army Horse Show team in 1930 and 1931 and he had been a reserve for the 1932 Olympics.

A graduate of the Advanced Equitation Course, the top military cavalry course in the army, Reed played polo and show jumped. He and his wife Janice had no children, but Reed doted on his polo ponies and rapidly rose up the ranks until he shipped out to England in 1943 at the head of the 2nd Cavalry Group bound for the coming invasion of Europe. He missed horses passionately and hadn't ridden since an occasional hack in between breaks from the hectic pre-D-Day training program in England. His two chestnut polo ponies, Tea Kettle and Skin Quarter, were safe at home at the Reed family place at Stanford Hill, Richmond. In many ways, Hank Reed shared much in common with his commander, General Patton, who had represented the United States at the 1912 Stockholm Olympics. With a strong background in running, fencing and shooting, Patton had finished fifth in the first modern pentathlon. But it was at riding that Patton really excelled, being like Reed a highly accomplished polo player.

Colonel Reed beckoned Captain Sperl over to the map table. Something interesting had occurred requiring Sperl's particular skills, he said.

"Corps wants a priority snatch mission, Sperl," said Reed, leaning over a map of the Czech borderlands. It was an order that had trickled down to him from XII Corps headquarters. "They have received some intel that a Kraut air force unit is stranded here"— Reed indicated a point on the map called Dianahof near the town of Waier,* just inside the Czech frontier. "It's an old hunting lodge in the forest. The Krauts number about twenty men and they're babysitting a whole bunch of records and files that Corps wants. Your orders are to proceed to Dianahof and *persuade* their commander to surrender to us. The *priority* from up above is to keep the documents safe, at all costs," said Reed. Sperl nodded.

---

* Now Rybník.

"Do you think that you and your team can handle it?" asked Reed with some concern.

It was an ideal IPW mission, and the prize that awaited Sperl at Dianahof could be of immense value to the Allied cause.

"Yes, sir," replied Sperl. The very nature of IPW work was fraught with dangers, and Captain Sperl had had his fair share of close calls in the campaign across Europe. But as he chatted more with Reed it was clear that the material at Dianahof should be worth the risk of dipping behind enemy lines. Reed told him to make his plan, brief him and be ready to leave on the mission the following day, April 26. If Sperl had worries, he didn't share them with Hank Reed. In his line of work, often only daring action could secure the prize. It was part and parcel of the job he'd been selected for.

Later that evening he would coin a humorous name for this mysterious little mission: Operation Sauerkraut.

CHAPTER 2

Colonel "H"

"We must live for the school. Offer our lives to it.
Then, perhaps, little by little, the light will grow from
the tiny candle we keep lit here, and the great art—
of the haute école—will not be snuffed out."

Colonel Alois Podhajsky

"I must speak to your commanding officer, at once," demanded the smartly dressed German air force officer who had just wound down the rear window of his staff car. A young GI had his carbine leveled at the vehicle, while the other members of the small 42nd Cavalry Squadron forward outpost covered him.

"Do you understand, young man," continued the bespectacled German officer to the young trooper, "it is a matter of the *utmost* urgency."

By the early afternoon of April 26, 1945, Captain Sperl and his small IPW team had been almost ready to roll out to Dianahof and the stranded German unit with its small goldmine of intelligence files when a radio message arrived at the 2nd Cavalry's HQ at Vohenstrauss from a 42nd Squadron outpost reporting a strange encounter.

A German staff car, with a white flag tied to its aerial, had just been flagged down. Far from simply surrendering, the officer in the backseat repeatedly demanded to speak to a senior American officer. Colonel Reed ordered that the car be escorted through to his HQ at once.

A few minutes later the large black Mercedes, its paintwork flecked with mud up to the door handles, sedately swung into the dirt front

25

yard of the farmhouse and stopped. An escorting American jeep pulled alongside, a GI standing in the back covering the German car with his .30 cal. machine gun. A young Luftwaffe driver climbed cautiously from behind the Mercedes' wheel and gingerly opened a rear door, conscious of the weapon pointed at his chest. Out clambered a short, middle-aged Luftwaffe lieutenant colonel, dressed in a blue greatcoat, cap and dirty jackboots. Reed had called for Sperl, and now the captain strode confidently over and saluted the senior German officer.

"Herr Oberst," said Sperl formally, using the German form of colonel. The colonel returned his salute.

"I wish to speak to your commanding officer," announced the German in his own language.

"Please follow me, sir," replied Sperl fluently, leading him over to where his men had erected the IPW tent the day before. Colonel Reed watched the German suspiciously then turned and went back inside the farmhouse and returned to his paperwork.

*

"Please, Colonel," said Sperl politely, indicating that the German should sit on one of the camp chairs set around a small green map table, its surface dominated by a black manual Imperial typewriter and a sheaf of papers in a buff folder. The colonel removed his cap, revealing a receded widow's peak, and settled himself on the chair stiffly. Sperl looked him over. The German was aged about fifty and sported a little toothbrush moustache similar to Hitler's.

"How can I help you, Colonel?" began Sperl in a friendly tone.

"I must speak to your commanding officer on a matter of the greatest urgency," replied the German in an agitated voice.

"Before we get to that, what is your name and rank?"

"Walter H., Oberstleutnant, Luftwaffe," sighed the German, refusing to divulge his surname.

Sperl, unsatisfied with the German officer's answer, repeated his question several more times, but he adamantly refused to give his surname. To an experienced interrogator like Sperl it seemed probable that the German's reticence indicated that he was involved in intelligence work of some sort.

"Turn out your pockets, please," demanded Sperl. The German sighed, then stood and started rooting through his greatcoat and tunic pockets, tossing various items on to the table in front of him. The German carried no identity papers—another intelligence "flag" in Sperl's meticulous mind. Picking up the colonel's leather wallet, Sperl carefully rifled through it. No family snapshots, just some black-and-white photographs, of *horses*. Sperl was no expert, but the white horses in the pictures looked beautiful *and* expensive.

"Why do you have these, Colonel?' asked Sperl. The German shrugged and repeated his demand to speak to Sperl's commanding officer. The colonel clearly had something to hide. Sperl pressed him for a while until the German finally and rather unwillingly addressed the issue of the photographs. Sperl thought that he had seen and heard a lot of crazy things since landing in Normandy, but the story that poured forth from the agitated and impatient German was both extraordinary and intriguing in equal measure.

*

Half an hour later Sperl strode across to Reed's HQ leaving the mysterious Colonel Walter H. under close guard in his tent. In his right hand he carried the collection of horse photographs. Entering Reed's makeshift office, he placed the photos on the colonel's desk blotter. "I think you might find these interesting, sir," said Sperl, straightening up.

Reed put down his pen and stared at the photos.

"Those are some fine steeds, Captain," said Reed. "Lipizzaners, if I'm not mistaken." The look on Reed's face was almost wistful as he gazed at the small images. Reed suddenly snapped out of his reverie and looked up at Sperl sharply.

"Where'd you get these, Captain?" he demanded.

"Off that Kraut air force colonel, sir," replied Sperl, a broad grin creasing his face. "And there's a story that goes with them that I think you ought to hear."

*

Lieutenant Colonel "Walter H." stared at the small badge consisting of a tiny "2" over a pair of crossed sabres that Reed wore pinned to one collar of his olive-drab shirt showing his cavalry arm of service. The opposite side displayed the silver eagle of a US Army colonel.

"Do you like horses, Colonel?"[1] asked Walter H. in excellent though strongly accented English.

"I do," replied Reed, meeting Walter H.'s keen gaze.

"Do you know anything about the famous Spanish Riding School of Vienna? The Lipizzaner stallions?"[2] asked the German, smiling slightly.

Reed nodded slowly, holding up two of the photographs that Sperl had taken from the German's wallet. "I know *of* them," replied Reed simply.

"Excellent," replied Walter H., rubbing his tired eyes. "They are the purest breed of horse in existence today, Colonel."

Reed, who had ridden just about every breed of horse in creation, could easily visualize the Lipizzaner. The name conjured in Reed's equestrian mind the noble white prancing stallions of Vienna, a unique and precious equine artefact that reached back to a far nobler age of warfare.

The Lipizzaner is not an especially big horse, but it is strong and compact, with a wide, deep chest, broad croup and muscular shoulders of the Baroque type. It has to be compact and strong in order to perform the difficult and unnatural moves of *Haute École*, the highest form of classical dressage that survives in the world. Their line of descent goes all the way back to the primeval ancestors of the Arabs. The Moors brought their horses with them to Spain and crossbred them with the ancient race of Spanish horses to create the

Iberian Horse known as the "Andalucían." The cleverest, sturdiest and noblest of spirit, and the quickest to learn, they were soon renowned all over Europe. These were the horses from which the Lipizzaner is descended.

Years of intensive training of both rider and mount is necessary to reach a standard deemed good enough for public performance. And what a performance. The level of training is startling to outsiders, but necessary to train a Lipizzaner stallion for the arena. It consists of three distinct stages, each lasting several years.

The first stage is called *Remontenschule* or Forward Riding. The four-year-old stallion is taught to be saddled and bridled. He begins on the lunge to teach him obedience and strengthen his muscles for the moves to come. He learns how to walk, trot and perform counter-transitions, but it is two or three months before a rider gets on him. Once mounted, the rider teaches the horse to walk in straight lines in the arena, to teach him to respond correctly to the rider's aides: his spurs, bridle and whip. The goal is to develop free forward movement in the ordinary gaits. This process takes about one year to complete.

Next comes *Campagneschule* or Campaign School. The young stallions are placed with experienced riders. They are taught how to ride in turns and circles in all gaits. The purpose is to develop impulsion, improve the stallion's natural paces, promote self-carriage, and make the horse supple and flexible, and gradually develop his muscles. The stallion learns to bend correctly in the neck and body. He learns to shorten and lengthen his gait and perform lateral movements, mostly at the trot. Before the end of this phase of his training, the horse is introduced to the Spanish Riding School's famous double bridle, which gives the rider much greater control over the horse's movements.

The final and most difficult stage in the stallion's training, taking several years, is *Hohe Schule* or High School. The rider gradually pushes the horse to perfection in straightness, contact, suppleness, collection, and impulsion, to produce improved gaits. The horse learns some of the famous moves of the Spanish Riding School—the pirouette, passage, and piaffe. The stallion is then assessed to see if he is suitable for "airs above the ground," the most famous "dancing" moves performed by Spanish Riding School Lipizzaners. Not every stallion reaches this pinnacle of training, but for those that do, the amount of time and effort that has been channeled into the horse represents many years of intense study. The Lipizzaners of the Spanish Riding School are living, delicate treasures—the white gold of Vienna.

Lieutenant Colonel Walter H. abruptly decided to drop the pretense and told Colonel Reed his surname—Holters. He revealed that he was the commanding officer of Dienststelle Ost, a secret air force intelligence outfit that had retreated from the Eastern Front carrying years of files, reports and photographs about the Red Army. Ordered south to the Alps by headquarters in imperiled Berlin, Holters' unit was stopped by a severe lack of fuel at Dianahof, just inside the Czech frontier near the town of Waier. Holters had ordered his men to bury packing cases stuffed full of valuable records in the grounds of a hunting lodge that he had commandeered at Dianahof while he tried to decide how best to proceed. It was while visiting local German units in the area that Holters had stumbled upon an extraordinary find. As Captain Sperl listened, he realized that Dienststelle Ost was the very unit that he had been ordered by XII Corps to capture intact—incredibly, the Germans had reached out to the Americans first, saving him the trouble.

"You have looked at these, Colonel?" asked Holters, pointing at the photographs of the horses. Reed nodded. "You will agree that they are quite remarkable animals?"

Reed looked again at one of the photos and felt his stomach flutter. Staring at the proud white Lipizzaner stallion, his graceful lines and strong stance betraying his noble heritage, Reed felt a fierce wave of nostalgia sweep unexpectedly over him. How long had it been since he had been in the saddle? Nine months. Holters passed him the other snapshot. "Beautiful," murmured Reed wistfully. In that moment he could have reached into the photo and touched the stallion's warm coat, run his hand along his back, feeling the strong muscles moving just below the skin. He would feel the great chest rising and falling under his flat palm. He would lay his ear against the stallion's flank and listen to the steady drumming of his big heart and breathe deeply the smell of him, that odor of horse that was at once as familiar to Reed as fresh air and as comforting as the happiest of childhood memories, a smell that had seemingly always been a part of his life until the dark nightmare of the last nine months. Reed discovered that he ached for that smell, to run his hand down the stallion's forehead to his big soft black nose, to murmur pleasant inanities into his ears instead of issuing orders and directions to men, orders that so often resulted in their deaths. At this moment, hunched over black-and-white photographs of horses in a musty green tent halfway across Europe, Hank Reed had never felt so far from home or so far from his life's passion.

"Colonel?" Reed was suddenly jolted out of his private thoughts by Holters' voice. He looked up at the German officer, a sad half-smile on his war-weary face, his eyes slightly misty and far away.

Holters told Reed that he had taken the photographs himself.[3] He explained that since evacuating his unit to the hunting lodge at Dianahof, he had grown friendly with the local German stud commander and visited the stables regularly to view the animals and to chat about horses.[4]

For Holters, his visits to the army stud had been a reawakening of his own long cherished enthusiasm for horses. After years on the Eastern Front, the stress and responsibility of his job had suddenly found an outlet as he had stood watching the horses being exercised or had wandered through the stables breathing deeply the glorious smells of hay, dung and polished leather tackle. During those private moments he had been back on his family estate, riding across the rolling East Prussian countryside, a powerful mount carrying him forward confidently and gracefully, the fresh Baltic wind blowing in his face as he urged the horse into a wild gallop. Like Reed, Holters' enforced separation from horses had been a difficult adjustment to make. The stud had become an oasis for the German, and he had drunk deeply from its equine waters, thoughts of war and duty slipping to the back of his overburdened mind for a few precious hours. He had begun to care deeply for this private time away from his responsibilities, and to take an active interest in the stud and its occupants. What had begun as a hobby, snapping away with his small Leica camera, had soon become an obsession as he had faithfully recorded each extraordinary horse for his private files. His intelligence officer's mind had soon grasped both the significance of these particular horses as well as their beauty and dignity. There was also something else—their innocence attracted Holters after six long years of war. These horses represented something as yet unsullied by the degradation of combat and suffering. They were of the world of peace and harmony, living relics of a far saner age.

Holters leaned closer to Reed and began to tell him about the Lipizzaner breed, of which he now considered himself an expert.[5]

"Where were *these* photographs taken?" asked Reed, interrupting Holters.

"At Hostau," replied Holters.

"Hostau?" asked Reed, his eyes turning to Captain Sperl.

"Yes, sir," said Sperl. "It's a German Army remount depot." The town of Hostau was small, with barely a thousand residents, its pretty German-style houses clustered along a narrow and steep main street that led up to a small plaza beside St. Jakobus Church, a yellow-colored building with a red-tiled roof and pointed steeple. Just beyond the church stood the princely castle—really more of a French château than a medieval fortress, an opulent two-storey white mansion arranged in two wings forming an L shape with a formal courtyard and garden. The castle had been commandeered by the local German military command for use as a headquarters. Opposite the castle was the stud, first established in 1915. Comprising 460 hectares, it was privately owned by the princely family Trauttmansdorff. The Austro-Hungarian government had leased the land in order to house parts of its official stud, and later, when the land became part of Czechoslovakia, the state had used the farm for its horse-breeding program. The German Army had taken over the horse stud at Hostau in October 1938, initially using it to supply horses to its cavalry regiments. All that soon changed.

"The Germans have moved hundreds of horses there from all across Europe, including the breeding Lipizzaner mares," said Captain Sperl.

"For what purpose?" asked Reed, fascinated.

"To create the perfect horse, Colonel" replied Colonel Holters simply. "As our armies advanced across Europe scientists gathered only the most pure examples with the intention of creating the finest horse that ever existed for the Reich."[6]

Colonel Hank Reed was both astounded and mystified. He knew that the Germans held strong and troubling beliefs about race, but hadn't realized this extended to animals. An "Aryan horse"—the idea seemed preposterous to him, but it was clear that Holters was sincere.

Reed leaned back in his chair and crossed his arms, one eyebrow raised quizzically at the German. Holters didn't look fazed by Reed's reaction. In fact, it was soon clear that he believed completely in what he said.

"At Hostau are the brood mares for the Spanish Riding School in Vienna, Colonel," said Holters, his eyes alive with happy memories. "There are other Lipizzaners, including stallions, from Italy and Yugoslavia. Also, about two hundred of the most famous racehorses from across Europe, and a hundred of the finest Arab stallions."[7] Holters paused. "One such is Brantome, the French racehorse," he said. Brantome was a thoroughbred, one of several seized from Baron de Rothschild's stud outside Paris in 1940, explained the German.

"Brantôme was winner of the French 2,000 Guineas, the Prix Royal-Oak, and France's premier race, the Prix de l'Arc de Triomphe." Holters reeled off his facts expertly. "He has *also* raced in the Ascot Gold Cup in England several times." The Germans had established all of these horses at Prince von Trauttmansdorff-Weinsberg's stud opposite his family castle in Hostau.[8]

For Reed, the idea of selectively breeding horses was nothing new, it had been occurring for thousands of years, but the scale and goal of the program appeared superficially impressive. The brains behind it, explained Holters, was Gustav Rau, an equine expert who had convinced the Nazi leadership that he could create a "super horse" for Europe's new "master race."

The small and balding Rau had served in the cavalry in World War I. A horse breeder rather than a scientist, the sharp-tongued Rau had ingratiated himself with the Nazis soon after their seizure of power and actually toured the United States in 1938, inspecting American horse-breeding facilities. But his theories had been worked out in the 1920s, before Hitler came to power, when he seized upon a plan to revitalize the German horse-breeding program that had languished following the depredations and horrors of the Great War, which had killed half of all the horses in Germany.

The Wall Street Crash of 1929 and the resultant Great Depression that followed had ushered Hitler into power in Germany, but it had also caused the export of much of Germany's remaining horse stock. It was Rau's belief that the Nazis could stop the rot and get Germans back interested in breeding horses, and that he would be the man to show them the way. Rau had received no scientific training. His theory was simply to breed closely related horses with each other in order to create excellent offspring. The new Nazi Minister of Food and Agriculture, Richard Darré, an ideologue who promulgated a theory of "blood and land," appointed Rau Chief Equerry of the state of Prussia in 1934. Slowly but surely climbing the greasy pole of Nazi politics, Rau set about putting his theory to paper, publishing

Horsebreeding in the National Socialist State in 1934. His theory appealed strongly to the social Darwinism of the Nazis—horses, like people, could be bred to create the finest specimens. If Britain bred the finest Thoroughbreds, and Poland the greatest racehorses, then Germany would excel and create the finest warhorse. Rau's trip to the United States in 1938 confirmed what he already suspected—that European horses, like its people, were "superior."[9]

In 1939 the 65-year-old Rau was given the opportunity of putting theory into practice on a national scale when he was appointed *Oberlandstallmeister* or "Chief Equerry" of the Reich and tasked with requisitioning, breeding and developing the warhorse of the future.[10] German expansion across Europe would provide Rau with the bloodstock needed to fulfil his plan. Rau had also been appointed a colonel in the army's quartermaster department. He had an undeniable talent for working the system to his own advantage, and it was commented that "Rau's decisions were often prompted by what was going on behind the scenes, and he often sacrificed his expert knowledge to diplomatic intrigue."[11] One such example was the Nazi equine eugenics program.

"Rau is not well liked," grimaced Colonel Holters, tapping ashes from his cigarette onto the floor of Sperl's tent, "but he is quite brilliant when it comes to horses." Rau had quickly identified the Lipizzaner as the "purest" horse in Europe. He had decided that it would form the base bloodstock from which the new horse would be created. Rau and his special army unit of veterinary surgeons, geneticists and technicians had plundered the great horse collections of Europe for material to experiment on. He had also re-established the Polish horse-breeding industry in 1940, centered on the great stud at Debica.

Eventually Rau's empire encompassed fourteen stud farms across Europe, with one even built on the grounds of Auschwitz Concentration Camp. SS officers from the camp, on their rest days from genocide, rode the Arabians on the 400-acre site. The horse-breeding program was massive—the German Army required 6,000 fresh horses each month during the height of the war, and with increasing fuel shortages, more and more horses were pressed into service hauling supplies and ammunition.

Rau had focused in on the Lipizzaners early in his program after a visit to the Piber Stud, where he was unimpressed by the facilities and felt that the potential of the animals was far from being realized. The stud, established at Piber Castle in 1920, provided all new stallions to the Spanish Riding School. Before the break-up of the Austro-Hungarian Empire at the end of World War I, Lipizzaner horses had been bred at Lipica in present-day Slovenia. The evolution of the empire into many separate countries had meant that the large herd of mares at Lipica was broken up and sent to form new studs in Austria, Italy, Hungary, Czechoslovakia, Romania and Yugoslavia. Through their occupation of most of these countries, the Germans had gained access to fresh stocks of Lipizzaner horses to augment those of the Spanish Riding School. Rau had brought in stocks of Lipizzaners from Yugoslavia and Italy and established a carefully worked-out breeding plan. This move had brought him into direct conflict with the director of the Spanish Riding School: Colonel Alois Podhajsky.

CHAPTER 3

Action This Day

*"It is probably wrong to permit any highly developed
art, no matter how fatuous, to perish from the earth.
To me, the high-schooling of horses is certainly more
interesting than either painting or music."*

General George S. Patton

In June 1942, Podhajsky had been horrified to learn that Rau planned to use the Lipizzaner mares as bloodstock to create a new army horse. For a time, the Nazis had protected the Spanish Riding School and used it as a propaganda showpiece and later as a morale booster for the war-weary Viennese. But the exigencies of war had meant that something had to give, and when the Piber Stud, where the Lipizzaner mares and foals were kept, was requisitioned by the army to breed pack animals in 1942, Podhajsky had faced a shortage of new stallions for the School.

Rau had left the Spanish Riding School stallions in Vienna alone, but had moved the breeding herd to Czechoslovakia, merging it with the former royal Yugoslav and other requisitioned Lipizzaner horses at Hostau. When Rau's plans for breeding the animals had become known to Podhajsky, the colonel had sent strong representations to the authorities in Berlin demanding that such an atrocity be forbidden: "If the Lipizzaner strain is to continue to be preserved in the interests of the Spanish Riding School, then at all costs any experiments which might impair its suitability for the classic style of riding must be prevented."[1] But Podhajsky's missives had been ignored—Rau was too well connected to have his madcap experiments stopped by one Austrian colonel.

Podhajsky was also unhappy that Hostau was where the mares were being accommodated. Rau failed to understand that the horse was a product of the soil, and Hostau was completely unsuitable to raise a delicate breed like the Lipizzaner. The pasture was much too rich, and when Podhajsky hurried to investigate, he discovered that the soil was so deficient in calcium that a supplementary feed had to be given.

But what worried Podhajsky even more was the location of Hostau, deep inside a hostile occupied nation. "If the war were lost and the Greater German Reich collapsed," wrote Podhajsky, "what was to become of the Lipizzaner in a 'protectorate' whose people were filled with a bitter and enduring hatred?"[2] Without the mares producing fresh pure-blood stallions the Spanish Riding School would wither on the vine and disappear, and with it 500 years of irreplaceable Austrian cultural heritage.

Gustav Rau was happy, using the Lipizzaners for a series of experiments that he termed "line breeding." Horses that were closely related were bred with each other, often brother with sister, allegedly to preserve the breed and the good qualities of the single strain. In this way, Rau believed, the best characteristics of the horses would be enhanced, while others were eradicated. Colonel Podhajsky was further outraged when he discovered that Rau had been using three-year-old mares for breeding. They were too young. Podhajsky had again protested to Berlin that Rau's breeding experiments were useless and should be resisted, since the extensive records of the Piber Stud were a sufficient guide to the breed, "and the achievements of the Spanish Riding School gave the best proof of the success of the present strain."[3] On this occasion, Podhajsky had managed to win some concessions from Berlin, one of which was to be informed when any breeding using the Lipizzaner mares was to occur and his opinion taken into consideration. But Rau had ignored the restrictions placed upon him, and continued with "line breeding," using mares and some stallions from Piber, secretly breeding father with daughter. In January 1943 Podhajsky had managed to stop this, but Rau still bred from brothers and sisters. Podhajsky was later to write that the offspring of such unnatural unions proved useless for the Spanish Riding School.

*

Inside Captain Sperl's tent, Colonel Reed's eyebrows had arched in surprise at Lieutenant Colonel Holters' mention of Alois Podhajsky, for the name was familiar to him. Podhajsky's brother had attended the Cavalry School at Fort Riley, Kansas, at the same time Reed was studying there, and Reed had even ridden a horse that had been named "Podhajsky" in honor of the commander of the Spanish Riding School.[4] Furthermore, Reed had attended the 1936 Berlin Olympics as an observer from the army, and had seen Alois Podhajsky ride in the dressage competitions, winning a bronze medal in the individual.

Holters' tale was now nearing its end.

"Rau had 250 Lipizzaners and hundreds of Europe's finest racehorses and stallions under this program,"[5] said the German.

Colonel Reed shook his head in disbelief. It seemed that an incredible amount of time, effort and resources had been poured into Rau's madcap experiments, and to what end? Holters explained that with the collapse of the Eastern Front in late 1944, Rau's program had been abruptly terminated by Berlin. Other precious horses had been transferred from the program's satellite studs in Ukraine and Poland to Hostau for safekeeping, to prevent their falling into Soviet hands. There they had joined the Lipizzaners and Thoroughbreds already in residence.[6] Rau had decimated the numbers of Piber mares at Hostau during the last months by constant selling. Podhajsky knew little of what was happening, as communications between Vienna and Hostau were precarious at best—though he was aware that the number of barren mares was on the increase: they had become fat and refused to be served by the stallions. It was also known that some horses had been born with misshapen hooves—"so bad they were almost like goat's feet"[7]—a problem never encountered at Piber.

"Is Rau still at Hostau?" asked Reed, lighting up a Chelsea cigarette.

"No, Colonel. He is gone," said Colonel Holters. "And he *won't* be missed," he added with a wry smile.

Holters explained that professional army officers were running the stud in Rau's absence, with the horses in the care of two dedicated young veterinarians. Recently, more horses had arrived from the east. With the arrival of each new batch of horses more pressure was placed on Hostau's limited space and resources.

"Tell the colonel about the prisoners-of-war," urged Captain Sperl, suddenly changing the subject.

"POWs?" said Reed, sitting forward in his seat, "what POWs, Colonel?"

"There are also Allied prisoners-of-war at Hostau and its outlying stations. Americans like you. There are also British, Poles, Serbs and French. The Army uses them to help take care of the horses and for work in the forest."[8]

"How many?" Reed demanded.

"Maybe … one hundred fifty,"[9] replied Holters, meeting Reed's gaze.

After further questioning, it emerged that the Germans had formed the prisoners-of-war into several *Arbeitskommandos* (working parties) at Hostau to care for the horses that were spread over the stud and its three outlying farms and pasture totaling 1,500 acres. Colonel Reed knew that the Geneva Convention permitted non-commissioned personnel of the lower ranks to be used for work in agriculture and industry, but not in any industry producing war materiel.

Holters told Reed that the prisoners at Hostau had been sent from Stalag XIII-B at Weiden on the Bavarian–Czech border. This vast camp had housed 25,000 enlisted prisoners with most out on working parties before it was dissolved on January 22, 1945.[10] Two units that were positively identified were *Arbeitskommando* 3119, consisting of thirteen French prisoners and *Arbeitskommando* 5129 with seventeen Serbs. Others were also in the Hostau area. Another *Arbeitskommando*, Number 3770, was located in the nearby town of Weissensulz* and consisted of nineteen French. Along the border area were *Arbeitskommando* 7062, twenty-one POWs at Zwirschen working in one of the attached stabling facilities; and 5206 with sixteen Serbs at Eisendorf and a large concentration of unidentified prisoners laboring in squads of thirty in the forest near Waier.[11]

"What about the guards, how many?" demanded Reed, immediately beginning to form an assessment in his head.

"Not many," replied Holters, "perhaps a few dozen. They are from Number 3 Company, Landesschütz Battalion 804."[12] Sperl was making notes on a small pad as Holters spoke. Reed knew that Landesschützen represented a desperate last war measure on the part of the Germans. The units consisted of either older soldiers aged 35 to 45 who were unfit for front-line service, reservists or younger soldiers whose battlefield injuries kept them out of further combat.[13] They had only light weapons and were, in Holters' opinion, mostly "third rate." The Americans would also learn later that a column of over 300 Allied prisoners was slowly marching through the area after evacuating from the east.[14]

"Where exactly *is* Hostau?" Reed asked, turning to Sperl.

Sperl reached over and unfolded a map of western Czechoslovakia, laying it on the collapsible table between them, and pointed with his index finger.

"Here, sir, about fifteen miles east of our current forward outpost line."

Any operations in the vicinity of Hostau would be the responsibility of the closest 2nd Cavalry Group unit—in this case

---

* Today's Bela nad Radbuzou.

Lieutenant Colonel Thomas B. Hargis' 42nd Cavalry Reconnaissance Squadron.

Sperl's finger traced a wavy line that ran roughly along the Bavarian–Czech border.

Troops A, B, and C had crossed the Czech frontier on the morning of April 26 and halted just inside Bohemia, establishing a forward outpost line. "Troop A is at Eisendorf as Squadron reserve and currently inactive," reported Sperl. "Troop B has pushed forward to establish a line of foxhole positions running from the village of Rustin through Waldorf to Ples, with patrols forward of this line."[15]

Troop C, meanwhile, had run into intense opposition.

*

First Lieutenant Bob McCaleb, Troop C's recently elevated commander, had spearheaded his attack with 2nd Platoon backed up with a platoon of five Chaffee tanks from Company F in support. The GIs had moved forward cautiously on foot from their forward outpost positions at 0845 hours, moving through a line of booby-traps that they had emplaced on the edge of the woods.[16] The troop's 3rd Platoon was on the flank. It was preternaturally quiet in the forest, with hardly even a bird noise under the gloomy canopy. The Americans could almost feel the presence of Germans close by. Guessing that the Americans might cross the frontier, the Germans had laid small minefields and also erected stout roadblocks across the forest tracks that were in many cases liberally booby-trapped.[17] As the American squads located the roadblocks they called forward engineers to deal with any explosive charges. So far the Germans hadn't attacked, but as Troop C continued the advance they ran straight into a well-concealed ambush.

The silence of the forest had been suddenly rent by the ripping sound of an MG42 machine gun thundering into action, tracers flicking through the trees like red lasers or clipping off branches as the GIs hit the deck and returned fire from behind trunks or from natural hollows and ridges. German Mauser rifles thumped while the GIs' M1 carbines and M3 machine guns returned fire. It was difficult to see the enemy soldiers who were hunkered down in prepared positions amid the greenery and rocks. They were a mixture of regular army, air force and Hitler Youth.

The American squads went straight into the attack, refusing to allow themselves to be pinned down and picked off, the platoons maneuvering to try to flank the German positions as the squads leapfrogged forward covering each other. It had all been practiced in combat many times before and was second nature to the veterans. Technician Fifth Grade Chatterton and Private First Class McFarland fell wounded, their squads calling up medics, while the GIs closed to grenade range with the Germans. As Germans started to go down, they realized that the American attack was unstoppable and like gray wraiths the enemy soldiers evaporated into the misty forest, leaving behind many dead and wounded and a handful to be taken prisoner.[18] With night soon to fall it was decided to withdraw C from the forest—they would return on the morrow to reoccupy the positions they had just taken by force. Eventually, a line of static positions covered the villages of Sveta Katarina, Mlýnské Domky and Skarna with the usual patrols forward.[19]

The 42nd's flanks were tied in with their sister unit from the 2nd Cavalry Group, 2nd Cavalry Reconnaissance Squadron, on the left (north) and with a battalion from the 358th Infantry Regiment on the right (south).[20] Once again, booby-traps were carefully prepared and laid on the edge of the forest to forestall a surprise German attack and the men dug foxholes and waited.

*

"According to latest reports, the Red Army is about here," continued Captain Sperl with his map briefing inside the IPW tent at Vohenstrauss, "forty miles or so east of Hostau and approaching Pilsen from the east." Colonel Reed could immediately see how little

Czechoslovak territory remained in German hands. The Soviets were striking strongly into eastern Czechoslovak lands with the Germans barely containing them.

"In between is Indian country, sir," said Sperl, sweeping his hand over the map, "full of Wehrmacht and SS units from the German Seventh Army."

"Colonel," interrupted Holters, "I can see that you, like me, is a man who loves horses, no?"

Reed nodded. His reaction to the photographs must have made it obvious to the German.

"I consider it, how you say, to be *more* than a coincidence that you and I should meet, here, at this time," Holters continued. "Colonel, I have to tell you that the horses that I have shown you, the horses that I have come to care for deeply, are in *great* danger." Holters' face was a mask of concern as he spoke. "You must save those horses, Colonel, before it is too late."

"What danger are you referring to, Colonel?" replied Reed coolly.

"The Bolsheviks, Colonel, they are only two, maybe three days march from Hostau," said Holters, his lip curling in disgust as he cast a belligerent glance at the American map.

Reed looked again at Sperl's map. It was obvious that the German was right. It appeared a foregone conclusion that the stud would be swallowed up by the Soviets. And anyway, Reed knew that this part of Czechoslovakia had been promised to Stalin as part of the Soviet occupation zone after the German surrender. It was for this reason that General Patton had thus far been prevented from striking at Prague.

"I'm sorry, Colonel," said Reed matter-of-factly, "but my orders clearly state that I'm to hold the line here and advance no further east for the time being. It has already been decided that the area you are referring to will fall under Soviet control in due course."

Holters didn't take Reed's words well. For the first time his urbane façade slipped, his face turning red. "No, Colonel, I *cannot* accept that," he said excitedly. "If you don't rescue the horses they will *all* die, and the prisoners, your own countrymen, will probably die with them."

"What the heck are you talking about?" exclaimed Reed, his brow furrowing in concern.

Holters, his face still flushed, briefly explained what had happened to the Lipizzaners captured by the Soviets outside of Budapest. The Royal Hungarian Riding School had been evacuated just too late. Lieutenant Colonel Ceza Hazslinsky-Krull von Hazslin's column of twenty-two Lipizzaners had been engaged by Soviet T-34 tanks and forced to surrender. Red Army soldiers had simply shot eighteen of the stallions for rations, and also shot any of the grooms or riders who tried to intervene. The surviving four priceless animals were roughly placed in harness and forced to pull heavy ammunition wagons. None were ever seen again. At a stroke, the Royal Hungarian Lipizzaner stallions, descended from the same ancient bloodlines as their Austrian cousins, were lost to history, ending up as horse burgers for hungry peasant soldiers. The surviving staff were hauled off as prisoners-of-war to an uncertain fate.[21]

But Holters went much further. The small town of Nemmersdorf in East Prussia had been temporarily captured and occupied by Soviet troops on October 21, 1944. The story had been widely distributed to the German armed forces and population by Dr. Goebbels' Propaganda Ministry in order to stiffen the will to resist the Soviets after German forces had recaptured the town. The Soviets had raped dozens of women before killing them. Young children and even babies had been beaten, bayoneted, or shot along with most of the male inhabitants.

"But this is not all," continued Holters darkly. "The Bolsheviks also liberated an *Arbeitskommando* of fifty French prisoners-of-war. Do you know what your allies did next, Colonel? They stripped these Frenchmen naked and each one received a bullet in the back of his neck," said Holters, making a pistol with his right hand as he spoke, pressing his index finger behind his right ear.[22]

"Imagine, Colonel," continued Holters in a low voice. "Fifty prisoners murdered by their own allies." Sperl nodded solemnly as he listened, his eyes never leaving Reed's face. As an intelligence officer, he was more than aware of the dark stories that were emerging from the Eastern Front. Soviet propaganda made no secret of its desire to enthuse Red Army soldiers with a deep thirst for revenge against the Germans for their crimes in Russia. The Western Allies turned a blind eye to what they were learning of "Uncle Joe" Stalin's way of fighting the war.

Reed was both shocked and horrified. There were hundreds of Allied prisoners in the area with nowhere to go. The implications for both the horses and the POWs struck home like a thunderclap.

"Anyway, even if the Bolsheviks don't arrive before the end of the war, the horses will be lost," said Holters angrily. "The Czechs hate us Germans and they will surely confiscate them."[23]

An orderly entered the tent and laid out a simple breakfast of American K rations and real coffee. Holters crushed the butt of his cigarette beneath one jackboot. Reed had plenty of questions and Holters was happy to answer them all. Holters already had a strong sense that this American officer was different, that he might be prodded into action. As they ate, the three officers discussed the wider tactical situation in the territory between the US lines and Hostau.

With the front line as leaky as a colander, and with resources stretched to the utter limit, the Germans had established blocking positions at four locations astride the main roads leading to either Prague or Pilsen, including covering Hostau where not only the military stud was located but also an assembly point for collecting military stragglers.[24] The forces facing the Americans were the last scrapings available to the Germans. At the village of Rosshaupt* one weak battalion was covering the settlement and both sides of the road

* Now Rozvadov.

that ran from Vohenstrauss, through the town of Haid* all the way to the strategic city of Pilsen.

At Weissensulz, a town just northwest of Hostau, one small Volkssturm home guard defense unit was dug in west of the road from Eslarn, hidden among the trees. They covered the main road to the stud. In a natural depression between the towns of Waier and Stadlern was a Ski Infantry Battalion, and defending the town of Taus,** just thirteen kilometers south of Hostau, was another army battalion covering the important road junction. The men had loose contact to their north with Army Engineer Brigade 655, highly professional and experienced combat engineers now fighting in an infantry role.[25]

Hank Reed had little fresh intelligence on these enemy emplacements, but even before he had finished his simple meal with Holters and brought the stressful meeting to a close a thought had been planted in his mind—a thought that deliberate and decisive action was required. As Winston Churchill's personal motto stated, what was required was "Action This Day."

---

* Now Bor.
** Now Domazlice.

CHAPTER 4

White Gold

*"The 2nd U.S. Cavalry put a hold on the war ... while we
extracted a sliver of culture for the rest of the world."*

Second Lieutenant Louis T. Holz

Three men crouched beside the broad expanse of a large tree
trunk, their eyes furtive. On their backs were scruffy-looking
homemade backpacks. Their uniforms were grubby, damp and soiled
with leaf litter; their lean faces wore nervous expressions. Standing,
the trio pushed on through the dripping woodland, constantly
scanning the sides and rear. After a while they heard a challenge to
their front.

"*Halt*," demanded the unseen voice. "*Hände hoch!*" The men's
hearts sank when they heard those harsh German words. But then
their despair turned to surprise when the voice shouted out again,
this time in English. "You deaf, Krauts? Get your god-damned hands
in the air," The three men exchanged surprised glances before their
arms shot high above their heads and their leader cried out: "Don't
shoot, don't shoot, we're Allied prisoners-of-war." A few seconds
later American soldiers from Troop C, 42nd Cavalry began to emerge
from the undergrowth, as if spontaneously generating from the very
earth, their carbines pointed warily at the scarecrow-like figures.

The prisoners, two Brits and one American, could scarcely
contain their joy. Their emaciated, starved arms reached out to their
saviors. Laughing and crying, they poured forth their story to the
sympathetic GIs, of how they had managed to slip away from a long

column of prisoners that was resting at the small village of Schmolau,* just west of the town of Weissensulz. The column had numbered well over 300 men.[1] The two Brits were in the worst shape—they'd been prisoners on work detail since capture at Dunkirk in 1940. The GIs gave them food and cigarettes and had them sent to the rear for debriefing. Their story, if it were to be believed, would more than corroborate Colonel Holters' assertion that hundreds of Allied prisoners-of-war were in the vicinity of Hostau.

*

At the conclusion of the simple breakfast in Captain Sperl's tent, Colonel Hank Reed announced that he agreed with Colonel Holters that to simply allow the Hostau Stud, its precious horses and the POWs to fall into Soviet hands would be a sacrilegious act.[2] He knew, with a conviction that welled up inside of him, that something had to be done, and done fast. Although no firm plans had been made, and he had only a hazy idea of the enemy's strengths and intentions, he knew that action was required. But what could an American cavalry colonel do on his own initiative? He couldn't go gallivanting off into enemy territory without specific orders. He would have to inform the chain of command and press his case for immediate action. He could only hope that someone in higher authority would see the importance of saving the horses, not to mention the importance of releasing the POWs. But Reed already had a squirming feeling running through his guts that did not sit well with his breakfast. The Red Army was, according to Sperl's G-2 intelligence, only forty or fifty miles from Hostau, perhaps even closer. If the Soviets made a concerted push, it would only be two days at most, if the Germans fought stubbornly, before the whole exercise became academic and Stalin's forces were at the gates of Hostau. Reed was experienced enough to know that military operations took time to plan, to gather units and assign orders. But

---

* Now Smolov.

there just wasn't enough time. What Reed needed was a superior officer prepared to make a snap decision—today. In the meantime, Reed would try to put into place the necessary groundwork to assist with any putative rescue mission.

First, Reed reached a compromise with Holters. Reed knew the value to the Americans of Holters and his stash of intelligence material. Reed, after a private consultation with Sperl, laid a simple deal on the table: Holters and his men must surrender to the Americans, along with *all* of the documents in their possession. In return, the German colonel and his men would be kept together and immediately sent to the rear for detailed interrogation. It was hoped that they would agree to cooperate with the Allies concerning their intelligence-gathering activities in the Soviet Union, sharing all of their knowledge and assessments. If Holters agreed to these terms, then Reed would try to help the horses. No sooner had Reed finished outlining his course of action than Holters agreed in full.

What Sperl had christened Operation Sauerkraut on the night of April 25, the mission to snatch Dienststelle Ost, was back on. Captain Sperl would accompany Holters back to his unit and organize their surrender and the recovery of the buried files while Reed reached up the chain of command. Holters and Reed shook hands solemnly. The German colonel had come to the Americans with the intention of saving the horses that he had come to love, and so far the plan was working perfectly. As long as the problem was tackled quickly, there appeared a good chance that everything would come off okay. But the one thing Reed, Sperl, and Holters hadn't factored into their equation was the reaction of the German Army—it was an unknown quantity, but for how much longer?

*

"Establish your blocking position here at Taus, Captain," said Brigadier General Baron Treusch von Buttlar-Brandenfels to the young captain standing beside him in front of a map of Western

Czechoslovakia that was pinned to the wall at 11th Panzer Division headquarters. In brackets below the word Taus was the name of the town in Czech—Domazlice. The Germans, totally unbeknown to Colonel Reed and the American command, were making fresh dispositions just in case the US Army decided to plunge deeper into Czechoslovakia. Protecting the important industrial city of Pilsen, where armaments production still continued, was very important. Relying solely upon locally raised troops with inferior training and weapons was not the answer. Instead, highly trained and experienced forces from the 11th Panzer Division would bolster the thin forward line.

"You will reinforce the local defense battalion that controls the crossroads west of the town.[3] It is imperative to prevent any further advance by the Americans towards the city of Pilsen," intoned von Buttlar-Brandenfels, who had recently assumed command of the 11th Panzer, one of the last largely intact German tank formations on the Western Front, from Major General Wend von Wietersheim. "The rest of the division will move up to support you once our supply of petrol has been re-established."

Nine days previously the tall, handsome 45-year-old von Wietersheim had been relieved of command of the 11th Panzer and ordered to Berlin to take command of a Panzer corps there. None too thrilled at the idea of ending up a Soviet prisoner, von Wietersheim had pleaded illness and instead remained close to his former headquarters.

The German's thin crust of poorly equipped infantry and Volkssturm constituting the military region's garrison had some strong units behind it, should the Americans attack. Alongside the 11th Panzer was the 2nd Panzer, and both were excellent formations with plenty of combat experience, but by this stage of the war they were short of men, tanks and, most importantly, gasoline.

The severely depleted 2nd Panzer Division under the command of Colonel Karl Stollbrock was in the worse state of the two, and had been reduced by constant combat to just over 2,000 men and fewer than twenty operational tanks.[4]

It was the 11th Panzer Division which would be the biggest headache for General Patton if he were to thrust deeper into Czechoslovakia, as he still hoped to do. The 11th was near to its authorized strength, fielding just over 11,000 men.[5] Its nickname, eerily close to that of the 42nd Cavalry Squadron, was *Gespensterdivision* (Ghost Division) and it wasn't even supposed to be facing the Americans. It had been ordered by Seventh Army to transfer to the Eastern Front, by now just outside Prague, but a lack of fuel left it stranded in Bohemia, just inside the Czech frontier.

Once refueled, the 11th Panzer Division would move up to Taus. Though severely degraded by combat losses, in late March 1945 the 11th reported to German Seventh Army headquarters that it had two Sturmgeschutz IV assault guns, four Pzkpfw IV medium tanks and, most ominously for the Americans, fourteen large Panther tanks ready for action.

On completing the briefing the captain sprang to attention. "At your command, *Herr General*," he barked, one gloved hand touching the peak of his crusher cap in a punctilious salute.

Within thirty minutes the German battlegroup was assembled, the captain standing imperiously in the first half-track, which would lead a motley collection of camouflaged armored fighting vehicles, trucks and Kübelwagen field cars, engine exhaust fumes mingling with a low mist that hung over the forested roads. The vehicles, fueled with every last liter of available gasoline, were loaded with 500 men from the 111th Panzer Grenadier Regiment, the 6th Artillery Battery and a pioneer company, and prepared to advance towards Taus.

Inside the vehicles, the grenadiers sat wrapped up in greatcoats or camouflaged smocks, steel helmets and webbing, their rifles and machine guns between their knees ready for instant use. They were a proud bunch. If anyone was going to stop Patton it was going to be the hard young Panzer grenadiers who smoked and joked with each other in the backs of the vehicles, and not the third-rate reservists or home guards that littered every town and village along the frontier.

The war in the West had become a numbers game, pure and simple. The Germans didn't have enough men and armored vehicles to hold off the Soviet juggernaut and the Western Allies *simultaneously*—something had to give, and by April 1945 that was the western defenses of the Reich. Facing the Red Army in the east the Germans had 214 divisions. Facing General Eisenhower, Hitler could only spare 26. He could hardly afford to pull a division off the line in the east where the Wehrmacht, despite committing the majority of its strength, was still outnumbered about five to one in men and ten to one in tanks.

It didn't take a military genius to see that the defense of the remaining portions of the Third Reich in Western Europe could not be sustained for many more weeks with the small forces allotted the task. Hitler's only hope was that the Americans and their allies would not advance into territories still held by the Germans that were destined, because of the Yalta Agreement, to form part of the postwar Soviet occupation zone.

The 11th Panzer Division captain turned and glowered impatiently back down the column of reconnaissance vehicles and trucks waiting under the leaden sky. It was still cold and wintry, with occasional snow flurries and rain showers. Fortuitously, the bad weather had grounded Allied fighter-bombers, allowing him to move his vehicles by day. His right arm shot into the air and then fell with a cutting gesture. "*Kampfgruppe … Marsch!*" he bellowed, before turning to face the road in front, adjusting the Knight's Cross that he wore around his neck beneath a camouflaged jacket. The air was rent by the revving of engines and the peculiar rattle and whine of tracked vehicles as they started on the road to Taus and an uncertain reception. The captain smiled grimly and replaced his field cap with a steel helmet, tugging the strap under his chin as his half-track bumped and lurched along the muddy road. He knew that within days von Buttlar-Brandenfels would be crawling up the same road with the balance of the division, including the dozen or so remaining Panther tanks. The captain had seen to it that his Panzer grenadiers had been liberally supplied with Panzerfaust rocket-propelled grenades, making every German soldier a potential tank killer. His left hand gripped the armored glacis of the MG42 machine gun mounted at the front of the half-track to steady him, and he glanced impatiently at his wristwatch. The 11th Panzer was advancing west one final time.

*

At Hostau the war had yet to become a bloody reality. A week before Captain Sperl launched his mission to Dianahof, on April 20, 1945, Hitler's 56th birthday had been celebrated with a surreal parade. Some of the Lipizzaner stallions had trotted through streets that were bedecked with swastika flags as the local population applauded and cheered. The white stallions, with riders in their best uniforms, walked imperiously through the little streets, their heads set proudly, their movements graceful and flowing. The locals, used to farm animals and draft nags, gazed in awe at such fine horses. Mixed in among the townspeople were refugees from further east, including a smattering from Vienna who well knew the reputation of the Lipizzaners.

It was a final propaganda gesture to reassure the locals. This region, abutting Bavaria, was known as the Sudetenland, and most of the inhabitants were Sudeten Germans; the parade reassured them that Hostau and its environs was still German and would remain so. The Germans outnumbered the local Czechs by about four to one in the Sudetenland, but they also knew that they were considered to be unwanted interlopers in Slav lands. The Hitler birthday parade was made using Austrian and Yugoslavian horses, which would have struck the worldlier among the crowds as bitterly ironic. But at the end of the parade, as the clattering of hooves died away into the distance and the crowds dispersed to their homes and businesses, the grim reality of total war once more settled like a pall over the town. For all Dr. Goebbels' undoubted mastery of words, did anyone really believe that Hostau and its inhabitants, human and equine, would remain inviolate?

At Hostau, the war had seemed very far away for most of its duration, and even as forces gathered to intrude on the peace of the stud, the officers and men continued with their tasks as if nothing much had changed. But lately, they had been forced to face some of the realities of Germany's deteriorating military situation. That reality had been passing in front of the stud's main gate in depressing little columns of refugees for weeks now, all desperately trying to stay one step ahead of the vengeful Red Army.

The stud's smart two-storey white stable blocks, neat yards and fenced paddocks had witnessed an influx of animals, not only from Gustav Rau's outlying breeding stations but also sick horses from the refugee columns.

Commanding this ever-expanding equine refugee camp was 48-year-old Lieutenant Colonel Hubert Rudofsky. He was as horse mad as his would-be saviors Colonels Holters and Reed, so horse mad in fact that he had refused to learn to drive a car on principle, but Rudofsky was cut from very different cloth to his American counterpart. Though he wore the field-gray uniform of a Wehrmacht officer, he was a Sudeten German who'd been born close to Hostau and whose elderly mother, niece and nephew still lived nearby. Before the German takeover in 1938, Rudofsky had served in the Czechoslovak Cavalry, and the row of medal ribbons over his left breast pocket testified to his years of experience and service to two nations. He was a tall, bald, bespectacled and somewhat humorless officer and a decorated veteran of the Austro-Hungarian Cavalry in World War I. In the inter-war years Rudofsky had been the preeminent horse-breeding expert in Czechoslovakia, before commanding the great Polish stud at Debica for Rau. His colleagues would remember him as a man who was so conscious of his position and image that he changed his uniform three times a day in order to always appear immaculate before his men. He was usually seen carrying a silver-topped leather carriage driving whip—for his specialty was training carriage drivers. A deeply religious man, and a family friend of Prince von Trauttmansdorff-Weinsberg, whose military stud Rau had appropriated for his experiments at Hostau, Rudofsky was certainly no Nazi, just someone who kept his mouth shut and did his duty with precision. His value to Rau was obvious.

The horses at Hostau were exceptionally well cared for by this correct and conscientious man, and detailed records kept on each. Every Monday morning he personally inspected every horse in the stud, which was led out into the yard where Rudofsky's keen eye for detail and professional expertise missed nothing. Under his command, the Hostau Stud had produced a bumper crop of new foals for Rau's program, each being branded with a mark consisting of an "H" pierced by a dagger. Colonel Rudofsky's relations with the head of the Spanish Riding School, Colonel Podhajsky, were chilly. Rudofsky resented Podhajsky meddling in the welfare of "his" horses, and Podhajsky saw Rudofsky as essentially Rau's creature, and complicit in the disastrous breeding program.

*

In March 1945, after much wrangling and logistical problems, the remaining Lipizzaner stallions at the Spanish Riding School in Vienna were moved for their own safety to a stud at Saint Martin im Mühlkreis in Upper Austria, 228km southeast of Hostau and just northwest of the city of Linz, and the treasures of the Spanish Riding School packed up for safekeeping until after the war. Podhajsky stayed with the horses at St. Martin. But having the breeding mares so far away at Hostau, and outside of his supervision, was killing him.

*

One day in March 1945, Colonel Rudofsky was in his office at Hostau Castle, carefully updating horse records and reviewing the supply situation at the stud, located opposite the castle's gate, when one of the senior grooms tapped impatiently at the door.

"Well, what is it?" asked Rudofsky, barely glancing up from his paperwork.

"You'd better come at once, sir," blurted out the groom in an excited tone. "Russians, sir ... Russians are in the yard!"

"What?" demanded Rudofsky, jumping up from his chair in astonishment, a bolt of fear lancing through his core. How could Russians have arrived without any word from headquarters? It had to be a mistake.

"Yes, sir, the main yard," repeated the groom, his eyes wide. "Russians on horses."

Rudofsky pushed past the groom and looked out of his office window, perhaps fearing a Soviet reconnaissance unit.

"Cossacks!" Rudofsky gasped in a surprised voice as he viewed the strange visitors for the first time. He quickly snatched up his cap from the rack next to the door and strode outside.

There were a couple dozen of them, sitting astride sturdy bay or black Anglo-Kabarda horses, a famous Cossack breed from the Northern Caucasus. Seeing his approach, the Russian officer in charge flicked his riding whip to his tall black Kubanka cap in a casual salute.

"Prince Amassov," announced the Cossack officer to Rudofsky. The stud commander looked over his exotic visitor with interest. The prince was young and handsome, a blond moustache giving him the look of some silent movie star. He was dressed in the same field-gray German officer's uniform as Rudofsky, except for colored rank straps indicating a lieutenant colonel and a unit badge on his left sleeve that confirmed he was a Cossack in the pay of the German Army.

Thousands of Terek, Don and Kuban Cossacks were in the German Army. Their reasoning was simple. Stalin had oppressed the Cossacks before the war, and they felt no loyalty to Moscow and the Reds. These men yearned for independence, and when the Wehrmacht had first conquered their lands it had looked as though Hitler might give this to them. But by March 1945 it was painfully clear to the members of the German 1st Cossack Division that they had backed the wrong horse. They could only seek to surrender to the Western Allies and save themselves and their families, as to fall into Soviet hands would mean execution as traitors to the Motherland or banishment to a Siberian labor camp where you were as good as dead anyway.

Amassov's Cossack hat was adorned with the Nazi eagle and German national cockade, but he wore a Russian-style *shashka* sword hanging from his belt. His twenty-six men were dressed in an assortment of German Army uniforms and traditional Cossack clothing, including long black kaftans with cartridge pouches across their chests. They had Mauser rifles or Russian PPSh sub-machine guns slung across their backs, making them look more like a gang of brigands than professional soldiers.[6]

"Where have you come from?" enquired Rudofsky, admiring the Cossacks' fine horses.

"From Poland," replied Amassov without elaboration. "We have brought our horses with us."[7] Rudofsky was soon informed by his staff that as well as twenty-seven armed Cossacks, and their families, they had brought with them sixty Kabarda and Anglo-Kabarda mares with four stallions, eighty Don and Anglo-Don mares, also with four stallions, and a herd of thirty Polish ponies. Rudofsky was exasperated, but Prince Amassov was adamant—he demanded refuge for his men, families and horses at Hostau. With Amassov was his wife and fourteen-year-old daughter.

The Cossacks had fought honorably for the Germans, and now it was time for the Nazis to repay that service. Rudofsky's precise mind sensed disaster: adding another 178 horses to an already overcrowded facility was asking for trouble and feeding the horses and finding them places in the paddocks and in the stables would prove difficult. Plus there was the question of all these strange Russians to accommodate. But Prince Amassov and his band didn't look like the kind of men who could be easily refused. The prince's hard gaze betrayed a man of immense combat experience and toughness. Rudofsky would have to find room.

*

The stud now housed over 600 horses, far more than could be realistically stabled and fed, and the small staff of German soldiers and Allied prisoners-of-war was hard pressed caring for them. The Lipizzaners, Thoroughbreds, Arabians and Cossack horses were housed at the main stud at Hostau and at the facilities at the adjacent villages of Hassatitz, Taschlowitz and Zwirschen.*

Life at Hostau was an endless schedule of feeding, mucking out, exercising and grooming. The prisoners worked alongside the Germans, and many had formed close bonds with the animals that they cared for. Some labored with one goal in mind—the welfare of the horses, and their feelings for the animals often transcended the traditional enmities of war. Others, particularly Soviet and Eastern European prisoners, hated the Germans and yearned for release, and perhaps revenge.

Colonel Rudofsky's most important subordinate officers were the Hostau Stud's two German Army veterinary surgeons. Captain Dr. Rudolf Lessing was a tall, lean and handsome man in his early thirties,[8] with fair hair slicked back from his forehead and piercing blue eyes. He was a man who knew horses intimately, and a hard-working and loyal subordinate. He had been appointed senior veterinary officer at Hostau in January 1944. Previously, Lessing had been Gustav Rau's adjutant in Poland in 1942 at the great Debica stud farm. Lessing had assisted Rau with veterinary matters on the Eastern Front and had seen action there, dealing with wounded horses in the mud and filth, an experience that had marked him for life.

---

* Now Svržno.

After the east, Hostau was an oasis for Lessing, though perhaps a mirage may have been a more apt analogy. His wife and young daughter lived on site, along with Rudofsky's spouse and many other civilian non-combatants. In this strange reality, the officers went home each evening to spend time with their wives and children. But the cozy domesticity was proving to be an illusion—the families were now close to the front lines and vulnerable, bringing no peace in the minds of the officers at the stud. They performed their duties with one eye always on home and hearth and with a growing sense of unease.

Lessing's close colleague and deputy, Captain Dr. Wolfgang Kroll, was twenty-six and possessed of a gregarious personality and a strong appetite for adventure. That last attribute was about to be fully tested in ways that he could never have imagined. Working under these men were the grooms and stable hands tending to the horses and grounds, dealing with supplies, machinery and general maintenance. Aside from the noise of horses, any visitor to the facility would have heard a multitude of languages being spoken: German, Czech, French, Polish, Serbo-Croat, Russian and English.

The problem for Rudofsky and his staff was the encroachment of the war in all its ugliness into what had been an equine paradise far from the realities of the conflict. Lessing and Kroll met with the refugees from the East daily, as they tended to the civilians' horses as well as the remnants of Rau's Nazi breeding program. The distress and exhaustion of both the civilians from the East and their horses were harrowing. "So far we had been completely unaware," recalled Lessing in later years. "We thought: well, we sit here relatively well. We really did not suffer any distress and were basically spared from the war, because we had not been bombed. But now … we got for the first time a concrete idea of the things that were happening outside."[9]

For the veterinarians, the state of the refugees' horses was gut-wrenching. Many had lost shoes, while others had terrible suppurating sores from hauling overloaded wagons. Ill-fitting harnesses on emaciated horses meant dreadful wounds caused by incessant rubbing and slipping. Many of the horses were lame or partly lame, while some had inflamed pressure points on their withers (the ridge between a horse's shoulder blades). Pistol shots were heard at the stud on a daily basis, as the veterinarians put down the worst cases.

This harrowing reality extended to the dirty, ill and destitute human refugees, and Rudofsky allocated what little space he could spare for them to rest in barns or outside in the yards. Most didn't want to linger too long at Hostau—they knew the Red Army was only a few days behind. Most limbered up their tired horses after an inadequate rest and pushed on to the American lines and safety. More than one among them warned Rudofsky and his staff that if they had any sense they would follow on before "Ivan" arrived at the gates. The "safe world" of bucolic Hostau was now a thing of the past.

But the escape routes to the West were becoming progressively blocked by the German military. Shortly after the Hitler birthday parade, Colonel Rudofsky, as ranking officer in the town, was ordered to inspect the erection of anti-tank barriers close to the Bavarian border and in Hostau. Their object was to stop the American advance. Some Reich Labor Service (RAD) troops were assigned the task of building the barriers,[10] but Rudofsky, knowing that militarily they presented little impediment to American tanks, convinced the local Nazi officials overseeing the work to leave the barriers open for the time being—Rudofsky needed the large numbers of refugees and their horses that were building up at Hostau Stud to keep moving west to relieve the overcrowding and strain on resources.

*

Colonel Podhajsky and the Spanish Riding School stallions faced as dire a situation as that at Hostau in their billets at Arco Castle outside Saint Martin im Mühlkreis. Refugees had flooded the village from the east, and in common with Colonel Rudofsky's command, the area was full of Soviet and Polish prisoners-of-war and displaced persons who had no love for the Germans or their allies. The food situation was so dire that several refugees had told Podhajsky that the prized Lipizzaner stallions should be shot and used for food. Podhajsky could only turn away ashen-faced and fearful. If push came to shove he and his handful of twenty barely armed men could do little to protect the horses from a hungry mob. Discipline was holding, but for how much longer? Like Colonel Rudofsky at Hostau, it was uncertain which army would arrive first—the Americans or the Soviets. Vienna had fallen to Stalin's forces on April 13, but the US Army in Bavaria was less than 100 miles to the west. There was nowhere left to run to— Podhajsky had to face the reality that the Spanish Riding School *would* fall into enemy hands—the only question was whether the Americans would beat the Soviets to the castle and the horses and staff would be spared. Communications with the stud at Hostau, where nearly all the Spanish Riding School's breeding mares were situated, had been intermittent until they completely failed due to enemy action, leaving Podhajsky with no idea of what was happening. It would be a disaster of historical magnitude if the Americans liberated Saint Martin im Mühlkreis and saved the stallions, only for the Soviets to capture Hostau and kill or haul off east the School's mares, without which no new stallions could be bred, leaving the ancient Lipizzaner bloodlines severed and the School to wither and perish.

*

"*Mein Gott,*" exclaimed Colonel Rudofsky, ducking involuntarily as he sat behind his desk in his office at Hostau Castle on April 26, 1945. The loud detonation caused the windows to rattle in their frames. He jumped up quickly, wrenched open the door and stumbled outside in time to see a plume of black smoke rising from one of the nearby paddocks. Horses were whinnying in terror and crashing about inside their stalls or charging madly around the paddocks. Several grooms and prisoners were lying flat on the ground, covering their heads with their hands, buckets and brooms abandoned in haste nearby. Rudofsky dashed through the castle gates and across the road to the stud.

"Alarm!" yelled a sergeant at the top of his voice. He ran over to where Rudofsky was standing wide-eyed.

"Take cover, Colonel. We are under artillery fire!"

The sergeant's words were barely out of his mouth when a ripping noise filled the air, sounding like an express train coming on at full speed.

"Take cover!" screamed the sergeant, pushing Rudofsky down as another shell arrived with a terrific detonation. The war had finally arrived at Hostau.

CHAPTER 5

Operation Sauerkraut

"It would be a great shame if these unique animals
fell into the hands of the Bolsheviks."

Lieutenant Colonel Walter Holters

"Got your chopper, soldier?" Captain Ferdinand Sperl asked his driver, as he climbed into the passenger seat of "Chez Stubby," his battered and worn jeep, on April 26, 1945.

"You bet, Cap'n," replied the grinning IPW 10 noncom, pointing to the Thompson sub-machine gun that was tucked in beside his seat.

"Right ... let's move out," ordered Sperl. Operation Sauerkraut was a go. Sperl, his driver and a couple of his men in the back of the jeep would take the surrender of Dienststelle Ost deep in the Bohemian Forest at dusk.

Squeezed in with Sperl's men and their weapons was Lieutenant Colonel Holters, bundled up against the cold in his Luftwaffe greatcoat and cap. The first part of Sauerkraut was a reconnaissance mission to the hunting lodge at Dianahof where the valuable intelligence trove was buried. If Sperl was happy with what he found at Dianahof, phase two would entail the safe removal of the documents and the German personnel to the American lines.

The jeep bumped its way along mountainous roads and tracks, Holters helping to direct the driver. The Americans were twitchy, constantly scanning the dark forest, alert to movement and well aware that they had already passed behind the German lines.

"Here we go," said Sperl, turning to speak to his men and Holters in the back of the jeep. "Stay sharp," he added, his hands tightening around the stock of his M1. The driver slowed to a crawl as a German sentry post appeared, barring the road ahead. Two Luftwaffe soldiers unslung their rifles and stared at the American jeep that had appeared unexpectedly around a corner in the forest road. Colonel Holters jumped down from the jeep waving his arms and engaged them in heated discussion for a few seconds. Eventually, the NCO in charge of the checkpoint slung his rifle, saluted and ordered the other man to stand aside. Holters jogged back over to the jeep and struggled aboard.

"Okay," said Sperl slowly, "let's move out." The driver gunned the engine and the jeep passed slowly through the checkpoint, the two sentries staring at the Americans as they passed. The jeep powered on, its engine noisy in the eerie forest, every man aboard the vehicle aware of how vulnerable they were to enemy fire should they drive into an ambush.

Sperl knew that the really unknown factor in this operation to save the horses was not so much the regular German Army; rather it was the Waffen-SS. The army was still dangerous and some officers and men were clearly still spoiling for a fight with the Americans, but many were either going through the motions of following increasingly desperate orders or actively looking to surrender. But the Waffen-SS, as political soldiers, had their fates ultimately tied to the survival of the Nazi regime, and remained fanatical even in the face of defeat.

And with the added problem of a heavily armed Kampfgruppe from the army's 11th Panzer Division firmly ensconced at Taus, only a dozen miles from Hostau, the chances of Sperl running into elements of either unit was high. By taking secondary roads and trails to Dianahof, Sperl at least avoided any confrontation with the handful of army battalions and Volkssturm that were entrenched in positions—at mercifully large intervals—to cover the main roads.[1]

*

Lieutenant Colonel Hubert Rudofsky got slowly to his feet, brushing dust and dirt from his previously immaculate uniform. The shelling of the stud at Hostau had stopped as abruptly as it had begun. A cloud of smoke and dust drifted lazily across the grounds from the impacts, but no more shells appeared to be coming. Reports arrived that the horses were all okay—by a miracle the shells had landed in unoccupied fields close by or in the grounds of the castle.

Rudofsky was alarmed to see that the sudden barrage had considerably shaken the Volkssturm and Hitler Youth representatives who had been working on the stud's defenses. They were running around, shouting and behaving in a generally unmilitary fashion. Everyone waited tensely, but no more shells arrived.

Who had been firing? It must have been the Americans, as they were thought to be the closest. But why target Hostau? Probably ranging shots or strays, thought Rudofsky hopefully. As the firing was not concentrated, it clearly did not herald an attack. But it gave everyone at Hostau pause for thought. If those shells had landed on the stables or amid the horses out to pasture, the consequences would have been horrific. Normality slowly returned to the stud, but the artillery fire unsettled Rudofsky. It didn't appear to bode well for the future.

*

The hunting lodge at Dianahof was impressive—a three-storey white building set atop a 1,800-foot-high wooded mountain ridge. It had belonged to Count Coudenhove-Kalergi before being requisitioned by the mysterious Colonel Holters and his men.

Captain Sperl's jeep came to a halt before the grand entrance and everyone jumped down stiffly, carrying their weapons. Drawn up beside the entrance drive was a collection of German air force trucks and a Kübelwagen field car, their gas tanks dry. Several German officers and men came out of the house and stood eyeing the steel-helmeted and heavily armed Americans with suspicion.

Holters motioned for Sperl and his men to follow him inside. Their boots rang loudly on the entrance hall floor as they trooped into what had once been the Count's long dining room. Holters motioned that the Americans should sit at the large dining table, around which already sat many of Holter's personnel, including some female clerks. Several large candelabra burned brightly down the middle of the polished table, giving the rather gloomy room a warm and inviting glow as Holters laid out Colonel Reed's surrender terms to his staff. There was an animated discussion among the Germans before Holters turned to Sperl.

"Captain, as soldiers we have all taken an oath to the Führer," said Holters, standing at one end of the long table, the flickering of the candles glinting off the decorations pinned to his left breast pocket. "We cannot surrender without resistance."

"I understand, Colonel," replied Sperl slowly. Holters and some of the other German officers desired to have an "honorable" end to their wartime service. After all, many still had family in Germany within reach of the Gestapo, which still functioned. Sperl discussed the matter at some length, in the process forming a novel plan.

"So, it is agreed," recapped Sperl in German. "I shall return to the American lines, gather more of my men, vehicles and fuel, and return here. I shall then 'attack' the lodge. After a suitable display of gunfire, you can surrender. If anyone comes looking, they will find evidence of a battle having taken place. The records and German personnel will then be evacuated as agreed."[2] In the meantime, Sperl demanded that Holters order his men to excavate the buried crates and stack them outside the lodge ready for collection when he returned with the task force at dawn the next day. He had no intention of lingering for a moment longer than he had to. Colonel Holters nodded solemnly. All those around the table appeared to be in agreement.

Minutes later, as the Germans formed work parties for the excavation of the crates, Sperl's jeep roared away from the lodge and disappeared into the forest.

*

"Jesus Christ!" Sperl exclaimed, as incoming rounds pinged off the side of his jeep. He was on his second trip to the hunting lodge, bringing with him a small task force for the purpose of retrieving the crates and personnel. Behind him on the winding mountain road German bullets stitched across the dirt or thumped against the armor of two M24 Chaffee tanks that the 42nd's CO Lieutenant Colonel Hargis had detached to assist Sperl's return mission to Dianahof. Sperl, shouldering his M1 as his driver hit the gas, loosed off a volley into the trees, but he couldn't see any enemy. Behind him, the machine guns on the tanks and two M8 armored cars joined in, hosing the woods with indiscriminate fire.

The little task force, a couple of trucks and some more jeeps huddled in among the armor, did not stop but pushed on to the lodge, quickly leaving the German firing behind. They had been lucky—the enemy fire had been wild and inaccurate and none of the Americans had been hurt.

A mile or so later and Sperl's jeep led the column through a now-deserted sentry point and pulled up outside the lodge. Sperl immediately jumped down from his jeep and rushed over to where Colonel Holters and some of his men were standing with anxious expressions on their faces.

"You heard the firing, Colonel?" said Sperl. Holters nodded, noticing the bullet scars on the American vehicles.

"We must be quick, Captain," replied Holters, his eyes nervously scanning the surrounding woods. Enemy forces could be closing on the lodge as they spoke—following the American task force's route. Holters glanced again down the line of olive-drab American vehicles, each emblazoned with a large white star on either side, some bearing dents or holes from bullets, and he worried even more. It was a puny force considering that German Panzers and SS troops were suspected to be in the area.

"Get those crates loaded!" yelled Sperl, pointing at the large pile of mud-encrusted wooden boxes, his carbine slung over his right shoulder, setting both his men and the Germans to the task. Working together at a feverish pace, the GIs and Luftwaffe men heaved and shouldered the heavy wooden crates into the American six-by-sixes, as the GIs called their large six-wheeled trucks. Others fueled Holters' Kübelwagen and some Opel Blitz trucks using US jerrycans brought up for this express purpose.

Sperl glanced nervously at his watch.

"Come on, let's move it!" he shouted, as he scanned the dark green forest that surrounded the house. Eventually, after what seemed like an eternity, the last crates were loaded and a sergeant ran over and saluted.

"Loading complete, sir," he said, rather breathlessly. In total, there were twelve truckloads of documents, representing an enormous cache of material.[3]

"Right, let's roll!" replied Sperl, clapping him on the back as he turned to find Colonel Holters.

"Please load your people on the German truck, Colonel," he said, pointing to the Opel Blitz. "You and the other officers can come in the jeeps and in your field car." Holters needed no encouragement—he was as eager to be away from Dianahof as Sperl and the GIs were.

Now all that remained was the "surrender." Sperl directed one tank, the trucks, jeeps and one armored car to start back down the mountain road towards the American lines while Sperl's jeep, with Holters seated once more in the back, pulled a safe distance away from the lodge. A Chaffee tank suddenly fired several 75mm high explosive rounds at the empty building, its windows imploding as the shells tore large holes in its formerly immaculate façade. Fires started to break out inside the lodge as the furniture and fittings caught alight. The tank ceased firing and the one remaining M8 Greyhound opened up, its 37mm cannon and machine guns thumping away to give the impression to any listening Germans of an exchange of fire between the American task force and Holters' unit. Honor satisfied, Sperl's jeep and the American armor headed for home as the hunting lodge smoldered behind them, a tall column of black smoke rising above the forest canopy. As his jeep thundered along the mountain road Sperl radioed ahead to Colonel Reed, telling him that the mission was a success and the prisoners were in the bag.[4]

*

The ultimate authority who would decide the fate of the horses and men at Hostau was not Colonel Hank Reed. Instead, the responsibility lay with the commander of the US Third Army, 60-year-old General George S. Patton.

Fortunately for Reed, his commanding general was depressed. He was depressed because it looked like the Germans were beaten and the war was going to end very soon. Patton loved war and he dreaded the peace to come. He was a man of immense energy and dash who had first tasted action in 1916 against Pancho Villa in Mexico. By late April 1945 the Third Army found itself sliding down the German–Czech border, forbidden by Eisenhower from advancing on the great prize of Prague. It looked like the Third Army's war, rather than ending with the triumphant liberation of the Czech capital, would instead involve trundling despondently into the foothills of the Alps gathering up demoralized German prisoners, while the Red Army snatched all of the laurels of victory. Patton wrote: "There is nothing of interest happening … The war is sort of dragging its end out to a non-spectacular termination … I feel lower than whale tracks on the bottom of the ocean."

So when one of Third Army's most daring and competent cavalry colonels radioed through a request for permission to rescue world-famous horses and Allied POWs beyond the American front line, Patton took notice. It was just the kind of mission he loved, but, being a realist, he would have to be careful to make sure that the operation was handled diplomatically.

Colonel Reed waited nervously for Patton's reply to trickle down through the long chain of command via Third Army then XII Corps and finally 2nd Cavalry Group, pacing up and down smoking cigarettes inside his farmhouse headquarters at Vohenstrauss, girding himself for a refusal. It seemed only logical, what with the Third Army's changed mission and the deal with the Soviets concerning the postwar occupation of Czechoslovakia.

"Radio message, sir," said a voice at his elbow, instantly breaking his reverie. Reed turned and found a young headquarters corporal waiting just inside the door, a pensive expression on his face. Reed followed him straight through to the radio room, where the operator was hastily writing down a message on his signal pad.

"Well?" asked Reed, bracing himself.

"Message reads: 'Get them. Make it fast. You will have new mission',"[5] read the clerk carefully.

"God damn!" exclaimed Reed ecstatically, "we're in business. Send the acknowledgment."

It was no secret in Third Army that General Patton loathed communists. His loathing for the Soviets had been considerably heightened as early as December 1943, when Free Polish leader General Anders had briefed him about the 1940 Katyn Massacre, in which the NKVD had shot thousands of Polish officers and intellectuals and then tried to blame the crime on the Germans. "If I ever marched my corps of two divisions in between the Russians and the Germans," Patton had declared at the time, "I'd attack in *both* directions!"[6] Later, in 1945, at an important dinner, Patton had given voice to these feelings again. "At dinner I stated that in my opinion Germany was so completely blacked out that so far as military resistance was concerned they were not a menace and that what we had to look out for was Russia. This caused a considerable furor."[7] Preventing the world's most famous and valuable horses from falling into Stalin's hands was an aim entirely in keeping with Patton's anti-communist and anti-Soviet views.

The window of opportunity for sorting out the problem at Hostau would be measured in only a few hours, judging by the last part of Patton's message about having a new mission. An "eyes and ears" outfit like the 2nd Cavalry Group could expect to be in the vanguard once Patton moved again.

It was not an official order from Patton, but rather "off the record." There were no further details and it was clear that Colonel Reed had some latitude of action. Patton would look the other way while Reed acted. It would be up to Reed to decide in what form the mission would be framed. If Reed was successful and the horses and POWs were brought into Allied lines Patton could take his share of the credit. And, importantly for Patton, if it went wrong his comment would be that some dumb cavalry colonel had "gotten lost in Western Czechoslovakia." There would be no official blessing from Patton.[8]

Reed was delighted—he was out on a limb but he felt that saving the horses was far more important than his own reputation. As he was to say later, "We were so tired of death and destruction; we wanted to do something beautiful."[9] Saving the beautiful horses at Hostau would be a very special end to his regiment's nine months of unremitting slaughter and destruction across the breadth of Western Europe.

Reed could now consider making firm plans. It was more than a little daunting. Risking his men's necks this late in the war was to be avoided if at all possible. It was imperative that he found some solution that would minimize the danger to his young, war-weary troopers but still bring in the big prize.

After Captain Sperl, following the successful completion of Operation Sauerkraut, had delivered Colonel Holters intact to Reed's headquarters, the German immediately volunteered to help. He drafted a short note and handed it to his orderly, telling him to take it to Colonel Rudofsky at the stud, and to wait for a reply. Reed and Sperl stood outside the farmhouse and watched as the German orderly, suddenly no longer a prisoner, mounted a borrowed bicycle and cycled off in the direction of Hostau. It seemed an incongruous beginning to such an important operation. For now, Reed could do nothing but await the outcome of his opening gambit.

*

Colonel Rudofsky glanced briefly at the note of which he had just taken delivery, then called Captains Lessing and Kroll, the two veterinary officers, to his castle office for a meeting.

The three officers sat around Rudofsky's desk, a black-and-white photograph of Adolf Hitler, his eyes looking down balefully at the men, hanging on the wall behind the colonel's chair. Rudofsky explained whence the note originated and then read it aloud to the two veterinarians.

"I send you these lines with the request immediately to send one of your officers, authorized by me, here to discuss the transfer of the horses to Bavaria as fast as possible." Rudofsky paused and Lessing and Kroll exchanged glances, Kroll raising one eyebrow but saying nothing. Rudofsky cleared his throat and continued. "It would be a great shame if these unique animals fell into the hands of the Bolsheviks," he read. "I have the opportunity to safely escort you and the horses through the lines. This matter needs, however, your immediate response. Nobody should learn anything about this except you, because the threat of betrayal is everywhere. Signed Lieutenant Colonel Holters, etc, etc."[10] Rudofsky finished reading and leaned back in his creaking wooden chair, adjusting his steel-rimmed Himmler-style glasses. He and Holters had chatted on many occasions, and the Luftwaffe officer had shown great concern for the fate of the horses. His last conversation with Holters before they had parted still rang uncomfortably in the loyal stud commander's ears:

"Vienna has already fallen to the Ivans, Rudofsky," Holters had said passionately, using the German Army slang term for Soviet soldiers. "The Red Army is just outside Pilsen, less than 60 kilometers away. For God's sake, Hubert, they will be here before you know it!

74

You must make contact with the Americans. They are not far—just over the border to Bavaria. Perhaps you can deliver the horses to them. It's your only hope."[11]

"I'm not in the treason business, Holters!" Rudofsky had snapped back at the time, horrified by the idea of voluntarily surrendering to the enemy, but Holters' comments about the Soviets had nonetheless unsettled him. Holters had continued to press his point, casting a gesture towards a paddock where several white Lipizzaner mares were standing quietly or grazing contentedly, black foals nuzzling at their teats for milk or prancing around playing, all long legs and awkward, jerky movements.

"You know that I've spent most of the war in the east," Holters had said, his face flushed with anger and frustration. "The Bolshevik swine care nothing for horses. When they arrive here they will slaughter them on the spot and fry them up as steaks to feed their hungry troops!"[12] Rudofsky had tugged at his stiff uniform collar, which suddenly felt too tight.

"You are in the *greatest* danger, and you must act *now* to save them!" Holters had pleaded angrily, his eyes flashing beneath the visor of his air force cap. With this angry exchange Rudofsky and Holters had parted company for good.

After Holters had left the stud, Rudofsky, seriously upset by the glimpse of the grim possible future that Holters had forced him to confront, had contacted his headquarters in besieged Berlin asking for instructions. It was the natural response to the unfolding crisis— Rudofsky wanted clarification from higher command, to shift the responsibility for deciding the fate of the horses and its people to someone else. He had sent a request by radio directly to Veterinary Corps General Dr. Curt Schulze,[13] who commanded all veterinary and stud services in the German armed forces, at the Bendlerblock, the army high command building in central Berlin where Count von Stauffenberg's plot to topple the Nazis had come apart in July 1944. The reply had been brought into Rudofsky's office by the signals clerk, handwritten on a flimsy, and placed before him. There was only one stark sentence: "*Stay put, at all costs!*"

"Is this it?" Rudofsky had asked.

"Yes, Colonel. That is the complete transmission."

"Dismissed," Rudofsky had muttered under his breath, the clerk quietly withdrawing from the office. Rudofsky had been even more upset by the order from Berlin than by Holters' words. To suggest that the stud do nothing when faced by imminent enemy envelopment appeared to signal that either Berlin failed to understand the parlous nature of the situation at Hostau, or else it no longer cared.

"Well, *meine herren*, I'd like to hear your thoughts on Colonel Holters' 'offer'," said Rudofsky, brought back to reality by Holters' new message offering salvation in Bavaria, addressing his two veterinarians Lessing and Kroll. "He's been a frequent visitor here as you well know."

"If it's a genuine offer, I think we are duty bound to reply," said Lessing immediately.

"He's right about the Ivans," interjected Kroll. "They could be here any day. God help us all then."

"I can't see any harm in at least doing what the note suggests and finding out more, can you, sir?" said Lessing.

Rudofsky nodded slowly. "I agree. Our first priority is the safety of the horses. That was what we were all sent here for. But do not forget: there are stallions that have to be led. And what do I do with the mares?" The crisis that was unfolding at the Hostau Stud was happening at just about the worst possible time in that it was foaling season. Half of the mares were heavily pregnant, the others already with foal, the silky black coats of the youngsters in marked contrast to their gray-white mothers. A move now would put their young lives at risk. Rudofsky went on: "It is a matter of impossibility to simply march with these horses from one day to the other thirty kilometers with them. And quite apart from that, I have been commanded to stay with the stud on this spot."[14]

But Lessing and Kroll were both relieved by Rudofsky's changed attitude. For weeks now they had been watching German troops preparing the area around the town for defense, planting mines and setting roadblocks, while roving patrols of soldiers had increased as the numbers of refugees shuffling past the stud had also multiplied. The refugees brought with them horrific stories of what the Red Army was doing to the towns and villages that it conquered. It appeared that the horrors visited on the town of Nemmersdorf were being repeated a hundredfold in the east. Unnervingly, stories also now abounded of the Soviets shooting German prisoners on the spot, and it seemed certain that if the Red Army took Hostau, the horses, and the men who cared for them, would probably all suffer horribly together. It was deeply unsettling, but Lessing and Kroll had tried to put all thoughts of the imminent arrival of the Soviets to the backs of their minds and instead concentrate on ministering to the horses. But Lessing often found his mind wandering to his wife and young daughter who lived in his quarters at the stud. He felt sick, panicky and helpless when he considered them. Rudofsky and many of the other soldiers at the stud shared this deeply private panic.

Rudofsky was torn. Holters' note made no mention of the Americans, which was one thing. But an officer like Rudofsky, no matter how panicked he might have felt on the inside, was not inclined to question his orders, however ridiculous or ill-conceived they might have been. He had taken an oath of loyalty to Hitler, and though he was no Nazi, Rudofsky had no intention of breaking his word.

"Lessing," said Rudofsky with new-found determination in his voice, "I want you to go. The note says that our officer is to proceed through the forest to a hut marked on this attached map." Rudofsky opened out a German military map that Holters had sent with his orderly, the route clearly marked with a red wax crayon. "A forester at the hut will then guide you to the Dienststelle Ost HQ. Take one of the grooms with you."

Lessing nodded. So Rudofsky was seeing sense. When headquarters had told Rudofsky to sit tight, it had been clear to Lessing and Kroll that their commanding officer had not been happy. This sudden communication from Holters, coupled with the recent artillery fire, had spurred him to action.

One thing that surprised Lessing was that Rudofsky had chosen him to go and meet with Holters. He couldn't help thinking that this was more a job for his adventurous young friend Dr. Kroll—but that was probably why the colonel had asked him instead: perhaps he wanted a calmer and more mature officer to undertake such an important mission.

"Be ready to leave in an hour," added Rudofsky.

Lessing nodded and stood. There was much to prepare for the journey. His stomach danced in nervous anticipation of the unknown.

CHAPTER 6

Plenipotentiary

"If you know a horse, you depend on him and if he was going to do something bad, you could depend on him to do that too. I always understood horses better than I did people."

Captain Thomas M. Stewart

Captain Lessing and a groom left the stud at Hostau on horseback, to ride to meet Colonel Holters at his headquarters at Dianahof. Following a dirt road for a few miles through the dark woods, Lessing found the specified wooden hut without difficulty.

A Sudeten German forester came out to greet them. Ominously, he told Lessing that the Americans had already taken prisoner the Germans that they wanted to meet. The hunting lodge at Dianahof had been attacked and it was still burning. He told Lessing that in order to reach the agreed rendezvous point he would have to cross into American territory. Dr. Lessing paused to think. Considering their limited options at the stud, perhaps it was wiser to continue to Holter's last reported position and see what the Americans could offer. Rudofsky might not like it, but Lessing made up his mind. He decided to continue on alone.

"Wait here until I get back," he ordered the army groom, adding honestly: "I don't know what's going to happen."[1]

Lessing switched to a motorcycle provided by the forester and rode on for several miles before stashing the valuable bike in some undergrowth, continuing on foot towards where he believed the American lines to be. He felt elated to be doing something positive, and now when he thought of his family that feeling of dread in the pit of his stomach felt a little less acute.[2]

*

Foxholes, strung out along the edge of the fir forest at irregular intervals, punctuated the hilly green countryside. Inside each, a helmeted American soldier crouched, weapon pointed east. Further back were concealed M8 Greyhound armored cars and jeeps, carefully hidden beneath trees with their heavier weapons loaded and ready. Occasional puffs of cigarette smoke wafted lazily from each two-man position, while the soldiers' field radio crackled. The troops looked tired and dirty, their faces adorned with two or three-day stubble, eyes ringed with black, khaki greatcoats flecked with mud and leaf litter. Gloved hands rested on M1 carbines, Thompsons and M3 Grease Guns, the light, short-range weapons issued to reconnaissance cavalrymen.

"Kraut!" hissed one of the young privates suddenly and within seconds the helmeted heads had retracted down in their foxholes like turtles retreating into their shells. Carbines were pressed into shoulders; cheeks settled against cold wooden stocks and a careful bead was taken on the German officer who had staggered unexpectedly into their midst.[3]

"*Hände hoch*, Fritz!" shouted an American corporal, his eyes never leaving his carbine's sight that was squarely zeroed onto the German's chest. The corporal signaled a buddy with a flick of his hand. The GI rose awkwardly from his foxhole, adjusted his dented steel helmet with one gloved hand and faced the tall, slim German.

Dr. Lessing, his field-gray tunic, riding breeches and black leather jackboots spattered with mud from his long journey, straightened up, his eyes watching the American soldier cautiously from beneath the visor of his crusher cap, a small homemade white flag flapping lazily from a stick he held in one gloved hand. The most important mission of Lessing's life had begun.[4]

After giving himself up to the American patrol, Lessing was taken under guard to the farmhouse at Vohenstrauss that was being used as the 2nd Cavalry Group's temporary headquarters, where Colonel Reed greeted him warmly.[5] As the German officer walked through the farmhouse, American officers and men stopped their work to stare, intrigued by their special visitor from the other side of the lines.

Lessing was somewhat taken aback by Reed's disarming manner. Over a pleasant meal, cocktails and plenty of Chelsea cigarettes, the German gradually relaxed and talked horses with the American colonel. Reed, in turn, explained that Colonel Holters and his Dienststelle Ost personnel had been sent to the rear for detailed interrogation, but that he had agreed with the Luftwaffe colonel about the necessity of rescuing the horses and liberating the prisoners-of-war in the vicinity of Hostau. But before that could happen, said Reed, he needed the complete cooperation of the German authorities at Hostau. "The whole atmosphere betrayed objectivity, beneficence, and understanding," wrote Lessing of his meal with Reed, "so much so that I actually was not aware of facing an enemy."[6]

Lessing was relieved by Reed's decision to rescue the stud and more than a little amazed. Although he had absolutely no authority from Rudofsky to negotiate with the Americans, he pressed on regardless now that the situation had been clarified. "For me," he later said, "only one thing was decisive at this hour: to know, here I have a conversation partner with whom I can talk about the matter in all openness."[7]

During the conversation, Lessing impressed upon Reed the fear of a Soviet arrival at Hostau and the peril that the horses and staff faced. "The Russians don't understand much about horses," Lessing said, shaking his head mournfully. "They don't bother much with bloodlines."[8]

"Well, Captain, I have a proposition for you," said Reed, putting down his fork. "If you can bring the horses *and* the POWs through

81

the forest to the American lines I can guarantee that the horses will be well protected and afforded safe passage to our rear areas."[9]

Dr. Lessing's face lit up at Reed's words, but his jubilation was short-lived as he remembered the problem they faced.

"That is a kind offer, Colonel, believe me," replied Lessing. "But it is an offer that we at the stud regrettably cannot accept or comply with." Colonel Reed looked nonplussed. "You see, Colonel, it is the foaling season. We cannot possibly attempt to move the mares at this time."[10]

Now that Reed understood Lessing's position he was also a little frustrated. He had hoped that the operation could be kept simple, and the risk to his men and to US–Soviet relations minimized as a result. He was not keen on sending any of his men or vehicles behind the German lines at this late stage of the war, certainly in the kinds of numbers that would be required to make an impression at Hostau.

"Allow me to suggest a counter-proposal, Colonel," said Lessing, gauging Reed's silence carefully. "Bring your men to Hostau. We won't shoot at your soldiers. We're practically unarmed. Come with your unit and occupy the stud."[11]

Reed grimaced. It sounded like a damned fool proposal. Though General Patton and Third Army command was turning a blind eye to the rescue operation,[12] Reed knew that elements of two Panzer divisions were in the general area, along with a miscellany of shattered units and local defense battalions, not to mention diehard SS. Captain Sperl had been lucky not to have faced more serious opposition during the extraction of the Dienststelle Ost personnel and files.

Reed said nothing for a few seconds, his mind racing through the scenarios that surrounded the problem. After a while, he spoke again.

"I'm sorry, I can't do that, Captain," replied Reed honestly. "For one thing, I'm not allowed. You see, the United States has an agreement with the Russians. The area where you are situated is to become part of the Russian zone. Our operations are limited to other sectors of the line."[13]

Lessing was not to be dissuaded. He told Reed that his decision came down to a simple choice. Either the Americans went to Hostau, or the Soviets would kill the horses—and, based on the horrific stories that he had heard from refugees, most likely the German staff as well and perhaps even the POWs who worked alongside them. It was virtually the same story that Colonel Holters had told Reed.

Tough calls were the price of higher rank, and Reed was never one to shy away from a difficult decision. He sat back and gave the matter some more thought while Lessing waited anxiously.

"I have a suggestion, Captain," replied Reed. "I'll give you one of my best officers, Captain Stewart. He can return with you to Hostau and he can negotiate with your Colonel Rudofsky and we can see if there are any possibilities to find some way to get the horses under American control."[14]

Lessing initially demurred, requesting that a more senior officer of field rank, at least a major, should be sent. Reed could not spare any, and anyway, the officer sent would need to be a competent rider. Stewart was ideal in this regard. "Since I was only a captain at the time," Stewart was to write, "I suggest that my selection for the job points more to the fact that our majors and lieutenant colonels were not expendable than to any diplomatic prowess on my part."[15]

Finally Captain Lessing agreed to Reed's proposal to send Stewart, reaching across the table to shake the colonel's hand. A bridge had at last been crossed.

*

"*Herr General*, this *is* a surprise," said Colonel Rudofsky, saluting stiffly. Since Dr. Lessing had left on his secret mission much had changed at Hostau.

"Where are your veterinarians?" said Brigadier General Schulz irritably and without preamble, returning the salute. "You have two, do you not?" The general had recently been appointed to command the remaining local defense forces covering this sector of Wehrkreis XIII, the military district in this part of the Reich.[16] He had established his command post in Hostau Castle, where the stud also had its offices.

Schulz had had a bad run of luck lately. Since being appointed to Wehrkreis XIII he had had to retreat on several occasions as his threadbare defense units had been defeated or pushed further into Czechoslovakia from Bavaria. One of his last actions before arriving at Hostau had been a doomed defense of Vohenstrauss, ironically Colonel Reed's new headquarters. Schulz had managed to gather just seventeen men to fend off the American thrust at Vohenstrauss, personally leading the defense. By some form of miracle the general and his half-platoon of veterans and raw recruits had held up the Americans for a day, buying time for higher headquarters to establish fresh blocking positions on the border. Schulz had narrowly avoided being taken prisoner by Reed's men.[17]

Now Schulz was at Hostau, commanding one reorganized battalion and the remaining regional defense troops in the sector west of Weissensulz and Hostau.[18]

Rudofsky answered Schulz's question concerning his veterinary surgeons, a sick feeling of worry in his stomach. "They are probably on the farms to treat horses there."

"When they come back, report to me!" hissed Schulz.

"Yes, *Herr General!*" barked Rudofsky, more than a little confused as to why this infantry officer was interested in two veterinary surgeons.

"Report as soon as the officers are here," repeated Schulz darkly.

"Yes, *Herr General!*"

Alarmingly, Rudofsky had recently discovered that Dr. Kroll had left the stud without orders and gone out looking for his friend Lessing, leaving Hostau bereft of any veterinary surgeons.

"That will be all, Colonel. *Heil Hitler!*" said Schulz in a bored tone, raising his arm in a half-hearted Nazi salute.

"*Heil Hitler!*" barked Rudofsky, crashing his heels together as his right arm snapped out in the "German Greeting" that had become mandatory in the Wehrmacht since the failed bomb plot against Hitler at the Wolf's Lair the year before.

*

Colonel Reed was sitting at a folding writing desk doing paperwork when Captain Stewart entered.

"Tom," said Reed, "thanks for coming." Also in the room were two regimental staff officers, Major Alexander Fraser and Major John Likes, along with Captain Sperl and Dr. Lessing.[19]

Reed looked closely at Captain Thomas M. Stewart, the 42nd Cavalry Squadron's S-2, or military intelligence officer. Of average height but strong-looking, his brown hair was cut short and his face was very pale. His eyes had dark smudges of exhaustion beneath them, and weariness was etched deeply into his young face. *My God*, thought Reed, *this boy's had a rough time of it and no mistake*. And the truth was that Stewart, like so many of the young men of the 42nd, *was* exhausted, both physically and mentally. Too many men had been lost and the survivors had suffered many near misses. Their nerves were in tatters after weeks of intense combat.

"Take a seat," said Reed. "Smoke?"

"Thanks, sir," replied Stewart, taking the proffered cigarette, flipping a Zippo lighter to its tip.

"How are you feeling?" asked Reed in a fatherly tone.

"Fine, Colonel," replied Stewart lightly. He didn't look fine, but then again who among them did, thought Reed. He decided to cut to the chase.

"This is Captain Lessing," said Reed. Lessing smiled and nodded. Stewart stared back at him blankly.

"I've asked you here because I have a problem that I think you could help me with," opened Reed.

"I see, sir," replied Stewart without emotion.

"We recently captured a German air force colonel who told us a rather extraordinary story," said Reed. For the next few minutes

Reed outlined what Colonel Holters had said about the horses and POWs at the Hostau Stud, and the grave danger that they were in. He also explained Lessing's role in the story. Stewart perked up a little when Reed described the horses. Stewart, scion of an old Scots-Irish family from Winchester, Tennessee, and the son of a senator, undoubtedly shared Reed's passion for horses. Reed was now determined to bend that passion to his own purposes. A graduate of Sewanee Military Academy and the University of the South, Stewart was rather a bookish sort but possessed of a sharp sense of humor that made him popular with his brother officers and the enlisted men.

"The thing is, Tom, I need an officer to go back to Hostau with Captain Lessing here and negotiate with the German CO," said Reed. "I'm not ordering you to go, you understand?"[20]

Stewart understood. He knew Reed well enough to know that this was not a decision that he would have taken lightly. Stewart was the squadron's intelligence officer, so he was a natural choice. And after listening to the story of the stud and the perilous situation it faced, he also understood the urgency of the mission.

"I'm not going to downplay the danger, Tom," said Reed. "Between our lines and Hostau there are a lot of Krauts who haven't yet got the news that they've lost the war. I also can't send any of our guys with you, so you'd be completely on your own in Indian country."[21] Stewart's facial expression didn't change.

"What are my orders, sir?"

"The objective is quite simple," continued Reed in a conversational tone. "Negotiate the peaceful surrender of the horse depot." Reed spent a few minutes outlining how Stewart should deal with the negotiations, before he added ominously: "Be careful. If you give any sign that you understand German, the results might be fatal."[22] Stewart understood perfectly. The Germans were nervous and jumpy and would be less inclined to discuss the issue in his presence if they felt that Stewart was gathering covert intelligence on them or the military situation around Hostau. Stewart took a long final drag on his cigarette before crushing it out in an empty tin can.

Reed turned to Lessing. He made it abundantly clear that Stewart must be returned to American lines within twenty-four hours or Reed and his unit would come looking for him, and a lot of Germans might die.

Tom Stewart dressed in the smartest uniform that his brother officers could scrape together, including a rather ill-fitting service jacket.[23] It was important that Stewart look "official" and it was the best that could be managed in the field. Major Alexander Fraser, Captain Sperl and Major John Likes carefully prepared German-language notes explaining Stewart's position as an emissary, as Dr. Lessing had warned Reed that the American would have to pass through German checkpoints to reach the stud.[24] They read:

> The bearer of this letter, Captain THOMAS STEWART is an emissary to Col. RUDOFSKY and has my authority to arrange the handover to the American Authorities of the horses in the vicinity of HOSTAU. He is sent through the lines as an emissary under the protection of Stabsveterinär LESSING, representative of Col. RUDOFSKY who I am returning through my lines. Charles H. Reed, Colonel, Cavalry Commanding.[25]

Lessing and Stewart then returned to the 42nd Squadron headquarters, which, according to Stewart, was abuzz with the news that Stewart was going to meet a German general.[26] But the atmosphere was soured somewhat by the 42nd's commander, Lieutenant Colonel Hargis, who placed a paternal hand on Stewart's shoulder. "You know, you don't have to go,"[27] murmured Hargis glumly. It didn't exactly inspire confidence.

*

At Hostau, Colonel Rudofsky was suddenly summoned again to General Schulz's office an hour after his first probing interview.

"So, where are your veterinarians?" demanded Schulz, his voice hostile.

"Well, I have not seen them," replied Rudofsky warily. "They must be out in the villages treating cows, or horses or pigs. There is no veterinarian in Hostau, our veterinarian, whom we had here, is incarcerated, and …" but before Rudofsky could finish his sentence Schulz cut him off.

"You are dismissed!" barked the general in an impatient tone. Rudofsky stumbled outside, fearful that Schulz had discovered the reason for Lessing and Kroll's absences from their posts. With his hands shaking and his stomach in a knot of nervous tension, Rudofsky stalked off to his own office, his mind turning over the problem. He was also very concerned by news from the Eastern Front—Soviet forces were definitely threatening Pilsen, less than fifty miles east. Any serious breakthrough and T-34 tanks could be coming over the nearby hills in only a day or two.

CHAPTER 7

Duty

*"I am here first and foremost for the horses. And it is
my duty to do everything possible to save them."*

Captain Dr. Rudolf Lessing

Tom Stewart and Rudolf Lessing had begun walking through
the Bohemian Forest late on the evening of April 26, 1945,
their breath pluming in the chill air, their path lit by a bright moon
that emerged from time to time from behind scudding clouds.[1] The
road was a ribbon of moonlight in the dark forest.[2] Stewart felt very
exposed, his right hand often falling to his only protection, a holstered
World War I .38 cal. revolver on his belt, referred to by his men as
Stewart's "Assault Gun."[3] He glanced at his companion. Lessing wore
his field-gray officer's uniform and cap, a Luger pistol in a brown
leather holster at his waist, his black jackboots crunching along the
hilly path. Stewart didn't know why, but he thought he could trust
this particular German. The affable Lessing had a quiet dignity about
him that others soon noticed. He had certainly impressed Colonel
Reed, and Reed's judgment was always sound. Dr. Lessing was keen
to get on as quickly as possible, Colonel Reed's twenty-four-hour
deadline for Stewart's safe return at the forefront of his mind.

Stewart looked about him as he trudged on. The forest on each side
of the path was of dense Norway spruce. It brought to mind Grimm's
fairy tales, which had sent him scurrying beneath the blankets in fear
as a young child. God alone knew what might be hiding in those trees
waiting to ambush them. Every rustle of a branch, creak of a trunk or

the sudden bolting of some nocturnal animal set his heart racing. Nine months of combat had honed his senses to a razor point. Normally any sound this close to the enemy lines would have sent him diving for cover, thumbing off the safety to his carbine as he did so. But now his fate was in the hands of this German officer whom he'd only just met. Until an hour ago they had been dread enemies.

Stewart tried not to think of what might happen should they run into an SS patrol—waving a piece of paper in the faces of the Third Reich's most loyal and brutal troops would probably not save them both from a bullet in the back of the head. Stewart continued along the path. *Add some snow*, he thought, *and I could be back in the Ardennes*. He shivered a little at the thought. The 2nd Cavalry Group had had a rough time of it during the Battle of the Bulge, and Stewart's outfit had suffered badly along with everyone else.

After a few miles Lessing suddenly stopped, raising his hand to Stewart. He began looking around the immediate vicinity, seemingly searching for something. Stewart tensed and waited, his hand hovering over his holster, until Lessing whispered for him to come closer. Lessing pointed behind a thick tree.

"Transport, Captain," he said in a fierce whisper, smiling. Stewart relaxed a little. It was a gray-painted army motorcycle propped against the tree.[4] The two men climbed aboard, Stewart riding pillion. Lessing kicked the bike to life, the noise of the engine sounding loud enough to wake the dead in the silent forest, but before Stewart could complain they were off, bouncing along the muddy track, the bike's blackout-screened headlamp throwing out a feeble light that barely illuminated the trees that rushed past on either side.

After a while there came the sound of an airplane overhead, the drone audible above the motorcycle's engines. Lessing pulled up abruptly and switched off the ignition and cut the headlamp.

"That isn't necessary," whispered Stewart over Lessing's shoulder, "it is only your old 'Bedcheck Charlie'—we've long since stopped paying attention to it."[5] Stewart was referring to a German light aircraft which had been droning harmlessly over the American positions every night for some days. But Lessing was not convinced.

"You are mistaken," said Lessing, "it is one of yours and they will strike at anything."[6] Lessing's fear was common enough among German troops in the last weeks of the war, as Allied fighter-bombers prowled the skies over enemy lines virtually with impunity, shooting up trains, convoys, individual vehicles and troop concentrations. The Germans had come to fear and loathe the "*Jabos*" that dealt death from above.

Stewart decided not to argue with Lessing, and they waited until the plane's engine disappeared into the distance before Lessing kicked the bike back into life.

Lessing and Stewart rode quickly to the forester's hut. The forester greeted them both warmly and, lighting their way with an old lantern, led them round to the barn where Stewart could make out two horses standing in the gloom. The smell was reassuring: the comforting odors of hay, horse and polished leather tackle.[7]

"We go now, Captain," said Lessing urgently, as he led out a large chestnut thoroughbred and quickly mounted up. He indicated to Stewart that he should take the other horse. Stewart would ride a rare jet-black Lipizzaner stallion, broad-chested and standing around fifteen hands. "As I approached to check the cinch [the girth for a Western-style saddle], he became very unruly," recalled Stewart, "as if auditioning for Leigh's mustang. There in the lantern light, my companion remained silent. I resolved to mount without a stirrup, hold leather, and if tossed, try to land in the hay." He needn't have worried. "Once mounted, he became as quiet as a lady's palfrey. I later learned that he put on the wild act for any new rider."[8]

Once Stewart was mounted, the American could feel how responsive and well trained the animal was. "I have never ridden a horse more responsive to leg pressure and the lifting of one's body weight. The bridle was almost unnecessary."[9]

"He is a special horse, Captain," said Lessing quietly as he reined in beside him. "He was the favorite of King Peter of Yugoslavia."[10] Stewart grinned and then trotted after Lessing. For the first time since arriving in Europe he felt like a proper cavalryman. And to be riding a royal horse, no less, well, that was just the limit.

As they made their way steadily through the forest, Stewart realized that he had never felt this connected to a horse before—it was as if the animal was reading his mind, such were its delicate and careful movements. The road ahead was dark, with a steep tree-covered embankment on one side and a black sheer drop on the other. "The forest was so thick through there you felt like you were riding through two walls of darkness,"[11] recalled Stewart.

Suddenly, blocking the road was an abatis, a barrier made of sharpened stakes that would have looked more at home on a medieval battlefield than in a quiet Czech country lane in April 1945. "I rode up and observed that it was not more than three feet high on the side next to the cliff and only some six to eight feet wide,"[12] wrote Stewart. However, the Germans often booby-trapped such obstacles with mines or stick grenades. Stewart reined in the Lipizzaner stallion and stared at the barrier. He knew he was going to jump—it was just instinctive after so much hard riding across Tennessee in his youth. He had to do this. "Backing off, with head up and hands low in my best imitation of the cavalry school's forward seat, I committed us to the barrier ..."[13] Stewart's mouth was beside one of the Lipizzaner's large ears, one gloved hand resting on the animal's black neck.

"We're going to do this, boy," Stewart whispered in his warm Southern drawl, the horse's ears flicking back as he spoke. "You ready?" Stewart patted the Lipizzaner's neck before touching his heels to the horse's belly. The stallion, his breath pluming from his big nostrils like a steam engine in the chilly night air, took off like a rocket, charging down the distance to the abatis. Stewart barely heard Rudolf Lessing shout out a warning. "He doesn't jump!"[14] yelled the German, before Stewart and the stallion were airborne, sailing over the wickedly sharp stakes to land with Olympic precision on the other side.

"He did jump, though," recalled Stewart, "and with a stretch of at least three feet to spare."[15] Dr. Lessing sat on his big chestnut Arab shaking his head. It was true what they said—all Americans were cowboys at heart.

After Stewart had jumped, the more cautious Lessing worked his way around the abatis over the high ground on their left, before they both set off once more for Hostau.[16]

*

Stewart glanced at the luminous face of his watch. It was 2am on April 27, 1945. Dr. Lessing reined in his horse and pointed along the road, which sloped down and through open fields towards a cluster of two- and three-storey buildings and a tall church spire in the moonlight. The moonlight reflected off the sloping roofs of the houses, giving the whole place the look of a large model, somewhat unreal and as quiet as the grave.

"Hostau," whispered the German veterinarian. Stewart stiffened in his saddle and nodded.[17] He involuntarily touched his breast pocket where the "official" letter of introduction from Colonel Reed was safely stowed. It was showtime. He took a deep breath to calm his nerves and urged his mount into a trot as he followed Lessing towards the unknown.

At the first checkpoint before entering Hostau, Dr. Lessing reined in his horse, handed the German sentry his identity papers and explained his business. The sentry was hardly able to tear his eyes off the American officer sitting astride the beautiful black stallion; much to Lessing's amusement, Stewart rode "Western-style," with the reins in one hand just like a cowboy. The sentry checked Lessing's credentials by torchlight and then gave him the road.

As Stewart rode on he could clearly see General Schulz's defensive preparations around the town. The moonlight illuminated German soldiers in slit trenches dug behind barbed-wire entanglements or sandbagged machine-gun nests, the muzzles of fast-firing MG42s poking threateningly out, with the occasional glow of a cigarette breaking the monochrome of the night. Stewart's military eye took careful note of the scattered defenses and he was relieved not to see any tanks or self-propelled guns.

Passing through the town, the two men rode up the steep main street towards the stud opposite the castle. As Stewart approached, his first impression was of ordered stable blocks and paddocks, and huge numbers of horses grazing under the moonlight. It was eerily quiet when the two men rode up to Lessing's quarters and stiffly dismounted. The door opened and out stepped a German officer— Stewart reacted instinctively when he saw the black MP40 machine pistol that the German cradled in his hands, reaching for his holstered .38.[18] But before Stewart could draw his revolver, the German offered his hand.

"This is my colleague, Dr. Kroll," explained Lessing quickly.

Gustav Kroll nodded and shook Stewart's hand, his face a mask of concern. He had abandoned trying to find Lessing and had returned to Hostau some time earlier. Lessing took Kroll aside and the two men talked hurriedly in urgent whispers. Then Lessing's pretty young wife appeared. Speaking in German, she told her husband that he must go immediately to see Colonel Rudofsky. Everything at Hostau had changed.

After hearing about the arrival of General Schulz from Kroll, Lessing was understandably worried. It looked as though the plan to rescue the horses could be in peril because of Schulz's presence. "I'm sorry, Captain, but you must remain in my quarters until I have spoken to my senior commanders," Lessing said to Stewart. "My wife will hide you." He spoke again to his wife in German, and the young woman quickly ushered Stewart into the darkened house.[19] Lessing would decide later if it were safe to bring an American officer before Schulz.

When he met with Colonel Rudofsky, the stud commander told Lessing that Schulz intended to defend the town from the enemy, to the death if necessary. Lessing knew about the earlier defense preparations, but until the arrival of Schulz he had not believed that they would actually be used in anger. Surely they were for show—another pointless propaganda exercise to instill belief in the people? Lessing rounded on Rudofsky and in no uncertain words told him that Schulz's plan was total madness. The troops were too few in number or quality and they lacked sufficient heavy support weapons or armor. Any defense would mean the end of most of the horses as well. He also told Rudofsky that Colonel Reed had offered to help save the horses. Rudofsky, a blank look of resignation across his face, threw up his arms in frustration. Events were moving beyond his immediate control.

"My hands are tied, Lessing," he responded angrily. "If I try to negotiate with the Americans, or let on that one of them is here, then all three of us risk being shot for treason."[20] Lessing pressed him further. Rudofsky finished by suggesting that Lessing tell Schulz everything himself. They could only hope that the general would listen to reason.

Lessing returned to his quarters and informed Stewart that things were not looking good. There was every chance that Stewart would end up as a prisoner-of-war rather than as US Army "plenipotentiary." Lessing's wife was deeply alarmed for her husband's safety, and as he made to leave to meet Schulz, she kissed him passionately and held on to him for a few moments, unsure whether she would see him alive again. Lessing knew that Schulz was well within his rights to have him shot for treason or handed over to the Gestapo as a traitor to the Reich. But Lessing's duty to the horses that he had so assiduously cared for was uppermost in his mind. He had to change their fate, and he wouldn't rest until he had done so. He was also equally determined to ensure that his family would not fall into the hands of the Soviets. In this regard, he would have the backing of every German at the stud.

When Captain Lessing stepped into General Schulz's office in the castle his worst fears were confirmed. The general was almost hopping mad. He shouted and railed at Lessing, calling him a traitor several times and threatening to have him hanged or shot for opening negotiations with the Americans. He lectured him on obedience and discipline. Lessing stood rooted to the spot, a mounting fury growing inside of him, until he could contain himself no longer. In an extraordinary breach of military protocol, Lessing also exploded in anger.

"Obedience, *Herr General*, discipline?" yelled Lessing, his uniform spattered with mud, his face grimy from his long and difficult mission. The outburst cut Schulz off mid-flow, the general open-mouthed at the younger officer's audacity.

"*I* cherish those things!" roared Lessing. "But *I* am here first and foremost for the horses. And it is my duty to do *everything* possible to save them." Hardly pausing for breath, Lessing continued to rail at Schulz. "It is no longer a question of winning the war—if we were going to do that we should have done it four years ago. Now it's too late!"[21] Lessing's treasonable words reverberated off the office's walls. In the outer office several staff officers stood listening to the exchange through the closed door, casting alarmed glances at one another. Lessing's blood was up and his tired eyes burned with a fury he himself hadn't thought he possessed. He almost dared Schulz to pronounce judgment upon him. Lessing felt almost purged—the Nazi propaganda and lies had been hard for an intelligent person to stand, and he had finally given full vent to his frustrations.

When he finished, the atmosphere in the office was one of ominous and dread silence. Lessing stood rooted to the spot, blood pumping in his ears, waiting for Schulz to do something. Instead of screaming for the captain's immediate arrest, the general simply stared back at him, his gaze blank and confused. He had probably never been spoken to in such a manner before. Perhaps he feared that others of his staff shared Lessing's unorthodox opinions about the future course of the war, or that the men that he was intent on pitching into an unwinnable battle in defense of Hostau were also flirting with disobedience, even mutiny. Schulz sank slowly down into his desk chair and said nothing. Lessing, slightly out of breath, stared at him, his hands clenched into fists by his sides.

After a pause that seemed to last for several minutes, Schulz spoke again, this time in a low and exhausted voice. "Well … *maybe* you're right," he said slowly. But some of his old spirit quickly returned. "But only the corps commander can decide this," he muttered. "I have to bring it before him."[22] And once again that would mean Lessing doing all the work.

The meeting over, Dr. Lessing glanced at his watch, grimaced and muttered an oath beneath his breath. Wehrkreis XIII Headquarters was at Schloss Gibacht, the ancient castle of Prince Windisch-Grätz, located just outside the town of Kladrau,* twenty-four miles from Hostau.[23] Lessing realized that he was in danger of not fulfilling Colonel Reed's deadline for the return of Stewart. Fortunately, Dr. Kroll bravely volunteered to take a stallion and ride to the US lines and explain the situation personally to Reed. After completing this mission, Kroll planned to ride back to the forester's hut and wait for Lessing and Stewart.

In the meantime, Lessing briefed Stewart about the situation and told him to remain in hiding. Stewart would spend hours in a back room in Lessing's quarters, drinking coffee and wondering whether he was less of a plenipotentiary than a prisoner-of-war. Lessing marched outside to where Kroll had procured transport for his mission. He mounted an army motorcycle combination and set off, determined to make the commanding general at Schloss Gibacht see sense.

---

* Now Kladruby.

CHAPTER 8

"*Adolf ist Kaput!*"

"The war is not yet lost!"

Lieutenant General Karl Weisenberger

When he arrived at Schloss Gibacht, now used as German regional headquarters, Dr. Lessing parked his motorcycle outside the main entrance, showed his pass to the guards and then marched directly into the entrance hall, his boots ringing on the flagstone floor. He was directed up the grand staircase to see Lieutenant Colonel Trost, a staff officer, who after a hurried conversation appeared to grasp the significance of Lessing's mission. Trost quickly ushered Lessing in to see the commanding general.

Lieutenant General Karl Weisenberger, a tough-looking 64-year-old who wore steel-rimmed glasses and sported a severe iron-gray short back and sides haircut, was the German general who had been handed the unenviable task of trying to fend off General Patton's probes into the border area between Germany and Czechoslovakia. Wehrkreis XIII initially had been so short of equipment that not a single artillery gun was available.[1] But it was feared that Patton might yet strike east directly into Czechoslovakia, maybe even towards the important cities of Pilsen and Prague. The borderlands had to be held—at any cost.

Weisenberger sat hatless behind his large wooden desk, a Knight's Cross, Germany's highest decoration for gallantry, at his throat. Hitler had bestowed it on him personally in 1940 during the French Campaign. On his right breast pocket was pinned the German

Cross in Gold, awarded for the other French campaign, the bloody battle for Normandy in August 1944. The Führer glowered down at Weisenberger and Lessing from a large oil portrait on the office wall, his light gray eyes appearing to frown on the strange little meeting, as they did in every military and Party office across what remained of the Third Reich.

Not that the flesh-and-blood Führer now bore much resemblance to his heroic portraits. If Lessing and Weisenberger could see the man who now shuffled about the gray concrete corridors of his bunker, forty feet beneath the bomb-cratered Reich Chancellery garden in Berlin, they would have seen a shambling, food-stained, rheumy-eyed wreck, stooped and prematurely aged by illness, fatigue and military defeat. Yet the Führer had determined to fight to the last, his daily military situation conferences growing more stressful and pointless each time the generals and Party leaders appeared before him. Up above, the Red Army had encircled the Reich capital and was fighting its way grimly through the ravaged city towards Hitler's last bolthole. Large German formations were already surrendering across the Reich, while on what remained of the Eastern Front others sought to disobey Hitler's orders and disengage from the fight against the Soviets to try to reach the British or American lines, there to surrender.

Standing beside Weisenberger's desk holding a sheaf of papers was his harried chief of staff, Colonel Götz Benneke. Outside, telephones rang constantly and teleprinters rattled out orders and reports like machine guns. Harassed staff officers dashed about with files in their hands. The information that trickled in from the front was confused and discouraging. The German Seventh Army, the force assigned to defend Czechoslovakia, had only depleted and battle-worn units. They were doing what they could to slow the Soviet encirclement of Prague, but it was a losing battle and everyone knew it. A strong push by the Red Army and its T-34 tank columns would be loose in the relatively flat land between Prague and Hostau and the horse stud. Weisenberger's task was not to fight the Soviets; he was to prevent incursions into western Czechoslovakia by the Americans—effectively to guard the back door.

Before Dr. Lessing had arrived, Weisenberger had been in conference with Colonel Benneke, discussing the current state of the defenses in his region. There had finally been a little good news concerning artillery. Some 150mm Howitzers had been discovered in the Skoda Works in Pilsen and assigned to Weisenberger's command along with a regiment of two battalions of infantry sent as reinforcements. Some new battalions had been formed from stragglers and four battalions made up from unemployed Luftwaffe ground personnel from local air bases, though they were not trained in infantry tactics. The experienced Engineer Brigade 655 had been subordinated to Weisenberger's front, extending his line three miles to the north.[2] General Schulz's battlegroup had not been reinforced and remained emplaced in the sector west of Weissensulz and Hostau.[3] Colonel Baer's Ski Infantry Battalion still covered Waier, Stockau and the entrances to the Bohemian Forest west of Taus.[4]

But news had also arrived that morale appeared to be deteriorating markedly. Weisenberger blamed the fact that these units had been cobbled together from stragglers or battle-broken formations. "The men didn't know each other nor their officers, and all age groups and all degrees of training were represented."[5] Baer had recently telephoned from his command post to report that desertions had reduced his battalion to no more than a company in strength. Weisenberger was also concerned at what would happen when the Luftwaffe combat units were committed to action—they would probably not last very long against battle-hardened American soldiers.[6]

Dr. Lessing stood stiffly before Weisenberger's desk, his cap tucked under his left arm, and repeated his story once again, but he noticed how Weisenberger's exhaustion-ringed blue eyes grew suddenly wider behind his spectacles as Lessing recounted the American offer, and his feelings about the pointlessness of continuing the war when Germany had so evidently lost.[7] Weisenberger suddenly slammed his fist down on his desk hard, making his pen tray jump, cutting Lessing off mid-sentence.

"You can't just go out on your own and begin negotiations for surrender with the Americans," he barked in a horrified tone. "The war is not yet lost!"[8] Lessing thought that Weisenberger knew far better than he the parlous nature of the German position, but Lessing refused to believe that the Red Army or the Americans were going to be stopped by Schulz's ragtag assortment of battle-shattered units and elderly reservists and Volkssturm at Weissensulz and Hostau. Lessing knew that all along the line about one thousand German soldiers *a day* were giving themselves up to Patton's Third Army alone, desperate to avoid being taken prisoner by the Soviets. No one was keen on dying for Hitler at this stage, with the exception of some of the Waffen-SS.

Lessing, exhausted and increasingly frustrated by the reckless and misguided attitudes of his superiors, stood his ground and as with General Schulz, he impertinently challenged Weisenberger's comment that the war was not yet lost.

"Really, General?" demanded Lessing, the old fury rising in him once more. "'Berlin remains German'; 'Vienna will be German again'—we heard it only recently on the wireless. But … do *you* believe that? I do not: I've been listening to such beautiful sayings for twelve years." Weisenberger looked horrified. "What we do here is madness!" continued Lessing. "Shall we continue with this madness, and now, at the end, destroy all that has hitherto remained whole?"[9]

Lessing fell silent, his right hand tightly clenched around his gloves. Weisenberger had gone pale, and said nothing for a minute, as he mulled over Lessing's impassioned words. Lessing knew that the interview could only go one of two ways—either the old campaigner would give him what he wanted concerning saving the horses, or he would order Lessing's immediate execution for defeatism.

"All right," said Weisenberger slowly, after a heavily pregnant pause, "do what you should, Captain."[10] Weisenberger evidently had more pressing matters to attend to than arguing horses with this angry young veterinarian.

"Well, what are you waiting for?" growled Weisenberger, when Lessing didn't move, his iron Prussian composure returning. "What *more* do you want?"

Lessing knew the military mind, and he knew Schulz's potential to still derail the operation. He insisted that Weisenberger, as the commanding general, give him official permission in writing.

"I cannot give you a written order," countered Weisenberger, clearly reluctant to commit treason to paper. "That is a matter for General Schulz. He is the responsible sector commander. So we will not pass over his head." Lessing began to speak, but Weisenberger cut him off by raising his hand. "But I'll call him," said the general patiently. "Send the American captain back to this Colonel Reed and let him tell him to come in God's name and occupy the stud. We will not shoot."[11]

As Lessing was leaving the castle Colonel Benneke caught up with him and unexpectedly thrust a piece of paper into his hand. Weisenberger had changed his mind and put something in writing informing Schulz that the matter of the horses was his responsibility. The ball was now firmly in Schulz's court. Now it was just a question of convincing Schulz to take responsibility for the surrender of Hostau and its stud.

Lessing kicked the motorcycle combination into life in the castle courtyard and left, his back wheel spraying gravel in all directions as he gunned the engine. He sped back to Hostau as fast as he could, knowing that with each delay the Red Army came closer to the stud and its precious horses.

*

Before Lessing took Captain Stewart to meet with General Schulz at Hostau Castle, the two men decided to conduct a brief reconnaissance ride around the district. As they walked across the yard from Lessing's quarters to fetch their horses, a small group of eight or ten children were playing outside the stables, little kids of elementary school age. They were the children of the German staff. As the two adults approached, the children ceased their games and almost as one their right arms shot out and they yelled "*Heil Hitler!*" All but one little blonde girl at the very end of the line who didn't raise her arm in the German greeting, but who very politely said "*Grüss Gott*" ("Good day").[12] Lessing stopped and placed his hand affectionately on the little girl's head.

"My daughter Karen," he said to Stewart, his face beaming with paternal love. It was becoming increasingly obvious why Dr. Lessing was so keen to cooperate with the Americans.

After mounting up, Lessing and Stewart rode around the vicinity of Hostau. As they turned on to a country lane, slightly sunken with high thickets of greenery at the sides, they stumbled upon an extraordinary sight. Resting on both banks of the road were hundreds of Allied prisoners-of-war, mostly British and Americans. They were all very thin, their uniforms dirty and patched, and each man had at his feet a pathetic bundle containing his few worldly possessions. A few German guards, middle-aged men on reserve duty, were watching over them. When the prisoners spotted Stewart in his American uniform astride the great black horse, they surged forward, thinking that the relief had come—that they were finally free. But Stewart could only hold up his hand to calm and quiet them as his horse shuffled nervously.

"Delay your departure for as long as possible," Stewart shouted at the crowd of expectant faces. "Our troops will be coming through tomorrow."[13] The thin faces lit up at Stewart's words, but he could only hope that he wasn't giving these desperate men false hope.

*

When Tom Stewart stepped into General Schulz's office at Hostau Castle, accompanied by a weary Dr. Lessing, he was immediately struck by the German general's exhausted look. The stress of the past few weeks had made Schulz's disposition brittle and explosive, as Rudofsky had already discovered. Stewart wasn't that impressed with Schulz, writing that he was a "small, unprepossessing man seated behind a bare table."[14] Schulz was wearing a field-gray uniform with the red and gold collar tabs of a German general, his receding hair slicked back from his heavily lined forehead. The Iron Cross First Class was pinned to his left breast pocket along with a Wound Badge and an Infantry Assault Badge. These were combat decorations won the hard way. But Stewart's eyes were also drawn to the small round red badge emblazoned with a black swastika. Schulz was a Nazi Party member. So he was both a warrior *and* an ideologue. This could be a dangerous combination. Schulz's flinty eyes signaled wariness and annoyance. Arrayed behind the general were four immaculately uniformed German officers, including Colonel Rudofsky.

"General, sir, I'm Captain Thomas Stewart, 42nd Cavalry Reconnaissance Squadron, 2nd Cavalry Group, Twelve Corps, United States Third Army," announced the American, his voice a little shaky with nerves. He felt out of his league. He was only thirty, and was no trained diplomat or negotiator, just a junior combat officer. He snapped out a regulation salute as he spoke.

Schulz said nothing, and he didn't offer his hand. Lessing stepped forward and asked Stewart to sketch out the idea of turning the horses over to the Americans, as Colonel Reed had offered, Lessing translating Stewart's words for the general and his staff officers. Stewart then produced the document signed by Reed and placed it on the table in front of Schulz. The general briefly perused it before he turned to his officers and began an animated discussion. Stewart listened but Reed had expressly forbidden him from revealing that he spoke and understood some German.[15] It seemed that Schulz was particularly upset that Stewart had seen some of the military defenses as he had ridden into Hostau town. There was a discussion as to whether Stewart should even be allowed to leave, and for one awful moment Stewart thought that he was destined to spend the last weeks of the war a prisoner.

Things turned momentarily ugly when Schulz's chief of staff, a tall, blond, haughty-looking colonel, turned from the group and sneered at Lessing, accusing him of being an American agent. Lessing, outraged and incensed, shouted back: "Sir, I am *no* spy. I am a German officer."[16] Both men angrily took a step towards each other. Schulz quickly interjected, gruffly ordering the two Germans to cease and desist with such nonsense and gestured to Captain Stewart that he should sit. Through Lessing, Schulz told Stewart that they agreed on two things, that the horses should be saved, and human life preserved. But he still seemed hesitant to fully commit himself to the plan.

"We are aware that your reputation could be at stake and we don't want to do anything to jeopardize your standing in the army, or our intention of saving these horses from falling into the hands of the Russians," said Stewart, carefully trying to mollify a reluctant Schulz.

"How many Panzers can you bring, Captain?" Schulz asked suddenly in heavily accented though good English. Stewart was caught off-guard by the direct question and thought for a moment.

"You name the number, we are flexible; we can bring any number,"[17] replied Stewart confidently.

Schulz turned and conferred again with his officers, one commenting that Hitler had promised them a secret weapon. Others made *"Adolf ist kaput"* comments that seemed to bring general agreement among them.[18]

Schulz turned back from his officers and looked pointedly at Stewart for some time without speaking. Then the general sighed, nodded curtly, leaned forward and grabbed a pen and a pad of headed paper. He dipped the pen in a small inkpot and proceeded to scribble a note. He signed his name and then, using a Nazi eagle stamp, marked his signature in the official manner. Then he slid the piece of paper across the desk to Stewart. It was a safe conduct pass that would allow Stewart through Schulz's lines without hindrance. Then Schulz stood, smoothed his uniform and pulled on his service cap. Stewart also stood.

"Captain," said Schulz in a low voice.

"General," replied Stewart, saluting again. Schulz's right arm shot out in the Nazi salute, then he turned on his heels and stalked out of the office followed by his officers.

Stewart relaxed a little, letting out a long breath. Lessing stood beside him, twisting his riding gloves in his hands nervously. After a few minutes the chief of staff and another colonel entered the office once again.

"General Schulz has decided that there will be no defense of Hostau and the stud,"[19] he said stiffly to Stewart. "But, Captain, this *only* applies to the Wehrmacht. The SS are not under our control. We *cannot* vouch for their actions."

Stewart was worried—"unanswered was the question of whether we would have to fight our way through the first line of defenses,"[20] he wrote, referring to the German units emplaced at the border and in towns and villages along the road to Hostau.

Stewart thanked the colonel. He and Lessing had done it. The Americans had official German permission from both the enemy zone and district commanders to mount a local rescue operation. But Stewart knew all too well that the omission of the Waffen-SS from the deal, along with any Wehrmacht forces beyond the immediate vicinity of Hostau, was significant. The Germans clearly had no intention of opening a gap in their lines that Patton could exploit militarily.

It was time for Stewart and Lessing to return to the American lines to brief Colonel Reed. But Lessing was concerned that Stewart was exposed traveling through miles of German territory still full of hostile troops. He handed the American a German field cap and a camouflaged rain cape to wear over his uniform. From a distance the disguise might work. Lessing started the motorcycle, Stewart clambering into the sidecar, and off they went, hurtling at full speed down damp forest lanes, heading west to freedom.[21]

*

The 27th of April 1945 had proved a busy day for the 42nd Squadron. While Captain Stewart had been away on his mission, fighting had erupted at several locations along the front line. Troops A and C held the positions that they had occupied on the 26th, but reports began to flow back to Reed via the 42nd's CO Lieutenant Colonel Hargis that the enemy had in place considerable defensive positions. Even more ominously, patrols were also reporting engine sounds, including those of tanks or self-propelled guns, clanking and rattling unseen in the distance like prehistoric monsters.

Hargis decided to confirm what was happening by establishing an observation post atop Hill 615. Troop C was detailed with the task and carefully ascended the hill's tree-lined slopes until it reached the summit. The patrol was able to look for miles in every direction. The land undulated like a rumpled green rug, the mountains and hills marking the natural boundary between the old kingdoms of Bavaria and Bohemia.

Through field glasses the patrol soon discerned where the engine sounds had been coming from. Far below them on the reverse side of the hill, camouflaged German vehicles could be made out, some moving slowly down the country roads that snaked along the front line, while others sat stationary. Tiny black human specks, German soldiers reduced to ant men, went about their business; the Americans would glimpse them occasionally on the roads or in clearings and small fields. Colonel Hargis' orders to the observation post were succinct: observe the German positions and engage targets of opportunity. They didn't have long to wait for the latter.

"Able Two Zero, this is Hot Dog Three, over," murmured the forward artillery officer into his radio headset. He had been assigned to the Troop C patrol atop Hill 615. The young officer from the 512th Field Artillery Battalion had been observing the German movements and plotting their positions on his grid map in consultation with the Troop C patrol commander.

There was a little static, then the artillery battery responded loud and clear.

"This is Able Two Zero, go ahead."

"This is Hot Dog Three, fire mission. Enemy troops, estimated company size and two vehicles moving west." The officer gave the enemy grid coordinates and his own position. "Will adjust, over."

"This is Able Two Zero. Sending you one round WP."

At the gun line, the emplaced M2A1 105mm Howitzers waited. Only one gun fired, sending over a WP or White Phosphorus round that would produce a highly visible white cloud; this would be used to adjust the guns on to the target.

"Splash—how do we look, over?" crackled the artillery battery operator's voice. The forward observer, his binoculars to his eyes, watched the WP round release its white smoke.

"Able Two Zero—you were a bit short, up two hundred, left twenty, over."

"Roger, Hot Dog Three. On the way." A few seconds passed and then another white plume burst in the valley below the hill. "Splash!" called the operator. Already, the black human specks were running for cover, knowing what was to follow.

"This is Hot Dog Three. Fire for effect, over."

"Wilco, Hot Dog Three. Sending you ten rounds HE and five Willy-Peter … On the way … impact in ten seconds, over."

The 19kg high explosive shells began passing over Hill 615 and impacting with great clouds of dust and smoke in the valley beyond. In between the brown and gray explosions was a sudden flaring of orange flame as a German vehicle was hit, followed by a plume of dense black smoke.

"Able Two Zero, this is Hot Dog Three. Nice shooting. Target wiped out." It was a cold, mechanical procedure that dealt death from several miles away.

Once the firing ceased, a patrol from Troop C scouted ahead for results. A German half-track had taken a direct hit, the men inside blown to pieces or scattered around the camouflaged vehicle, their uniforms charred and still smoldering, while further along a road a three-ton truck had been destroyed. The scouts reported that the truck was loaded with two tank engines.[22] Panzer engines meant German tanks were close by. Probably forward elements of the 11th Panzer Division. It was a sobering realization.

*

"Halt!" screamed the leader of four middle-aged men who suddenly materialized in the center of the narrow country road after stepping from the thick trees. Three of them were armed with rifles, which they leveled menacingly at Captains Lessing and Stewart. Lessing hastily switched off the motorcycle's engine and raised his arms above his head.

Stewart's heart was in his mouth, his stomach a knot of tension. He too gingerly raised his arms. The ambush had happened so fast that Stewart hadn't had time to draw his revolver from beneath the German Army rain cape he was wearing.

From the outset, the Germans were jumpy and aggressive. "*Raus!*" ordered the checkpoint's leader loudly, gesturing with his pistol, and Lessing and Stewart slowly dismounted from the motorcycle combination. Three of the four men were dressed in a ragtag of civilian and army overcoats and Wehrmacht forage caps, with cylindrical field-gray gas mask canisters slung across their bodies. Lessing could see from their red and black armbands that they were Volkssturm people's militia. These emergency forces made up much of General Weisenberger's available manpower for static defense. Lessing also recognized their leader—he was a chemist in Hostau and the local *Ortsgruppenleiter* or Local Group Leader, the district Nazi Party bigwig. His brown tunic, breeches and cap, with its gold rank badges, had earned these Party functionaries, along with their esteemed superiors, the Gauleiters, the sarcastic nickname of "Golden Pheasants" among the population. On his left arm was the red Party armband. Many local group leaders had assumed command of local Volkssturm militia units, though they were often totally untrained in military tactics. Others were making themselves scarce to avoid arrest by the Allies.

"Amerikaner!" yelled one of the Volkssturm men, pointing his rifle excitedly at Stewart before Lessing had time to explain. The man stepped forward and wrenched up the rain cape to reveal Stewart's khaki service tunic beneath. The militia man stepped back, cocking his Mauser rifle as he did so with a harsh metallic click. One of his comrades came forward and quickly relieved Stewart of his sidearm.

Stewart stood still with his hands raised watching as rain dripped from the muzzle of the rifle that was pointed squarely at his chest. The eyes of the man behind the gun were cold. Stewart noticed that the man's finger had slipped over the rifle's trigger, taking first pressure. The focus of Stewart's world was suddenly reduced to the black hole at the dripping end of the rifle's barrel and the face of the German behind it. Lessing and Stewart had enjoyed good fortune on their travels thus far, but it now looked as though their luck had run out. Stewart watched in horror as the German's right eye narrowed along the rifle's sights. His finger tightened ever so slightly against the trigger ...

CHAPTER 9

The Road Less Traveled

"If it had not been for Col. Reed's knowledge, compassion
and understanding, the Lipizzaner mares would surely
have become horse burgers for the Russians."

Captain Dr. Rudolf Lessing

"Look, my friend," said Dr. Lessing slowly to the brown-uniformed local group leader, who still had his pistol drawn, "I have a certificate of authorization here." Lessing gently reached into his hip pocket and extracted General Schulz's note. "We are official *parliamentaires*. So put your weapons away again, and leave us alone."[1] The Nazi officer looked suddenly less confident. He replaced his pistol in its brown leather holster and examined the letter closely, the paper quickly spotting in the rain. Captain Stewart was still rooted to the spot, his eyes hardly daring to leave the man who was covering him with his rifle. It was clear that one false move and things would take a decidedly terminal turn.

"Move aside and let the American pass!" Lessing demanded impatiently in an authoritative voice. The local leader said nothing for a few seconds. He just stood in the rain gazing at the German and American officers. He was clearly weighing up his options. His eyes darted from Lessing to Stewart and back again in nervous indecision. His men kept their weapons trained on the two captives, but their eyes also flicked to their leader, awaiting orders. Suddenly the group leader licked his lips and thrust the letter at Lessing, who plucked it from his outstretched hand. He was obviously deeply suspicious of Lessing's motives, but a general's signature had triggered something in his obedient nature and he had decided to let them go. The immediate crisis had passed. Just before Lessing restarted the motorbike, a Volkssturmmann slapped Stewart's .38 revolver angrily into the American's outstretched hand.

It had been a close run thing, and both Lessing and Stewart knew that if it had been an SS patrol they would not have got off so lightly, pass or no pass. As the motorcycle combination trundled down the tree-lined track Stewart checked his .38 then shoved it back into its holster. It wasn't much, but it might prove the difference if he and Lessing ran into serious trouble again. It was all he had.

*

It was the evening of April 27, 1945, when Captain Stewart arrived back at American lines on foot. Dr. Lessing had taken him in his BMW motorcycle combination to the forester's hut, but Dr. Kroll had been nowhere to be seen. Stewart had made his own way back from there.

Captain Lessing had decided to wait for Kroll. He had lain down in the musty hay in one of the horse stalls and had tried to sleep. Though he had been on the go for over thirty hours, sleep refused to come. Instead, Lessing lay in the darkness with only the occasional movement of the horses for company, his mind turning over the incredible chain of events, nervous and with one ear cocked for any unusual sounds from the dark and forbidding woods outside the stables. He yearned for the sound of Kroll returning, but there was nothing, just the breeze gently rustling branches and the occasional call of some nocturnal animal in the undergrowth.

*

Captain Stewart was met by Corporal Pat Jose, the 42nd Squadron Courier, who took him by jeep to Lieutenant Colonel Hargis' command post. There Stewart reported on the details of his mission to Colonel Reed by radio.[2]

"How was it?" asked Reed.

"Interesting, sir, very interesting," replied Stewart laconically.

Reed was fully aware of the great risks that Stewart had taken, and the young captain discussed the journey out with Lessing and the reactions of Lieutenant Colonel Rudofsky and Generals Schulz and Weisenberger to his mission. Reed would later put Stewart forward for the Bronze Star for this brave service.

"Everything is arranged at Hostau, sir," said Stewart at the conclusion of his debriefing.

"I hope to God you're right," replied Reed ominously, the drawbacks to the rescue plan at the front of his mind. "You get some chow inside of you and some well-earned rack time, Tom," said Reed. "You'll be going back as Major Andrews' assistant tomorrow." Stewart was confused.

"I'm sending a task force to liberate the horses and the POWs,"[3] said Reed, clarifying his statement. Stewart was delighted at this news.

While Stewart had been away on his diplomatic mission, Reed had taken the precaution of assembling a small task force ready to take action if the Americans received the green light from the German authorities at Hostau. Due to forthcoming operational commitments, Reed couldn't spare much for the dash to the stud. Earlier he had called the 42nd's S-3, or Operations Officer, Major Robert Andrews, who had earlier led the attack into Asch, to his office to brief him.

"I can only spare you and the men for a couple of days, Bob," stated Reed. Andrews, his helmet tucked under his left arm, nodded solemnly.

"I understand, sir. What are your orders?"

"Captain Catlett's Troop A, suitably reinforced of course, will be your main force component,"[4] said Reed, referring to fellow Virginian 27-year-old Captain Carter Catlett's cavalry reconnaissance company. Catlett was a prewar star athlete who had been on a football scholarship at the Virginia Military Institute when he volunteered for the army, also playing baseball and basketball and running track and field. "I'm assigning Troop C as point. They will punch a way through the Kraut lines to objective three-oh-six here." Reed pointed down at a map of western Czechoslovakia spread on the green camp table before them. Andrews read the town name next to Reed's index finger.

"Weissensulz?"

"It's a one-horse burg three-quarters of the way to our target, here," said Reed, tracing a thin road all the way to Hostau. "C will secure the objective and halt until ordered forward. It will then proceed to liberate POWs at objective eight-oh-oh here," explained Reed, pointing to the small village of Schmolau next to Weissensulz. "Once C has secured three-oh-six, you pass through with A and take the point to the final objective at Hostau and the remount stud,"[5] said Reed. Andrews leaned close, making quick notes on a small pad in his hand.

"Because we need to maintain the element of surprise and we are pressed for time, I can't permit any forward reconnaissance of the route or targets," said Reed gloomily. Such a move ran contrary to the entire ethos of cavalry reconnaissance. But there was more bad news to follow.

"I also can't give you any certain information on the dispositions or strengths of hostile forces between three-oh-six and the final objective, so I'm also giving you a platoon from C as reinforcements to ensure that you punch through.[6] The balance of C will secure your supply route back to our lines."

Andrews nodded silently, his keen eyes poring over the map with a professional's gaze, taking in the topographical markers and contours.

"What about armored support, sir?" he asked, visions of Tiger tanks clamoring to the front of his mind. Andrews knew better than anyone that the area could be crawling with all sorts of nasty surprises, surprises that M8 Greyhounds and jeeps would not be able to cope with.

"I can spare a platoon from Company F," said Reed. The armored unit in each reconnaissance outfit didn't use the old cavalry title "troops." A platoon amounted to five small M24 Chaffee tanks. Andrews held his tongue. "You can also have a platoon of assault guns from Troop E,"[7] added Reed, helpfully. This would consist of just two 75mm Howitzer Motor Carriages, ugly tank-like vehicles with truncated gun barrels. The meager armor would be split between Troops A and C to give them some offensive edge. His total force would amount, at full strength, including himself and second-in-command Stewart, to 325 men.

"Look Bob, I know its not much of an army, but speed *is* the key. It's about eighteen miles straight through to Hostau and the stud." Both men leaned forward and went over the route again on the map in detail, Reed answering further questions.

"You may run into roadblocks or resistance in the villages and towns that you pass through," said Reed, "or the only Krauts you see might already have their hands up. It will be up to the point teams in the lead platoons to give the advance parties time to deploy in case of resistance." Andrews' concerned eyes retraced the thin route to Hostau.

"As you can see, there are no friendlies north or south of the targets," said Reed. "And there will be no further movements of our forces forward in this sector. So, to recap Bob, secure Hostau town, take the German surrender and set all-round security.[8] Organize the evacuation of the enemy POWs to our lines. Liberate any Allied POWs and also arrange for their safe evac. Once you are organized get on the radio and I'll start sending up every available truck to move the prisoners out. Part two of your mission is to secure and hold the remount stud beside Hostau Castle here," said Reed, pointing out the horse center on the map. "It is imperative that the horses and German staff are secured intact. I will come up myself once you have them." Andrews nodded thoughtfully.

It was decided that the point unit for Troop A would be 2nd Platoon, commanded by First Lieutenant William "Bill"

Quinlivan. Bill, from East Dubuque, Illinois, was the son of Irish immigrant parents and had enlisted in the old horsed cavalry at seventeen. He would have just twenty-eight men but be reinforced with two of the assigned tanks crewed by ten men from Company F. With the tough, combat-experienced Quinlivan would be specialists from the Quartermaster Corps' Remount Service.

The US Army Remount Service dated from the Civil War, and provided animals, primarily horses and mules, to army units. During World War II most of the Remount Service's efforts had been directed to operations in the China–Burma–India theater, New Guinea and the Southwest Pacific, where geography, flora and weather often inhibited the use of vehicles. Mules and horses were seeing extensive service in these campaigns by the United States, its British Empire allies *and* the Japanese. In the European theater of operations the requirement for animals was considerably less, with the US Army the mechanically best-equipped force in the field. But some horses and mules nonetheless saw service. The 6835th Quartermaster Remount Depot was the single unit responsible, and between June 6, 1944, and the end of May 1945 it requisitioned and processed 1,800 animals and issued 750, mainly mules, to the 513th Quartermaster Pack Troop.[9] One of the major tasks for the 6835th was processing captured German military horses and taking over the German horse-breeding establishments.[10]

Colonel Reed paused and sighed heavily, "I hate sending you blind like this, Bob, but I've no choice. Speed and aggression are our best weapons. General Patton has ordered me to 'make it fast,' and that's precisely what we're going to do."

Andrews understood. It was a big risk, but a risk worth taking, for the sake of the prisoners and the horses. He didn't relish the idea of barreling down an unknown road through bandit country, but if any force could do it, it was the 42nd, "Patton's Ghosts." It was the sort of crazy-ass mission that the regiment had been undertaking since Normandy.

The mechanization of the US Army was astounding in comparison with the state of the German forces arrayed against it, and was the Americans' greatest advantage in the fluid situation they faced. But the assignment bothered Andrews nonetheless, for the nature of the mission ran contrary to his training. To put it simply, the mission broke the cardinal rule of armored reconnaissance operations: "Sufficient strength is always sent to be assured of accomplishing the assigned mission."[11] It stated that in black and white in the field manual.

Andrews went to see Lieutenant Colonel Hargis, the 42nd's CO, where the officers from Troops A, C, E and Company F who would be taking part in the mission were assembled for initial orders. Objectives and routes were indicated by Andrews on a wall map, and then copied to all troop and platoon leaders; a detailed mission duration timetable was also drawn up, vital for logistical planning.[12] The supply sections needed to know how much fuel, ammunition and rations were to be loaded aboard the vehicles taking part. Nothing was left to chance. Once the task force left the American lines, it would be on its own and would have to sustain itself until resupply could be arranged.

Troop A, Andrews' main force component, was a typical late-war mechanized cavalry reconnaissance unit. At full strength it consisted of 5 officers and 140 men organized into a troop headquarters and three reconnaissance platoons. Each platoon was equipped with six Bantam jeeps, three mounting 60mm mortars, and three a .30-cal. machine gun. A few of the jeeps mounted German MG42 machine guns that had been "liberated" from the enemy. The rest of each platoon rode in three M8 Greyhound armored cars.

The M8 was the vehicle that had earned Third Army's reconnaissance units their nickname of "Patton's Ghosts," because the vehicle's engine was so quiet compared to other armored cars of the period that US troops were often able to surprise German forces, who didn't hear them until it was too late. The M8 was also fast, its 55mph top road speed earning it the nickname in British service of

"Greyhound." With a crew of four, the 8.6-ton six-wheeled armored car's main weapon was a puny 37mm anti-tank gun mounted in a small turret. Secondary armament was a .50 cal. heavy machine gun on the turret top and a coaxial .30 cal. machine gun beside the driver. Its light armor made it impervious to small arms and shrapnel, though it would not last long against a German tank and was very vulnerable to the new Panzerfaust. The M8 was later deemed "unsatisfactory" in a report by Colonel Reed, because its main gun was simply too light and its truck-type suspension "seriously limited its cross-country mobility."[13] It was, unfortunately, a rush job created in 1943 to face the Germans in North Africa.

What armored support Reed had given Andrews didn't count for much either. The Chaffee tank was popular with its crews, being reliable with great off-road performance. Most importantly, it stood a chance against German tanks, being armed with the much larger and higher-velocity 75mm gun normally found in the Sherman. But its main drawback, certainly against the Panther and Pzkpfw IV tanks that both the 2nd and 11th Panzer Divisions had in western Czechoslovakia, was its relatively light armor, which meant that it was no match for any late-war German tank or even the dreaded Panzerfaust. Another issue was the tank's main gun—mechanized cavalry leaders like Colonel Reed were of the opinion that a heavier weapon was ideally needed considering the size and armor of late-war German Panzers.[14]

The M8 Howitzer Motor Carriage was basically a 75mm artillery gun with a truncated barrel mounted in an open turret atop the body of an M5 Stuart light tank. The vehicle was designed to afford units like the 42nd close support against enemy fortified positions, and it could also act as mobile artillery. But as with the Chaffee, its light armor made it an easy kill for German tanks.

If one word summed up Task Force Andrews—as it was to be called, after its commander—that word was *light*. He was light on men, light on intelligence regarding route and enemy strengths and intentions, and his vehicles were light on armor *and* firepower. There were no Sherman tanks assigned to the force; he would have to make do with the little Chaffees. Major Andrews knew that if his little column was to run into a Tiger or Panther tank his Greyhounds, Chaffees and HMCs would be turned into so much scrap and a lot of his men would get killed.

When Andrews took his leave from Colonel Reed to consult with Lieutenant Colonel Hargis and to brief in detail the officers commanding A and C Troops and the individual platoon commanders, he tried not to think of another cavalry officer who had gone gallivanting into Indian country sixty-nine years earlier without proper reconnaissance or any idea of enemy strength. Andrews was determined that his mission was not going to turn into a latter-day Custer's Last Stand.

If Reed, Andrews, or any of the other officers involved in planning the rescue at Hostau needed a warning that the Germans were far from beaten, and still capable of aggressive and devastating use of their forces, they only needed to look at what happened to Task Force Baum one month before.

Task Force Baum, like Task Force Andrews, was named for its commander, in this case a big, tough, flame-haired New Yorker named Captain Abraham Baum of the 4th Armored Division.

In late March 1945 General Patton had received intelligence that several hundred US prisoners had been moved to Oflag XIII-B, an officers' camp near Hammelburg, Germany, around 40 miles behind enemy lines.[15] He was thrilled, declaring: "This is going to make the MacArthur raid on Cabanatuan look like peanuts."[16] Patton was referring to a POW rescue operation that General Douglas MacArthur had ordered in the Philippines when a special task force of US Rangers and Filipino guerillas had trekked thirty miles behind enemy lines and rescued over 500 starving and sick Allied prisoners-of-war from a Japanese camp near Cabanatuan City. The successful raid had garnered great plaudits for MacArthur and his command, and earned the envy of Patton.

Captain Baum was ordered to lead a task force of ten Sherman tanks, six M5 Stuart light tanks, twenty-seven half-tracks, and fourteen support vehicles to the camp through largely unknown German opposition, along a route about which there was no intelligence and on which no reconnaissance had been attempted. "The division is not to follow you," read Baum's stark orders. "You'll be on your own."[17] Once he had liberated the prisoners, Baum was to load them aboard his transport and retrace his steps back to US lines.[18] To use a common military term of the time, Baum's "ass was in the wind."

Undaunted, Baum set off on the evening of March 26, fighting through the town of Aschaffenburg, where he lost one Sherman and some other vehicles and successfully alerted the Germans to his presence. Soon Baum was to see a Luftwaffe Fieseler 156 Storch spotter plane shadowing his column, reporting his presence to German forces that were closing in to attack. As well as infantry, the Germans managed to deploy some Hetzer tank destroyers to deal with Baum's armor.

On the 27th, Task Force Baum rolled up at the gates to Oflag XIII-B, where after a short battle with the guards, they successfully captured the camp. By now, Baum's force had been reduced to 50 percent strength following a series of running skirmishes with German forces. He now realized that there were considerably more prisoners in the camp than he had been told to expect. He ordered that only two hundred of the more senior American officers would be permitted to ride on his remaining vehicles. The rest, all half-starved or ill, were told that they could walk. Most wisely decided to stay put in the camp.[19]

Task Force Baum started back on the evening of March 27, but it was soon realized that powerful German forces were closing in all around them. Taking refuge on a hilltop for the night, Baum determined to start off again at dawn on the 28th. But the moment the task force began to move it was struck from all sides by heavy German fire. In a very short period all of the remaining American tanks were knocked out, and Baum reluctantly ordered every man for himself, also abandoning all of his remaining transport. Just 35 men managed to walk back to American lines. Baum and 246 others were listed as wounded, missing or taken prisoner, while 32 men were dead.[20] The operation sullied Patton's reputation at SHAEF and in the press, though he managed to minimize the wider fallout through his staff's excellent damage control.[21] It wasn't helped that it was discovered that Patton son-in-law had been one of the prisoners in the camp, though Patton vigorously denied having any knowledge of this when ordering the operation.

The similarities between Task Forces Baum and Andrews were obvious: the high-value prestige target, the small numbers of men and vehicles—enough to get noticed by the Germans but not enough to have a chance of winning an engagement and making it back in one piece should the Germans fight—and the same long high-speed dash into the unknown without proper reconnaissance of the route or careful evaluation of the enemy. In fact, Task Force Andrews was expected to travel only eighteen miles, as opposed to the forty driven by Task Force Baum, but conversely it was entering an area where German Panzer divisions had been identified, and with the Americans bringing along even less firepower. Task Force Baum's ten Sherman medium tanks had proved no match for the Germans, so what was to be expected of five little Chaffees and a pair of Howitzer Motor Carriages was anyone's guess.

The 42nd's Troop C, commanded by First Lieutenant Bob McCaleb since the bloody battle of Asch, would take point during the initial attack into Czech territory, bursting open the German front line and racing forward to its first objective at Weissensulz. At the very tip of the point would be the reliable Staff Sergeant Joseph Carpenter leading 3rd Platoon. McCaleb, Carpenter and the other platoon leaders were not told about the ultimate objective, the capture of the horses at Hostau, just that the mission was part of a PW rescue. The recent "capture" of one American and two British prisoners-of-war by Troop C, while Captains Lessing and Stewart had been undertaking their careful negotiations, had confirmed that a large concentration of POWs was being held close to Weissensulz at objective 800, the village of Schmolau.[22]

*

Captain Lessing had spent the whole night waiting for Dr. Kroll at the forester's hut, but he hadn't shown up. As the first rays of dawn began to lighten the sky, Lessing made up his mind. He couldn't dally any longer. He would ride back to Hostau and help Colonel Rudofsky prepare for the arrival of the Americans, who he thought must be coming soon.

Mounting his horse Indigo, the same stallion that he had ridden with Captain Stewart on their original mission, Lessing started back. He was exhausted after so much travelling, arguing and tension, and a night without sleep had left him in a precarious condition. He was almost asleep in the saddle, the horse's regular movements lulling him. As he was riding through the village of Heiligenkreuz between Weissensulz and Hostau, Lessing passed in front of Baron von Dobirsch's manor house. Fortuitously, the baron was on his balcony and spotted Lessing. The two were old friends and the baron immediately urged him to break his ride and rest for a while.

Lessing told the baron that the Americans might be passing through in the next few hours. He had to get back to Hostau at once.

"You're completely exhausted!" protested von Dobirsch with almost paternal concern. The baron demanded that Lessing rest for a little while and eat something. Lessing couldn't disagree with the baron, for his mind was befuddled by stress and lack of rest. Lessing gave in, dismounted heavily and went into the manor house where the Baron's cook served him up a bowl of piping hot pea soup, fresh bread and a mug of steaming black coffee. As he slowly ate, Lessing chatted with the baron, a fellow horse lover whose own stables were full of both his own mounts and refugee horses blown in from the east. Lessing had visited often to minister to the horses and talk with von Dobirsch. The baron's eyes grew wide as Lessing described his adventures on behalf of the stud, and Lessing realized he could see something like hope in his friend's face.

At that moment a telephone began to ring insistently in the entrance hall outside the door.

CHAPTER 10

Enemy Situation Unknown

"Wir Kapitulieren Nie"("We Will Never Surrender")

Nazi slogan, 1945

The men of Troops A and C waited in their vehicles at their start lines, their company and platoon leaders glancing nervously at their watches while the men smoked their issues, rechecked their personal weapons for the thousandth time and tried to stay warm. The engines of the Chaffee tanks, Howitzer Motor Carriages, M8 armored cars and jeeps rumbled and growled as they idled, hot engine exhaust pluming in the cold air. H-hour had arrived. A light rain was falling and visibility ahead was poor, the roads slick with water.[1]

The low mountains that in the distant past had protected Czechoslovakia from invasion from Bavaria were thick with stands of timber that gave way at the lower altitudes to ancient fields and clearings. The forest was so thick that little light penetrated to ground level, giving the impression of permanent dusk.

Then a sound cut in over the burble of idling engines—from the west, a deep rumbling like summer thunder. The experienced soldiers among the platoons had heard this so many times over the past nine months. It was the percussion herald to an assault—played not on kettledrums but by the cold steel of American artillery.

On the 512th Field Artillery gun line far to the rear, the 105mm Howitzers mouthed shell after shell in a precisely timed opening barrage, the barrels slamming back on their recoil mechanisms as the gunners turned away, hands over their ears and mouths slightly open to protect against the concussion. More and more shells were fed into the hungry gun breeches, while piles of steaming brass casings soon lay abandoned in the mud around every weapon.

On the start lines the GIs instinctively glanced up at the leaden gray sky as the shells passed over with an insistent whine before dropping onto their pre-registered targets along the border area. "Kraut serenade," remarked the GIs, the slang term for a TOT (Time on Target) barrage designed to cut down the enemy before he could go to ground. The shells burst in the distance, the thumps comforting to the men waiting for the signal to advance. Colonel Reed was doing what he could for Task Force Andrews, helping them to kick in the door to Hostau with a short, sharp opening barrage along the troop lines. There was no reply from the German artillery.

The American attack would not come from one direction; rather, Colonel Reed had ensured that Task Force Andrews would approach Hostau in three small battlegroups. Troop C, under the able First Lieutenant Bob McCaleb, would make the initial thrust, advancing on Weissensulz, and then on to hopefully liberate what was understood from hazy intelligence to be upwards of 300 Allied prisoners-of-war in a column at nearby Schmolau. McCaleb would have half a platoon of Chaffee tanks to help. Staff Sergeant Joseph Carpenter, commanding Troop C's 3rd Platoon, would be spearhead, with McCaleb in the next M8 behind and the bulk of Troop C's platoons strung out in a fighting column.[2] The distance was believed to be about seven or eight miles to secure the prisoners.

Troop A, commanded by Captain Carter Catlett was to rendezvous with C at Weissensulz, and once Weissensulz was secure it would pass through C's positions and capture Hostau town from the north and secure the horse stud opposite the castle. Riding with A was Major Andrews, with Captain Tom Stewart as second-in-command.

Troop C would in the meantime establish patrols and checkpoints to cover the road back to US lines, designated the MSR (Main Supply Route). Troop B remained in position screening the villages of Rustin,

Waldorf, and Ples to the south, but would push out patrols to the east side of the forest and help secure Troop C's flank.

One element of Troop A would move on secondary tracks towards Hostau separate from the rest of the troop. This was First Lieutenant Bill Quinlivan's 2nd Platoon, reinforced by two Chaffee tanks from Company F. Bill had orders to follow the route that Captain Stewart had recently ridden during his negotiations with the Germans, bypassing Weissensulz. The plan meant that Troop A had two chances of getting to the stud: should one of its components become embroiled with the Germans, the other should make it.[3]

The task force would have to reach several miles into enemy territory to complete its mission,* with a single main road running from Bavaria through Weissensulz to Hostau to be secured and held open to permit the evacuation of the Allied prisoners, the horses and German POWs. It was a tenuous connection to the rest of the 2nd Cavalry Group and presented plenty of opportunities for any nearby German units to cut the link and isolate Troop A at Hostau or Troop C at Weissensulz, or both. Speed was of the essence—Reed had impressed this upon the task force leaders several times. Get in, get the POWs and horses, and hold the stud until relieved or given further orders.

Major Andrews looked again at his watch. The barrage ended as abruptly as it had begun and the thunderous detonations subsided, leaving only the rumbling note of the engines.

"Move out … repeat, move out," Andrews ordered over the radio, and within seconds the vehicles started to roll east. A low mist hung like a blanket over the dark Bohemian Forest as the men and vehicles of Task Force Andrews began their advance into the unknown. It was deeply overcast, adding to the oppressiveness of the countryside. Rain dripped incessantly from the tall firs and the American soldiers' helmets shone with wetness as they huddled in their jeeps or stood in the turrets of their tanks and armored cars.

---

* The actual distance was 18 miles—much further than they believed it to be.

Staff Sergeant Joe Carpenter's platoon was in the most vulnerable position. The formation march for all units was the same—by column along roads. Each platoon was arrayed exactly the same, in a time-honored and battle-tested formation. Leading was the point squad consisting of a .30 cal.-armed jeep, an M8, and a jeep carrying a 60mm mortar. The vehicles were spread out over about 150 yards. About half a minute behind the point section came the platoon's other two squads, arranged in the same vehicular formation and spread out over 500 to 1,100 yards.[4] On the front of the M8s were masses of tire chains hung on the bow plates as protection against Panzerfaust rockets.

Machine guns were manned on the M8 Greyhounds and jeeps while the turrets of the little Chaffee tanks traversed left and right as they jerkily surged forward, their commanders giving instructions to the drivers by radio microphone, standing with their heads and shoulders out of the open turret hatches.

*

The effects of the American artillery barrage were horrific. In the town of Waier the shells had arrived suddenly and without warning, catching both townspeople and local defense forces in the open. As the smoke and dust cleared, moaning and screaming mingled with the crackling of burning houses, as the wounded and stunned lay scattered about the streets. Bodies, and mangled body parts, were thrown all about. The Germans recorded that twenty-eight civilians were killed by shellfire.[5]

The local Volkssturm commander, Colonel Wastl, immediately ordered the rest of the civilians to their cellars until the inevitable arrival of the Americans. They ran in panic, mostly women and children and a few old people, pushing and shoving to get under cover before another barrage went up.

Eventually, the German defenses woke up to the American threat and opened fire.

*

"Contact!" came the familiar call crackling through the intercom headsets as Major Andrews' lead platoons pushed on. Within minutes of crossing the border, incoming fire was received by the point platoons of Troops A and C. Germans opened up with their fast-firing MG42s from concealed positions, with rifles joining in, the bullets smacking into the American armored vehicles and ricocheting off into the woods, red tracer rounds stabbing through the trees or across the open fields as the columns started to pull out into more open terrain. "Watch your spacing!" ordered the platoon commanders, conscious that bunched-up vehicles made for juicy targets.[6] "We got troops on the ground," crackled voices in the armored vehicle commanders' headsets as they strove to locate the enemy firing positions. "Get that machine gun," was the familiar cry and suppressing fire was ordered immediately, the tanks and armored cars returning fire with their heavy .50 and .30 cal. machine guns that thumped hollowly and slowly as their thumb-sized slugs shredded the German positions. Sometimes the tank guns joined in, their turrets traversing on to the target before blowing it to pieces with high explosive rounds.[7] "Cease fire—target destroyed."

"SOL," muttered more than one GI at the demise of a German position—those Krauts were "shit outta luck."

For the first mile or so of the advance Task Force Andrews was constantly assailed by small pocket of enemy resistance, and though it suffered no serious casualties, the advance slowed and much ammunition was expended eliminating the German front-line positions. Major Andrews, further back in the Troop A column and riding in one of the headquarters' M3A1 half-tracks, received a steady stream of reports from the lead platoons, and he was acutely conscious of time.

Many prisoners were swept up as the columns advanced and these had to be guarded or sent to the rear. In Troop C's sector, sixty-five Germans were captured at 1300 hours when the lead platoon rolled through the village of Vjezd su Krize.[8] Carpenter's 3rd Platoon took three prisoners at 1405 hours. These men helpfully informed Lieutenant McCaleb that there were three German officers commanding an infantry company dug in at Schmolau, the objective where the main concentration of Allied POWs was located, giving the Americans some idea of likely enemy resistance.[9]

*

In Waier, the artillery barrage launched by the German defenses had proved somewhat desultory, and now Volkssturm commander Colonel Wastl was horrified to see groups of his men fleeing out of town towards nearby high ground, many throwing away their weapons and ammunition as they ran when news of the approaching American column was received.

"Everything is lost!" cried one of Wastl's lieutenants, his eyes wet with tears of impotent fury when he reported to the Volkssturm command post. "Two hundred men have fled!"[10] The unwillingness of the Volkssturm to sacrifice themselves in battles that they had no hope of winning with the limited weapons at their disposal led to many either surrendering quickly to the 42nd Squadron's advance guards the moment they appeared or going to ground and waiting out the passing storm. Any serious resistance mostly came from the regular army or particularly fanatical Nazis among the Volkssturm or Hitler Youth.

The men of Troop C quickly took Waier's surrender. The mayor emerged, madly waving an improvised white flag at the approaching American armored vehicles. Two Allied prisoners-of-war, a Briton and an Australian, who the Germans were using as cooks in the building where the Volkssturm garrison was lodged, were hastily called forward by the mayor and his party. The British prisoner, a Londoner who spoke good German, translated the mayor's words.

"I, as mayor of Waier, surrender the place and assure that no

German soldier is left in the place,"[11] he said. An American officer climbed down from an M8 and the little ceremony was concluded with everyone lighting up cigarettes and shaking hands. Waier had been saved from serious devastation. In order to minimize US casualties, the Americans normally blasted any town or settlement that attempted to resist; here the local leaders had averted such a fate. An immediate curfew was imposed and the GIs dismounted from their vehicles to institute a weapons search.

A large number of Allied POWs were liberated from their working parties in the forest close by and the joyous news was immediately transmitted by radio back to Colonel Reed. Lieutenant McCaleb detailed a couple of squads to babysit the POWs and hold the road through the town until transport could be sent up to evacuate the prisoners into Bavaria.

*

"Town ahead," crackled Staff Sergeant Carpenter's voice in Lieutenant McCaleb's headset. McCaleb acknowledged his sergeant's warning from his position some 500 yards back in the column.

"Heads up everyone," broadcast McCaleb to his platoon commanders. Once clear of the thick forest the road wound down across rolling farmland towards a small settlement, really more of a village than a town. It was basically just a main street lined with two- and three-storey German-style houses and shops. From a distance it looked quiet. Carpenter asked McCaleb whether he should stop and send in a recon squad.

"Negative, Sergeant," replied McCaleb, against every tenet of cavalry reconnaissance. Speed was of the essence. They'd have to chance it. "Proceed."

Carpenter's M8, with a jeep front and rear, picked up speed and led the long line of American vehicles straight through the town. Weapons were pointed ahead and up at the windows that lined the road. Carpenter and McCaleb and the other GIs tried not to think of the ease with which they could be ambushed as the line of green vehicles snaked through the narrow medieval street, with most of the platoon riding in open-topped, soft-skinned jeeps that offered no protection. If the proverbial hit the fan McCaleb's command would be trapped like rats in a barrel.

The few Sudeten German civilians that the column surprised stood on the pavements or in doorways, their mouths agape in astonishment. They had clearly had no idea of how close the Americans were to their little town.[12] There were no soldiers in evidence, mostly just women with shopping baskets, old men, and young kids. Anyone left who was capable of bearing arms had already been drafted into the army or the Volkssturm. They stared at the Americans with undisguised hostility. The few Czechs among the populace were friendlier, smiling and waving at the Americans.

As the cavalry drove through the town one or two Nazi flags still fluttered from official buildings, and along one wall was painted in neat white letters the optimistic statement *"Wir Kapitulieren Nie"* ("We Will Never Surrender"). And then the troops were through and continuing on a good road across open countryside dotted with occasional farms and patches of forest. McCaleb consulted his map. So far all was going to plan. The Germans had stopped shooting at them, and in a little while the column should reach the outskirts of Weissensulz. There should be no further major settlements ahead until they hit Weissensulz.

*

"Column ... halt!" crackled the radioed order down the Troop C vehicles. The troop, with Staff Sergeant Carpenter's platoon still on point, came to a halt, vehicle brakes complaining as the heavy armored vehicles and little jeeps stopped. Precautions were immediately taken to defend the column during the temporary halt, with each platoon placing its vehicles under any available cover, such as roadside trees. In case of ambush or air attack, the vehicles were dispersed at least fifty yards apart from each other, and all main and secondary armament manned.[13] "Heads up!" was the common order among the sergeants and corporals to their squads as the column sat immobile deep behind enemy lines. The GIs looked along the barrels of their vehicle weapons and waited, or sat inside smoking and monitoring their radio sets for fresh orders. There was some grumbling among the enlisted men, conscious that German eyes could be watching their every move and perhaps preparing an ambush.

The town that they had passed through shortly before had seemed to make sense at the time; but now, going by the American military maps that they held in their hands, the expected next objective had failed to materialize when it should have.[14] It was evident to the officers of Troop C that they had taken a wrong turn.

The troop was now well into its cautious advance towards Weissensulz, and had already stopped several times to deal with pockets of enemy resistance. Officers and senior NCOs nervously scanned the road ahead and the surrounding fields and woods with their binoculars. It was easy to get lost—the country all looked the same, and the little roads meandered through multiple intersections or led to isolated farms or to tiny settlements. And of course there had been no opportunity to properly reconnoiter the route to Weissensulz before setting out.

Colonel Reed confirmed the halt order via Major Andrews over the radio net until the correct route to Weissensulz could be discerned.[15] The operation was too sensitive to permit one half of the available force assigned to wander off and attempt to feel its way to Weissensulz along any available road—it would have to be turned around and put back on the correct agreed route.

The advancing troops had to stick to the plan if at all possible for one other very important reason—cavalry reconnaissance officers were trained to react to any unexpected vehicles that appeared on their line of march as hostile, and if one of Task Force Andrew's two cavalry troops went off reservation and blundered into the other, the chances of a friendly-fire incident were high.[16] Staff Sergeant Carpenter was not happy with the enforced halt—he was champing at the bit to get moving again.[17]

In the meantime, a reinforced Troop A continued its own separate advance towards Weissensulz, and Lieutenant Quinlivan's platoon pulled further ahead on its own special and separate mission towards Hostau following Captain Stewart's horseback route. The advantage of this route avoiding all major highways and roads was quickly obvious to Quinlivan—his platoon encountered no opposition.[18]

At length, the radio confirmation came through from 2nd Cavalry Group headquarters to First Lieutenant McCaleb and the temporarily halted Troop C: "You are one town west of where you are supposed to be."[19] Maps were consulted again and the precise position of the troop recalibrated. The go signal that Joe Carpenter awaited with bated breath was finally transmitted.

"'Bout Goddamn time!" cursed Carpenter as he clambered back aboard his M8.

Within seconds, engines were restarted the length of the column, and men who had been standing around chatting and smoking beside the vehicles quickly jumped aboard. "Mount up!" yelled Carpenter, throwing away his cigarette and glaring down the column. "Move your asses!" Troop C was back in business.

*

"Three POWs captured at vicinity 598249 state that about ten enemy 600264 also others in woods southeast of town," ran a typical report from Troop C transmitted to Major Andrews as the unit crawled towards Weissensulz, now back on the correct road following its earlier temporary halt. As task force commander, Andrews was receiving a constant stream of situation reports, or "sit reps," from Lieutenants McCaleb and Quinlivan and Captain Catlett. This information was transmitted back to Lieutenant Colonel Hargis at

42nd Cavalry Squadron HQ and to Colonel Reed at 2nd Cavalry Group HQ at Vohenstrauss. "Road block at 568255. More enemy reported 621260 and 628238."[20] The coordinates were marked on the officers' maps accordingly and fresh orders issued as necessary. The situation was, to use military parlance, "fluid."

Weissensulz was close now. It was Troop C's 2nd Platoon that made first contact. A radio message back to headquarters merely stated that the unit was "involved in a small fire fight."[21] Heavy gunfire erupted from the woods close to the right side of the town, codenamed "Objective 306," as Troop C cautiously approached. German troops, mostly Volkssturm, were firing from slit trenches and small log bunkers, the bark of Mauser rifles and the occasional burp of machine guns rippling along the edge of the trees. The fire started to be directed against Staff Sergeant Carpenter's 3rd Platoon, the Germans trying to stop the point squad from advancing further. Carpenter immediately established a base of fire, bringing forward the platoon's other two armored cars. Bullets pinged off the M8s, which began to return fire at the German positions with their 37mm cannons and machine guns, while the platoon's 60mm mortars were offloaded from the jeeps and added to the barrage. A single 37mm shell from one of the M8s destroyed a hastily assembled roadblock.[22] The German positions were plastered with mortar bombs, the detonations pluming among the trees, flaying the trunks with shrapnel and cutting down any Germans not deep under cover. Carpenter's maneuver force, assisted by 2nd Platoon, left the road and outflanked the Germans on the extreme right flank, the combined fire of the armored cars, mortars and the dismounted troopers' personal weapons driving off the enemy without loss to Troop C. Some Germans stubbornly held on to their positions, returning fire as best they could with their infantry weapons, while others broke and fled.

Intelligence gleaned from prisoners had put the German force at the strength of one company but the resistance was heavy enough to cause Major Andrews and his senior officers some concern. Was the

German force the precursor to the arrival of some much larger and better-armed formation, or simply a token defense of the town? Either way, the little fight put the Americans even further behind schedule.

The bulk of Troop A arrived at Weissensulz as the Troop C fight was winding down, and the fresh forces under Captain Catlett helped to disperse the remaining Germans from their foxholes and bunkers. The overwhelming firepower that the Americans could bring to bear decided the issue. Troop C took prisoner twenty-five Germans who emerged waving white flags.[23] The remainder fled, or died in their positions.

"C asks 166 Engineers to have their truck return to C to collect POWs,"[24] came a message from Lieutenant McCaleb, desperate to be rid of the German prisoners and free up the manpower that was tied up in guarding them. Soon one of the engineers' big six-by-sixes was rumbling along the liberated road to Weissensulz to oblige.

At 1702 hours Troop C reported up the chain of command to Reed that Weissensulz was in its hands. Now it was necessary to liberate the POWs at Schmolau. "German officer prisoner-of-war states sixty enlisted old men guarding POWs at eight-oh-oh,"[25] reported McCaleb by radio to Major Andrews, giving the code number for Schmolau. It didn't appear that C would face much opposition from such troops, though it would have to be cautious, given the potential for so many unarmed prisoners-of-war to be caught up in a firefight.

Staff Sergeant Joe Carpenter and 3rd Platoon found the column of Allied prisoners right where they had been told they would, spread out along a lane near the village of Schmolau. The guards offered no resistance as the M8s and jeeps cautiously approached the hundreds of Allied prisoners, most laying down their arms or fleeing. Within minutes, hundreds of thin and bedraggled men crowded around the American vehicles, mostly weeping openly, and more than one GI among the liberators wiped away a tear of joy. The Troop C soldiers handed out whatever rations they had to the liberated British and American prisoners, as well as packs of Luckies. As the rest of C arrived on the scene, McCaleb organized a defense of the released prisoners, safeguarding them[26] while a handful of medics were brought forward to minister to the sick and the injured. Part one of Reed's plan had passed off without any significant hitch. Now there remained the problem of snatching Hostau and the horse stud.

Back at the 2nd Cavalry's headquarters at Vohenstrauss, Colonel Reed had been busy organizing a force of trucks ready to drive straight through and begin evacuating the liberated Allied prisoners and any captured German personnel.[27] One of the problems he faced was a shortage of trucks—as a cavalry reconnaissance squadron the 42nd had only nineteen trucks spread among its various elements, and those were busy hauling ammunition, fuel, food and supplies to its various troops.[28] He couldn't borrow trucks from the 2nd Squadron, as they were engaged elsewhere on their own operations. The only other appropriate vehicles were the handful of half-tracks that were used by the various HQ elements of the 42nd Squadron. Shortage of transportation was to prove to be a problem that would continue to dog the mission as it unfolded.

*

In Baron von Dobirsch's elegant dining room, Dr. Lessing was still tucking into his soup when the baron's manservant appeared at the door to inform his master that there was a telephone call for him. Lessing continued to eat, but was startled when the baron suddenly burst back into the room, his face split by a huge grin.

"One of my tenants reports that American vehicles passed by his house not five minutes ago." Lessing jumped to his feet.

"Where?" he demanded, pulling on his riding gloves.

The baron told him the location: a hamlet not far from Weissensulz.

"I have to go," announced Lessing. "I have to get back to Hostau and warn them."

"Of course, my dear fellow," replied the baron. "It's momentous news, truly momentous."

"Thank you for your hospitality," said Lessing, pumping the baron's hand.

"Have the Captain's horse brought to the front of the house at once," the baron ordered his manservant.

"Good luck, my friend," said Baron von Dobirsch seriously, "and take care of yourself. These are dangerous times." Lessing pulled on his service cap and nodded before striding out through the manor's main door where the baron's grooms were hastily preparing Indigo. He quickly mounted the stallion and tore off across the courtyard towards Hostau, the horse's shoes clattering on the cobblestones like machine-gun fire.

CHAPTER 11

Liberators and Saviors

"Not a single shot was fired at us."

First Lieutenant William Quinlivan

Colonel Rudofsky ran out from one of the stable blocks, where he had been conducting an inspection, at the sound of gunfire in the distance. It was different to the stray artillery rounds that had fallen on the stud two days before, badly frightening the horses *and* the Volkssturm defenders. This sound was different—flat bangs followed closely by the crump of explosions. Rudofsky, with some of his staff and grooms, stood in the courtyard, straining their ears and looking all about. More dull detonations followed.

"Panzers, Colonel," piped up one of the grooms, who had spent some time at the front. To the trained ear, the sound of tank guns was quite different from that of artillery. But where was it coming from? Were they American or Soviet tanks?

"There," said Rudofsky, pointing northwest as the firing started up again. "Its coming from the direction of Weissensulz." It was unmistakable. It had to be the Americans.

General Schulz appeared beside Rudofsky looking pale and agitated. He had hurried across the road from his headquarters inside the castle. The two officers briefly discussed the situation, Rudofsky noting that the general was even more blunt than usual.

"Where is Lessing?" Schulz demanded. Rudofsky shrugged his shoulders and said nothing. The young veterinarian and now plenipotentiary must arrive soon with news of the outcome of his

141

intense negotiations. Regardless, Rudofsky knew that he must make certain preparations for the imminent arrival of the Americans.

"Excuse me, General, but I have matters to attend to," said Rudofsky, who saluted, before stalking off towards his office closely followed by some senior members of his staff.

A few minutes later Rudofsky was informed that some of the defense force units were leaving. He emerged from his castle office to see Schulz's Mercedes drive past, headed south. The general was sat in the rear, his face a mask. The car's luggage rack was piled high with leather suitcases and baggage. So the gallant general had decided not to submit to surrender, at least not yet. Some of his troops did likewise and started pulling out of their prepared positions and filing into the countryside, undoubtedly aware that they lacked the weapons to take on American tanks. The stud at least was soon free of armed soldiers; the only military men left behind being Rudofsky and some of his grooms.

Suddenly, Rudofsky spied Dr. Lessing, weaving his way against the tide of soldiers who were hurrying away from the stud and the town's castle. He cantered over and reined in his horse beside Rudofsky before sliding exhaustedly from the saddle.

"Colonel," he said, saluting formally with one gloved hand. "I wish to report that American Panzers are about five kilometers away."

Rudofsky nodded curtly. He was happy with the confirmation. It made up his mind. He quickly briefed Lessing on the local situation and the departure of Schulz.

"We have preparations to make, Captain, and *very* little time," announced Rudofsky, once again all business.

*

Just fifteen miles southeast of where Rudofsky and Lessing were discussing how to surrender the stud, the balance of one of the most powerful remaining German units on the Western Front was crawling slowly up muddy country roads towards the town of Taus.

The 11th Panzer Division had been ordered forward to join the reconnaissance battlegroup that General von Buttlar-Brandenfels had dispatched a few days before. The division's orders were simple: block the American advance on the city of Pilsen.[1] Enough fuel had been organized to move the 10,500 men and thousands of vehicles into position, including its handful of serviceable Panther tanks, 45-ton behemoths whose wide tracks and wheels rattled and clanged eerily, petrol engines growling like angry big cats.

*

First Lieutenant Bill Quinlivan's head and shoulders were outside of his M8 armored car, which was following fifty yards behind the small detachment of two Chaffee tanks from Company F that were the vanguard of his single platoon's lonely advance to the stud. He had been separated from Troop A since beginning the advance that day, following Captain Stewart's more cross-country route. With Quinlivan was the rest of his platoon, divided into an Armored Car section and a Scout section. The Armored Car section, totaling Quinlivan and eleven enlisted men, consisted of two more M8 Greyhounds, their little turrets scanning all around. The Scout section, consisting of six jeeps and seventeen men, was the most vulnerable. Three mounted 60mm mortars, while the other three packed .30 cal. medium machine guns. With the ten men crewing the tanks, Quinlivan's force was only thirty-nine strong—not exactly much of an army.

The countryside was eerily quiet, but Quinlivan was taking no chances. The terrain favored the defender perfectly. Rolling fields undulated away into small valleys and hollows and the road system passed through open areas before abruptly plunging into dark stands of fir trees. The only advantage for the Americans was the fact that the Germans lacked the necessary firepower and manpower to defend the country properly.

Communicating with the tanks through his headset, Quinlivan

kept their speed down. He feared driving into an ambush. In fact, every fiber of his body was stiff and alert. Every few minutes he would raise his field glasses to his eyes and scan the rolling countryside ahead. Away from the still-wintry fields, the patches of forest and undergrowth—perfect positions to conceal German tanks or anti-tank guns—were difficult to penetrate with his field glasses. It was still raining, which reduced visibility considerably. He could almost feel hostile eyes watching his vehicles, perhaps even at this moment levering a shell into the breech of some hidden anti-tank gun and lining up a hapless victim. His column was a sitting duck on the narrow and rain-slicked road. The tanks covered both sides of the road with their turrets; black exhaust fumes pluming in the chill air.

Quinlivan's column passed nervously through a couple of small one-horse villages, slowing to a virtual crawl as machine guns and carbines were aimed at empty windows and down narrow alleyways between the solidly built German-style houses and barns. The danger here was from buried Teller mines—big dinner plate-sized explosives capable of crippling any Allied vehicle—and of course from handheld Panzerfaust rocket-propelled grenades. Hardly a civilian was seen. Any inhabitants had either fled into the woods or were hiding in their cellars or attics, waiting for the Americans to pass by. "There was no resistance," reported Quinlivan. "Not a single shot was fired at us."[2]

Quinlivan consulted his map. According to his present position, his unit was now close to Hostau and the horse stud but the terrain and trees obscured his line of sight. He quickly communicated this information over the radio net, warning his men to stay alert and ready for anything.

Suddenly, the tanks up ahead stopped and Quinlivan quickly drew the trailing column to a halt. The lead tank's commander reported a town ahead, below the crest of the hill on which the Americans sat. Quinlivan's M8 hastened forward to investigate. He raised his binoculars. It was unmistakable from the description he had been given and the map references—the tall church spire atop the hill, the white castle buildings beyond, the streets of colorful two- and three-storey houses that crowded the hillside.

"That's it, boys," said Quinlivan through his intercom. "Objective Three-Oh-Six." Quinlivan glanced at his watch: it was 1910 hours. But where in the hell were Major Andrews, Captain Stewart, and Captain Catlett with the rest of Troop A? They should have rendezvoused with him by now.

Getting on the radio, Quinlivan soon discovered that Troop A had been held up by resistance at Weissensulz but was scheduled to arrive very soon.[3] In the meantime, he was the ranking officer on the spot.

"Left stick, left stick," came a crackling warning in Quinlivan's headset from the lead tank commander to his partner Chaffee, "you got troops on the ground." Quinlivan swung his binoculars round. Sure enough, a group of field-gray figures, some riding in horse-drawn carts, could be made out on the opposite side of Hostau moving up a road or across fields. It looked as though the German garrison, or at least a big part of it, was running away.[4] The left Chaffee immediately turned to face the enemy, being joined shortly after by the lead tank, their big Cadillac engines growling and throbbing as they moved into a firing position, tracks gouging up clumps of earth and grass beside the road.

The tank squad commander sought immediate permission to open fire. Quinlivan decided that he would instead test the defenses and ordered fire to be opened upon some empty fields behind the town. Shooting at fleeing men was not his style. Sending a few shots over Hostau should reveal any German artillery or tanks that would naturally return fire at the targets silhouetted on the ridgeline.

"Roger ... firing now," came the tank commander's clipped and businesslike voice in Quinlivan's headset as he acknowledged the order and gave the gunners their instructions. Inside each tank a 75mm high explosive round was rammed into the open gun breech.

"Clear!" yelled the loaders, as the gunners took careful aim through their periscopes.

"Fire!" ordered each tank commander.

"On the way!" yelled the gunners, depressing their triggers, the breeches slamming back inside the turrets, rocking the tanks on their springs as the shells arched away towards Hostau.

*

Colonel Rudofsky reached up and took down the portrait of Adolf Hitler that hung on his office wall. He looked at the face of the man he had loyally served for so many years. Even now, it was difficult to break the bond to this man. Rudofsky, like all other Wehrmacht soldiers, had taken an oath of loyalty, not to Germany, but to the person of Adolf Hitler. An oath that stood until death, he reminded himself grimly. There was a knock at his office door.

"What shall we do about the flags, Colonel?" enquired a groom.

Large Nazi swastika flags flew proudly from poles outside some of the stud buildings. It would send the wrong message to their conquerors.

"Lower them and bring them to my office," he replied firmly. "Also, have white sheets hung from some of the upper windows of the buildings." It was important that the Americans understand that the stud was not a threat. The flag flying in the village remained up for the time being.

"*Jawohl, Herr Oberst!*" The man dashed off to comply with his orders. Rudofsky's eyes fell once more on the large photograph of Hitler that he held in his hands. Quickly, he jerked open the top drawer of the filing cabinet beside his desk and stuffed the photo inside, slamming it with a bang. It was the horses that counted, and only the horses. That was what Rudofsky had been sent here for in the first place. Politics did not concern him any longer.

As he slammed the filing cabinet shut, a loud detonation went off close by, rattling the glass in his office windows. It was followed by several more in quick succession. Within seconds he received an alarming report—American tanks were firing on Hostau.

*

"Dismounted enemy at 640180. Tanks fire ... Patrol now investigating,"[5] was the terse message received at 1730 hours from First Lieutenant Quinlivan by Task Force commander Major Andrews, who was moving forward with Captain Catlett's Troop A from the battle at Weissensulz.[6] A glance at Andrews' tactical map indicated that Quinlivan was engaging the enemy near the town of Hostau. Andrews was conscious that Quinlivan's little command was out on its own and that he needed to get Troop A through to support Quinlivan's single platoon as soon as possible, particularly now that firing was being reported close to the main objective. The task force hurried forward, covering the last few kilometers without incident.

One or two of the tank rounds that Quinlivan had ordered fired fell a little short of the German troop concentration, landing close to some houses at the rear of Hostau, damaging them.[7]

"Rounds complete," reported the officer commanding the section of two Chaffee tanks supporting Quinlivan's recon platoon, his transmission crackling with static in the damp air.

"Stand by," replied Quinlivan over the radio. He raised his field glasses to his eyes once again. Dust was still pluming into the air from the explosions beyond the town. German troops, on foot and in horse-drawn carts, continued to hastily depart from the other side of Hostau, but nary a hostile round was aimed at the American force atop the ridge. But still Quinlivan waited for a couple of minutes, trying to gauge the risks.[8] Another sweep of the objective revealed no apparent German intention to resist the American advance.

A few minutes later, Stewart and Catlett, along with Andrews and the other three platoons from Troop A arrived, linking up with Quinlivan's little outfit. Catlett took field command and proceeded to lead the unit down towards Hostau and the final prize.

*

Colonel Rudofsky, still immaculate in his uniform in spite of chaotic scenes at the stud following the American tank fire, the loud detonations in the vicinity of Hostau upsetting both the horses and the staff, walked briskly along the narrow country road that led from Hostau towards where the American tanks had been seen, his jackboots shining like black glass. Marching next to him was the rather more bedraggled figure of Captain Lessing, his field-gray uniform still splattered with dried mud from his hours spent in the saddle. Between the two German officers they carried an incongruous white bed sheet as a rather ersatz parley flag. Both men still wore their service pistols in holsters on their belts. They didn't speak, they just marched along the mostly empty country road hoping that they were doing the right thing and that everything would turn out exactly as Lessing had negotiated with Colonel Reed. The sounds of firing had abruptly stopped. The Americans should not be far away now.

*

"Column halt!" ordered Captain Catlett over the radio net. Two German officers were walking up the country road towards the head of the American column carrying what looked like a white sheet between them. The American vehicles shuddered to a halt and stood idling, engines rumbling. Weapons were pointed towards the two enemy officers.

"Well, I'll be damned," muttered Catlett, jumping down from his vehicle and pulling out his Colt .45 automatic.

"Cover me," he ordered his men. Rudofsky and Lessing had also halted to nervously await events. For a moment the two Germans and the American officer stared at each other, unsure of how to proceed. Then Captain Stewart arrived from further back in the column. The time had arrived for Rudofsky to surrender.

*

"It looks like the goddamn fourth of July!" exclaimed one of the astonished troopers inside Lieutenant Quinlivan's M8 as the little column of American tanks, armored cars and jeeps ground slowly through Hostau's main street towards the small plaza outside the entrance to St. Jakobus' Church. Along both sides of the road were locals and released prisoners-of-war, many of the latter overcome with joy.[9] American, British, Polish, and French prisoners, along with several other nationalities, crowded around the US vehicles, their uniforms tatty and outdated and their faces thin and strained from years of rationed POW diets. They whooped and hollered and reached up to shake the hands of the passing Troop A GIs, some even jumping onto the jeeps to catch a ride with the smiling and laughing Americans. From the windows of the buildings that lined the steep hill up to the church fluttered white linen sheets, pressed into service as makeshift surrender flags. The Sudeten Germans and Czechs treated the Americans more as liberators and saviors than as conquerors.[10] Some of the former POWs were singing—it was a raucous and unexpected reception, and the joy on both sides was infectious. But just as Catlett and his men had started to relax and be swept along by the outpouring of joy and goodwill, the lead American vehicle suddenly spotted German soldiers. Weapons were rapidly unslung and made ready for use.

The sight that greeted Catlett before the church was altogether more surreal than their overwhelming welcome. Drawn up in ranks several men deep was at least a battalion of Wehrmacht soldiers, the part of the garrison that had not run away. They slammed to attention as the American vehicles clattered to a halt and some of the troopers dismounted, carbines and Tommy guns at the ready.[11] Stacked neatly before each platoon of Germans were their rifles and machine pistols, while off to the side Prince Amassov and his Cossacks sat impassively atop their horses, haughtily surveying the strange scene.

Colonel Rudofsky and Captain Lessing took their places before the German forces, standing in front of a flagpole from which a large Nazi flag fluttered in the light breeze. Captain Catlett, accompanied by task force commander Major Andrews, Captain

Stewart and a couple of his platoon leaders, approached the formal gathering, conscious that their scruffy combat uniforms and dirty faces contrasted sharply with the solemn dignity of the occasion. The released prisoners and townspeople hushed and waited.

Rudofsky and Lessing brought their heels together and gave sharp military salutes, as did the other German officers.[12] As Troop A had taken Hostau, Captain Catlett would have the honor of accepting the German surrender, rather than Major Andrews.

"Lieutenant Colonel Rudofsky, as senior officer and commander of the German Army Remount Stud Hostau, presents his compliments, Captain," announced Dr. Lessing in loud and clear English, "and requests that you accept the surrender of the stud and the remaining garrison of Hostau town."

"I do," said Catlett, saluting.[13] He looked at the tall Rudofsky, who was still immaculate in his uniform, though his eyes looked tired and troubled. Lessing muttered something to Rudofsky, who reached down and unbuckled his leather holster, extracted his Luger pistol, reversed it and handed it butt first to Catlett. Lessing followed suit. Catlett handed the pistols to some American officers standing behind him, then saluted the two German officers, who also saluted. Then Catlett glanced up at the Nazi flag and back at Lessing, who understood what he wanted.

Lessing barked an order and two German soldiers stepped forward smartly and slowly hauled down the flag. Rudofsky and Lessing stood rigidly at attention and saluted once again as the flag was lowered. It was unhooked from the rope, neatly folded and handed to Rudofsky, who held the flag with both hands and then carefully handed it to Catlett. The American officer turned to his own men and asked for the flag that they had brought with them for this express purpose. It was quickly attached to the rope and winched up into position.

"Ten hut!" shouted one of the top sergeants, and the Americans all stiffened to attention and saluted as Old Glory unfurled into the breeze. For a few seconds all eyes, American, German, Czech,

(*right*) Colonel Reed in Europe as Commanding Officer of the 2nd Cavalry Group, 1945.

(*above*) Lieutenant Colonel Thomas B. Hargis, Commanding Officer of the 42nd Cavalry Reconnaissance Squadron (Mechanized), photographed at Neukirchen, Germany in 1945.

Courtesy Gary McCaleb

Captain Carter Catlett (left), commanding Troop A, 42nd Cavalry Squadron, with some of his men and a captured Nazi flag, 1945.

Colonel Charles H. "Hank" Reed, the officer who saved the Spanish Riding School in 1945.

Captain Thomas M. Stewart, who commanded the task force that held Hostau, beating off two determined SS assaults in the last days of the war in Europe.

(right) Hostau Church, outside of which the German garrison surrendered to the US 42nd Cavalry task force.

© Mark Felton

(below) Colonel Rudofsky (right) standing with Colonel Reed (second right) at the Hostau Stud, April 29, 1945.

Courtesy The Reed Museum and 2nd Regiment of Dragoons Heritage Center

(*above*) A young Lipizzaner stallion being shown to Colonel Reed and his officers at the Hostau Stud, April 29, 1945.

(*left*) Colonel Reed photographed with one of the Arab stallions from the Hostau Stud, May 1945.

American troops and German grooms watch as horses are loaded aboard converted trucks for evacuation from the Hostau Stud.

Horses from the Hostau Stud being driven in convoy. The vehicles consist of a mixture of American and German trucks hastily modified by Lieutenant Quinlivan and his platoon.

Intelligence officer Captain Ferdinand Sperl riding one of the horses that he helped to liberate at Hostau.

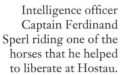

(*right*) Colonel Reed (center), and Lieutenant Colonel Hargis (right), commanding 42nd Cavalry Squadron, photographed riding Lipizzaners in Germany, 1945.

Courtesy The Reed Museum and 2nd Regiment of Dragoons Heritage Center

(*right*) First Lieutenant Robert McCaleb riding a Lipizzaner stallion in Czechoslovakia, 1945.

Courtesy Gary McCaleb

(*left*) Two of the NCOs who took part in Operation Cowboy, photographed by Captain Catlett in 1945.

(*below*) First Lieutenant McCaleb riding Aces High, a stallion that he brought back to the States with him at the end of the war.

Courtesy Gary McCaleb

First Lieutenant Robert McCaleb (left), officer commanding Troop C, 42nd Cavalry Squadron, and his radioman on May 8, 1945 near Myslív, Czechoslovakia. This photograph was taken a few minutes after the announcement of the end of the war in Europe.

Colonel Reed (center) photographed during a friendly meeting with the Red Army, contrasting with his first tense encounter with Soviet forces outside Hostau, Czechoslovakia in May 1945.

(*above*) The Hofburg Palace in Vienna, home of the Spanish Riding School.

(*left*) The Spanish Riding School's main arena, where the famed Lipizzaner stallions perform to this day.

Russian, British, French, Polish, and Serbian, settled on the Stars and Stripes before the watchers erupted once again into tumultuous and hysterical joy.[14]

Catlett and Andrews knew that controlling the situation was critical. Catlett quickly gathered his platoon commanders together. His orders were simple. He detailed one squad to keep the Germans under guard until somewhere could be found to secure them, and to take over the German weapons. His other platoons were ordered to establish outposts on all roads into Hostau. An all-round system of observation posts would be established, though because of manpower shortages, they would be very thinly held.[15]

"I want machine guns dismounted from some of the vehicles to cover the OPs," ordered Catlett. The tanks and M8s would be dispersed through the town to reinforce and cover these security points. "I don't want anyone getting in or out of this place without us knowing about it," said Catlett seriously. Major Andrews approved all these measures. Catlett, following regulations, also ordered the dismounted troopers to start digging prone shelters to protect against aerial or artillery attack.[16]

One issue was the large number of German prisoners who had been taken.

"Put fifty of the Peewees in the castle's cellars," ordered Major Andrews. The rest of the Germans were divided up into groups and locked in the cellars of six local homes and kept under armed guard. Andrews and his second-in-command Captain Stewart were concerned that the German soldiers might yet decide to resist, particularly if other German forces in the area made a concerted attack on the town. They outnumbered the Americans by at least three-to-one. The Germans' weapons were collected together and stored at another location, also under a strong guard. It amounted to a fair arsenal of rifles, machine guns and pistols.

*

"Come on, lets take a look at the horses, Bill," suggested Captain Stewart to Lieutenant Quinlivan. With all outposts now set and manned, the German POWs securely under lock and key, and American control over Hostau complete, Major Andrews and Stewart had decided to proceed with the final part of the mission—properly securing the horse stud and examining its contents. Andrews could only spare a handful of men for this task, for nearly every man from Troop A was manning the perimeter or on guard duty in the town, but every available officer and man who could be spared entered the stud's main yard opposite the castle.

Spread out behind the stud and beyond the castle there were paddocks and fields that were full of horses. The animals were grazing contentedly and barely lifted their heads to greet their saviors. Colonel Rudofsky and Captains Lessing and Kroll accompanied the Americans. Rudofsky and Lessing had been released by Catlett to return to the administration of the stud shortly after Hostau had been liberated, rather than imprisoned as POWs. The Americans needed them to continue at their posts.

The Americans, weapons in hand, warily scanned the yard and its several large buildings. Some German Army grooms and prisoners stood staring at them, a frozen tableau of men at work, some leaning on pitchforks where they had been moving hay, others with wire brushes for scrubbing the floors, one or two carrying buckets of water. The stable blocks were tall and very long sturdy brick and stone buildings with high set windows and large double doors to allow the horses to be moved about. Captain Stewart wandered over to the door of one block and felt instantly at home as the smell of horses greeted him. Inside, in the gloom, horses' heads turned to look at him from behind the bars of their stalls. Though considerably less luxurious than the stable blocks at the Piber Stud in Austria where the mares were usually housed, the blocks were immaculate and well-maintained, with the white horses well provisioned and groomed.

*

When Colonel Reed was informed of the capture of the stud he was ecstatic. He made an immediate report to Third Army headquarters through XII Corps, outlining to Patton the apparent value of the herd, and requested instructions as to its disposal. For the time being, Reed would have to wait for a reply from Patton as events elsewhere overtook those at Hostau. For Reed, his priority was to visit the stud in person and, as Third Army had put it, "use my own initiative."[17]

CHAPTER 12

No Way Out

"I am a Sudeten German. Here is my home."

Colonel Hubert Rudofsky

"300 horses found"[1] was the amazing message received by Colonel Reed from Major Andrews at 2050 hours on April 28, 1945. Andrews and his officers had just completed their first inspection of Hostau Stud. But this number, though impressive, was only the tip of the iceberg.

The American soldiers who had entered the stud spread out and carefully checked each building for any remaining enemy soldiers or weapons while Lieutenant Colonel Rudofsky and Captains Lessing and Kroll chatted with Major Andrews. Captain Stewart gave orders for a checkpoint to be established at the stud's entrance gate.

The problem for Andrews and Stewart was the sheer scale of the stud. Colonel Rudofsky explained that in addition to the main facility, which was clearly crammed with horses of every description, there were also three satellite facilities at the nearby villages of Hassatitz, Zwirschen, and Taschlowitz. In total, Rudofsky announced, the facility held over 700 horses. Dr. Lessing offered to show Stewart the other studs, and the two men, accompanied by a driver, went in a jeep to each site in turn.

Barely three kilometers from Hostau, the horse farm at Zwirschen was the closest to the main stud. Stewart's jeep covered the distance in just a few minutes, turning in to a narrow, sunken road between two high hedgerows that reminded the American captain of the

Normandy *bocage*. To the right stretched paddocks well stocked with horses. Stewart's jeep took a right turn on to Zwirschen's main street and halted. The horse farm consisted of a number of buildings similar to those at Hostau and took up a good portion of the hamlet. But it was obvious when Stewart and Lessing dismounted from the jeep that all was not well.

The Germans who, along with some locals, were supposed to be running the place, did not come out to greet the new arrivals. Some Russian POWs, forcibly drafted to care for the horses, had taken the arrival of the Americans as a signal to begin terrorizing their former masters and innocent locals alike, appropriating private property and generally throwing their weight around like a gang of thugs. Captain Stewart realized that he needed to show them who was actually in charge. An ugly incident followed, beginning with Stewart demanding the return of some stolen property and ending with the American officer knocking the Russian ringleader to the ground with a powerful right hook, then punting him in the rear end with his boot like a football.[2] Over the coming days, American officers would often be forced to resort to threats and even physical violence to control groups of surly and often outright mutinous groups of former prisoners from the east. American soldiers would soon be posted at the farm at Zwirschen to try to prevent looting, intimidation, and fighting.

As the little cluster of houses and stables was easily visible from high ground just outside Hostau, Zwirschen was clearly defensible and Stewart made a mental note of this before he began an inspection of the horses and their facilities. What was clear immediately was that the main stud at Hostau desperately needed these satellite facilities to ease the overcrowding.

*

At 2100 hours it was reported to Colonel Reed that First Lieutenant Quinlivan's 2nd Platoon had taken up position at the main Hostau Stud to guard the horses and staff.[3] This total force amounted to less than thirty men. The balance of Troop A manned blocking positions and observation posts around the village of Hostau and also threw out a series of screening patrols into the immediate countryside. The whole area was crawling with displaced German soldiers, some looking to surrender while others sought to continue the struggle.

With the coming of the night Colonel Reed reviewed the tactical situation of Task Force Andrews. Troop C maintained its control over the roads to Weissensulz, with a platoon reinforced by two Howitzer Motor Carriages and another platoon with three Chaffee tanks at the command post in Weissensulz town.[4] The rest of the troop was patrolling the miles of road between the Bavarian border and Weissensulz. Troop A was fully invested in the defense of Hostau and the stud and in providing a link along the road to Troop C at Weissensulz.

After the dash forward and the fighting, both troops radioed a requirement for gasoline—Troop A requested 40 gallons and C, 200.[5] This would be brought up to them in jerrycans aboard trucks, along with rations and more ammunition. The empty trucks would then load up with "sour Kraut" German POWs, as the Americans had nicknamed them, and any of the recently released Allied prisoners who wished to be repatriated, and begin ferrying them back to the American lines.

It was imperative that all Allied POWs be immediately sent to the rear. Most of the American, British, and French former prisoners were driven out. The others, the Poles, Russians, and Serbs, could not be returned to their own nations, so many decided to stay behind at Hostau and help the new conquerors. A few British and New Zealand prisoners also managed to avoid evacuation, preferring to remain at the stud. They would prove invaluable over the coming days. The main road through Weissensulz was to be busy all night long with American truck movements, making for an inviting target for any rogue German units.[6]

*

At St. Martin in Upper Austria, Colonel Alois Podhajsky prayed for the speedy arrival of the United States Army. The atmosphere in the town of St. Martin was darkening by the day, as huge numbers of refugees vied for what little food was available. Podhajsky had heard that many refugees were openly voicing the opinion that the Spanish Riding School stallions should be used to supplement their meager meat ration and the staff sent off to fight the enemy.[7] Podhajsky decided to take steps to place Arco Castle into a state of defense, not against the approaching Americans, but against the local population.

Using his few infantry weapons, Podhajsky set up strongpoints in the castle and its outbuildings. The little one- and two-man positions were connected to Podhajsky's office using field telephones, and they had overlapping fields of fire.[8] The stallions were moved to a closed courtyard, well out of sight of the locals.

The US advance appeared to have slowed, but American fighter-bombers totally dominated the skies overhead, pouncing down and bombing anything moving on the roads. Podhajsky remained prepared for the arrival of the American spearheads, and with his wife he prepared for their arrival. Getting rid of their Wehrmacht uniforms would be a priority, lest the Spanish Riding School staff be rounded up as prisoners-of-war and separated from their beloved horses. A secret room was prepared in Arco Castle, where civilian riding outfits, each carefully labeled, were laid out so that when the Americans arrived the riders could quickly change.[9]

*

Colonel Rudofsky stood waiting in the main courtyard outside one of Hostau Stud's long stable buildings on the morning of April 29, his first morning as a prisoner of the Americans since the arrival of Task Force Andrews the evening before. The whole situation made him very uncomfortable. He would finally be meeting face to face the man who was responsible for saving the horses and Rudofsky and his German staff and their families from the Soviets. And while he was grateful for their safety, to give themselves up to the enemy in this way just felt wrong.

Standing beside him were Captains Lessing and Kroll, the Cossack Prince Amassov, and a handful of other German staff. The air was still chilly and damp, with spring late this year, and Rudofsky was dressed in a long gray leather greatcoat, looking tall and somehow aloof from the unfolding proceedings. Guarding the entrance to the stud were two sentries from Bill Quinlivan's platoon. They suddenly stiffened and brought themselves to attention. Rudofsky watched as a jeep swung into the yard and squealed to a halt in front of Rudofsky and the other officers. A couple more jeeps followed.

Two things about Colonel Hank Reed immediately struck Rudofsky. Firstly, he was sitting casually beside his driver; and secondly, when he stepped down from the jeep he was a head shorter than the German colonel. Rudofsky was surprised by how ordinary Reed appeared, dressed in a dark green steel helmet without insignia, waist-length beige field jacket and with his khaki trousers tucked into his high lace-up combat boots. The German officers saluted and Reed returned their salutes before he looked around with undisguised pleasure at the horses and the buildings, clearly keen to begin his inspection. Captain Catlett moved ahead of him, presenting each officer in turn. Reed noticed, however, that Rudofsky looked uncomfortable, his eyes rather shifty. He was also, unusually for him, hatless, having removed his service cap so that he would not have to salute Reed.[10] He was also sweating profusely. Keen to demonstrate his goodwill, Reed walked along the line-up of Germans as if inspecting them before pulling a pack of Chelsea cigarettes from his pocket and offering one to each of the captives. When he reached Rudofsky, the German colonel grimaced. "*Nicht rauchen*," he said, "*chocolade bitte.*" ("Don't smoke; chocolate please.")[11] Several of the other German officers guffawed loudly at this.

"How many horses are stabled here, Colonel?" asked Reed. Rudofsky, replacing his service cap, consulted the careful notes that Dr. Lessing carried on a clipboard before replying.

"A total of 589, Colonel,"[12] replied Rudofsky. He gave Reed a quick breakdown of the total. There were 247 Lipizzaners, 64 Arabians, 144 Kabardiners, 75 Don horses, and 59 Panje horses.[13]

Rudofsky enquired whether Reed had brought a veterinarian with him, as they were very short-staffed. "Of course, Colonel," said Reed confidently, turning to one of a coterie of American officers who were standing nearby. "This is Captain Kalwaic," he said. But in reality, it was a bluff on Reed's part: Henry J. Kalwaic was indeed a medical man—only an MD rather than a vet.

A young Lipizzaner stallion, listed in Rudofsky's records as one of twelve three-year-olds at the stud, was led out for Reed's inspection, his white coat mottled with gray. As a groom held the stallion's halter, Reed and a group of American officers stood around admiring the animal's fine lines. Dr. Lessing, dressed in a field cap and greatcoat, was on hand to answer any medical questions as Colonel Rudofsky outlined the stallion's vital statistics and history with a professional pride and competence that replaced his earlier awkwardness in front of the Americans. The stallion's ears pricked back on his head at Rudofsky's familiar voice, his tail twitching. Next, an older breeding stallion, what the Germans termed a *"Hauptbeschäler"*[14] or "main coverer," was led out for Reed's inspection, his coat almost white and his shoes echoing on the yard's cobbles. Reed listened patiently and asked some direct questions. Once the stallions had been returned to their stalls, Reed decided to view the Lipizzaner mares and fillies, which numbered 159 animals.[15]

Once the inspection was completed Reed and his party moved back into the yard. "Colonel?" said Reed to Rudofsky, indicating that he should sit in the American's jeep, specifically the passenger seat. Rudofsky, taken aback at the American's generosity, clambered aboard while Reed climbed in the back and perched awkwardly on an ammo crate.[16] It was time for a tour of inspection of the outer stations and the paddocks, with Rudofsky as guide.

*

Around the time that Colonel Hank Reed was conducting his first inspection of the horse facilities at Hostau, Colonel Podhajsky at St. Martin received an important visitor.

Major General Erich Weingart arrived at Arco Castle after a long and very dangerous journey from Berlin in his gas powered army staff car. The middle-aged Weingart had been sticking up for Colonel Podhajsky and his horses for years during the battles with Gustav Rau, and Weingart had been a powerful friend to have. As Inspector of Riding and Driving at the Army High Command, Weingart had taken an active interest in the Spanish Riding School. Now, with the war almost over, he had felt compelled to take one last look at the stallions before he was captured. It was a melancholy occasion as Podhajsky accompanied Weingart on his tour of the stables. Afterwards, they walked together in the garden.

"You have found the best place imaginable to let the Front roll over you," said Weingart, adjusting his spectacles as he spoke. "I am not anxious about you, for the Americans will be coming, and with your Spanish Riding School you will succeed in putting these soldiers as deeply under the spell of your white horses as you have always managed to do with me."[17] Weingart agreed to help Podhajsky one last time: he would issue a written order removing the Spanish Riding School from the Wehrmacht. This should prevent Podhajsky and his staff being viewed as enemy soldiers when the time came.

As the two men walked and talked, artillery fire rumbled in the distance. The Americans were close now. Before he left, Weingart spoke of his bitterness against the regime that had brought his country to the point of total defeat.

"My life comes to an end with the occupation of Germany," stated Weingart bluntly, "for I have no longer the strength to begin again as in 1918. We generals will be accused of allowing ourselves to become Hitler's tools ..."[18] He spoke of how he felt responsible for having served a criminal regime, and the misfortunes that had befallen Germany. Weingart took his leave and Podhajsky watched as the gray-painted staff car drove away from the castle. He would never see him again. Later, Podhajsky would learn that General Weingart had ordered his driver to pull to the side of a country road. Weingart had gone a little way into the woods, pulled out his service pistol and shot himself.

*

"I've decided that only Hostau, Hassatitz, and Zwirschen will be occupied by American soldiers," announced Colonel Reed, returned to the main stud at Hostau from his tour. "Taschlowitz, which is the furthest east of the stations, seems inadvisable to hold considering that the Russians are close to Pilsen."[19] Colonel Rudofsky and the other German officers were alarmed when Reed confirmed just how close the Red Army had come to the stud. They understood that the Americans desired to avoid a confrontation with the Russians, and evacuating and abandoning the facility at Taschlowitz seemed prudent, so Rudofsky raised no complaints.

Reed had another problem that he had already discussed with Major Andrews. The "new mission" that General Patton had warned him about when he had first contacted the Third Army commander seeking permission to rescue the horses had materialized. The 2nd Cavalry Group was transferring south with orders to capture the Eisenstein Pass, a strategically important route for any invasion of Czechoslovakia. Major Andrews was to return with Reed to 2nd Cavalry Group headquarters later that day. The only forces that Reed could leave at Hostau would be Captain Carter Catlett's Troop A reinforced by just two Chaffee tanks and two HMCs, including Quinlivan's single platoon at the stud. Captain Stewart was ordered to take overall responsibility as the new task force commander.[20] Stewart did the math. At full strength, a cavalry reconnaissance troop totaled 145 men. With the addition of eight men from Troop E crewing the two HMCs and the ten men from Company F in the pair of Chaffee tanks, Stewart's army, including himself, amounted to a grand total of just 164 warm bodies. With this tiny force he was expected to secure the entire town of Hostau, plus guard the stud and two outlying horse farms. It was in total an area that covered several square miles, but the best that Stewart could do with such limited men was guard all the main roads into the Hostau area and conduct perimeter patrols. Keeping back any meaningful reserve in case of emergencies was not really possible.

Colonel Reed would be returning to his headquarters forthwith to begin organizing the evacuation of the horses from Hostau to Bavaria. To make this a success he needed Colonel Rudofsky's cooperation.

"You remain here at your post," he said bluntly, pointing a gloved index finger at Rudofsky, who had expected to be sent back to the American lines as a prisoner-of-war. "Make an exact list of everything that is in the stud—horses, carts, harness, saddles, forage, other material. All of this will be taken over by us and taken away."

"Colonel, we have some Cossacks here with their families and a considerable number of horses. Should I include them on the list?" asked Rudofsky.

"We have no interest in those horses," replied Reed bluntly. "They stay here. All the rest of the horses we carry out."[21] The American officer's tone was unmistakable—he was the master of Hostau now, and the Lipizzaners and Arabians were the property of the US Army. The message was simple: if Rudofsky still cared for these animals, then he was to get with the program and help the Americans evacuate them to safety behind their lines. There was little time and certainly no room for sentimentality. Prince Amassov and his Cossacks, though they had assisted Rudofsky well in running the stud since their arrival, were Russian citizens, regardless of which side they had backed. Politically, they and their horses were a hot potato that Reed had no intention of holding. He would instead cut them loose to fend for themselves.

"You'll get news before the evacuation is ready," continued Reed to Rudofsky. "You'll take the convoy across the border to Bavaria."

Rudofsky appeared rather put out at Reed's attitude, and glanced at Dr. Lessing, who was listening intently, before turning back to the American. He had good reason to take issue with Reed's order. He pulled himself up to his full height and glared down at the American from behind his round spectacles.

"Colonel" he said slowly, "I am a Sudeten German. Here is my home. I have a property only twenty-five kilometers from here. Also, a sick mother. If it does not have to be, I do *not* want to go."

Reed's face had hardened as he listened to Rudofsky. He looked up at the German officer and barked in a no-nonsense tone: "You are coming with us!"

Rudofsky was genuinely shocked by the American's aggressive attitude, so different from the man described to him by Dr. Lessing. The veterinarian was also slightly taken aback by the change that had come over Reed since they had last met.

"You are accompanying this convoy for the time being and will come to America with the stud,"[22] continued Reed. *America*, thought Rudofsky, alarmed. *This is not possible*. But looking at the thunderous expression on Reed's face, he decided to keep his thoughts to himself and not press the matter for the time being.

Before he departed for his headquarters at Vohenstrauss, Reed spoke to Quinlivan. He would be responsible for security at the main facility and its two satellite stations at Hassatitz and Zwirschen, which meant spreading the troops very thin on the ground, while Colonel Rudofsky, now technically a civilian, would continue to command the stud and its personnel.[23]

With the evacuation of the former Allied prisoners ongoing, Rudofsky had to make do with his original German soldiers, plus some former Volkssturm, Hitler Youth and the Cossacks to try to keep the place running normally until the horses could be evacuated to safety. When and how that was to be achieved was yet to be settled by Reed, as operational activities further south, part of the American advance on Pilsen, would take up most of his time for the next few days.

Task Force Andrews was now re-designated Task Force Stewart. The name of the commander may have changed, but the situation the GIs faced at Hostau was still dire. They were eighteen miles behind German lines, a tiny American island in a sea of German troops, connected to the Allied lines by a single long and thin umbilical road that for long stretches was barely protected. Stewart and his men now babysat the most valuable horses in the world, spread over three different sites, with minimal resources, minimal ammunition and supplies and little hope of relief if the worst happened. Hostau was one step away from becoming a twentieth-century Alamo.

In addition to checking that all of the road blocks and observation posts were in position and manned, a further vital thing that Stewart did was to radio through to XII Corps headquarters requesting the creation of a "no-fire area" based on the rectangle of Czech land that incorporated Hostau and the two other horse farms. No artillery fire was to be permitted inside this protected area, regardless of the operational situation on the ground.[24] It was a big risk, but if push came to shove Stewart would have to rely on his own organic firepower—the two 75mm HMCs and the 60mm mortars of Troop A.

It was plainly clear to Stewart and the officers of Troop A that however carefully they sited their defenses and husbanded their limited manpower, they had to find more men, and fast. And Stewart already had a brilliant solution in mind. He had spoken to Rudofsky and the other German officers, including Prince Amassov, and it was clear that some of the troops formerly under their command felt that keeping the horses safe was now *the* priority, a priority higher than politics. More pragmatically, many viewed their work as a way to ingratiate themselves with the Americans and perhaps win a ticket out of Hostau when the time came to move the horses. Stewart suggested that Rudofsky and a hundred of the Germans deemed politically reliable should be rearmed, field-expedient, from the large stock of captured enemy firearms then held under lock and key.[25] Prince Amassov immediately volunteered his men as well, even though

Colonel Reed was not at this stage prepared to give the Cossacks a free pass to Allied lines.

The Germans at Hostau had surrendered to the Americans without firing a shot, and should the enemy retake the town, they would be asked to account for their passivity, regardless of the deal that Captain Lessing had secretly forged with Generals Schulz and Weisenberger, particularly so if it was the SS that showed up. These Germans had to be trusted, but Stewart judged the situation carefully when handing arms back to them. He needed trained soldiers, and many of the Germans had tied their fates to the survival of the rescued horses. The horses were their guaranteed way into American captivity rather than a Soviet gulag. The remainder of the Germans, those deemed suspect or uncommitted to Stewart's cause, continued to be shipped out to Bavaria on trucks sent up by Reed or left in the town under secure lock and key.

However, even with this extreme measure, there were still not enough men. Some of the released Allied prisoners-of-war, particularly the Poles who had nowhere to go, and a handful of Brits, French, and Americans, also demanded arms.[26] "Stewart's Foreign Legion" thus came into being, one of only two occasions during the Second World War when American and German soldiers fought side-by-side.*

The "Foreign Legion" was dispersed into small multinational squads and used to bolster Troop A's guard posts and positions. Soon the incongruous sight of battle-hardened GIs occupying positions alongside field-gray clad Germans in coal-scuttle helmets and former Allied prisoners in British battledress or French kepis appeared around the entire perimeter.

---

* The other was in early May 1945, when a small group of American GIs with one Sherman tank defended Schloss Itter, an Austrian castle, from the SS. The castle had been used to imprison prominent French military and civilian leaders until the German guards changed sides and fought with the Americans in defense of their famous prisoners. See Stephen Harding, *The Last Battle* (Boston: Da Capo, 2013)

Stewart had been wise to take this course of action, for hostile eyes *were* watching Hostau—and watching very carefully indeed.

*

In a dense patch of woodland just beyond the thin American perimeter an officer stared intently at Hostau through black field glasses. Over his field-gray uniform he wore a camouflage smock, and his helmet too was covered with a layer of camouflage, allowing him to blend in well with the surrounding foliage. He dropped the binoculars from his eyes and signaled to his small observation party with one gloved hand to withdraw. As he turned he picked up an MP40 machine pistol that lay beside his knee. The black collar of his tunic caught the weak early spring sun and the lightning runes insignia flashed dully before he and his men carefully withdrew silently deeper into the woods to confer. On the left cuffs of their gray uniforms each man wore an embroidered black band with a single word picked out in silver Gothic script—"*Deutschland.*" The SS had arrived.

CHAPTER 13

The Alamo

*"However grave the crisis may be at the moment, it will,
despite everything, finally be mastered by our unalterable
will, by our readiness for sacrifice and by our abilities."*

Adolf Hitler

"Message from Troop C, sir," said Stewart's radio operator.
Captain Stewart had been taking a few minutes rest on a bed
inside the wing of Hostau Castle that the Americans had taken over
as a temporary task force base.[1] The Troop A Headquarters section,
which Stewart was using as his own task force HQ, was set up in the
castle, including the administration, supply, and mess section.

Stewart was exhausted—he had been on the go since Colonel Reed
had appointed him to command the task force. There was so much to
do. Trucks and half-tracks still thundered up and down the road from
the 2nd Cavalry Group headquarters just across the border in Bavaria,
bringing in supplies to Weissensulz and Hostau and carrying out those
liberated Allied prisoners-of-war who wanted to leave. Two half-track
loads of Germans had also been removed, with the remaining German
prisoners who had not volunteered for Stewart's Foreign Legion still
under lock and key in six cellars throughout the town.[2]

Stewart had visited all of the positions prepared by Captain Carter
Catlett's Troop A both in and around Hostau. Now snatching some
much-needed shut-eye, Stewart was jerked back into reality by the
signaler's urgent voice. He sat up in bed, fully clothed and with his
boots still on.

"What time is it?" asked Stewart groggily, running a hand through his tousled hair.

"Oh-one-forty hours, sir," replied the signaler. A new day had begun since Stewart had hit the hay—April 30, 1945. Though Stewart and the other members of the US Army occupying Hostau would not even remotely suspect it, today was the day that Adolf Hitler would die.

"What's the message?"

"It's from Troop C's CP. The MSR has been cut, sir," replied the signaler, referring to the Main Supply Route back to Bavaria.

"Show me," demanded Stewart, following the man back through into the makeshift radio room where a tactical map was pinned to the wall. A stout block of felled trees had brought all vehicular movement to a halt on the road between Hostau and the American front line.[3] Troop C's command post (CP) was now cut off from its 1st Platoon at Weissensulz.

The sudden establishment of the roadblock during the hours of darkness demonstrated to Stewart that the American presence so far from their own lines was well known to the Germans, and that hostile forces were attempting to pinch off that bulge into their lines. Closing down the MSR, the route over which all supplies and fuel arrived for Troop A at Hostau, also meant that the liberated prisoners and German POWs could not be evacuated. Was it the prelude to an attack?

It was decided not to try to remove the roadblock until daylight, as the Germans routinely booby-trapped such obstacles and combat engineers would have to be sent up to deal with it. For the time being, Hostau was effectively marooned.

Stewart took immediate steps to alert Captain Catlett, who in turn warned all of his patrols and guard positions to keep their eyes skinned. Something was definitely brewing. Stewart stepped outside the darkened castle and put on his steel helmet. He looked up at the overcast night sky, rain falling refreshingly on to his face. He glanced at the luminous dial of his wristwatch—daylight in about four hours. Hostau's main street was deathly quiet—just the occasional cough from an American on sentry duty. The stillness was almost eerie— it was too quiet for the experienced combat soldiers of Troop A. It wasn't normal. What the new day might bring for Stewart's beleaguered command was anyone's guess.

*

Confirmation of the presence of an SS unit in the area arrived by radio from 2nd Cavalry Group HQ shortly after sunup on April 30, 1945.[4] It made for chilling reading for Captains Stewart and Catlett and their fellow officers. XII Corps had learned of the presence of the III Battalion, SS Panzer Grenadier Regiment "Deutschland," logging it as an advance guard for the fearsome 2nd SS Panzer Division "Das Reich."[5] The regiment had been sent west following heavy combat against the Red Army near Vienna to the Passau region of the Austrian–German border to help hold off the Americans. Passau was lost on April 29 and the remnants of Regiment "Deutschland" appeared to have scattered into rudimentary combat groups, with one moving northeast into western Czechoslovakia.

Compared to General Weisenberger's ragtag assortment of army and Volkssturm formations, these SS were very much in a league of their own. The formidable 2nd SS Panzer Division "Das Reich," renowned as the best division in the entire German armed forces, had earned an appalling reputation for brutality during the Normandy campaign, most infamously the killing of 642 men, women, and children in the French village of Oradour-sur-Glane in June 1944.[6]

SS Panzer Grenadier Regiment "Deutschland" had its own horrific reputation for bestiality to add to its genuinely impressive military feats of arms. In Normandy, the regiment had shot fifty-seven civilians in cold blood following an Allied attack on June 11, 1944. The Panzergrenadiers had gone on to kill eleven in the little village of Trebon; nineteen, including two young children, at

Pouzac; and twenty five, including eleven women, at Bagnieres. The unit epitomized the Waffen-SS—it was suicidally brave and coldly efficient in combat but inhuman towards its enemies, making for a terrifying combination. And now those selfsame soldiers were close to Hostau and the men protecting the world's most valuable horses.

By now, Colonel Reed and most of the 2nd Cavalry had withdrawn from their positions and headed south towards the Eisenstein Pass, northeast of Regan, as per Patton's order. Only Troop A remained at Hostau along with the two Chaffee tanks from Company F and the pair of Howitzer Motor Carriages from Troop E. Occupying the 2nd's vacated positions was the 97th Infantry Division's 387th Infantry Regiment, its three battalions moving into position during the night of April 29/30. They would assume responsibility for guarding some of the MSR, with Captain Catlett's Troop A taking over some of the responsibility for the area around Weissensulz and through to Hostau, as Troop C was gone, further stretching Stewart's already thin manpower reserve. The 387th was now responsible for furnishing supplies to Stewart's task force.[7] Also, the regiment provided flank protection, taking over the towns and villages just inside Czechoslovakia that the 42nd had liberated a few days earlier.[8]

The roadblock that the Germans had set during the night of April 29/30 was investigated in daylight by a patrol from the 387th Infantry and discovered not to be booby-trapped. It was broken up and hauled aside, allowing for the trucks to Hostau to resume running again.[9] But the fear remained that the Germans might try the same tactic again, perhaps in multiple places simultaneously.

Further enemy activity was reported close by along the line, demonstrating to Stewart that the enemy was far from beaten. Nine miles northwest of Hostau a reconnaissance squad from the 386th Infantry Regiment was ambushed, losing two killed and several wounded during an ugly exchange. At the same time, a battle broke out on the road to Klenc, eleven miles from Hostau. The 3rd Battalion, 358th Infantry suffered two killed, thirty-eight wounded and Panzerfausts knocked out two supporting tanks. The question was: would the Germans also strike in the middle, at Hostau?

"I'm sending Verry to the 387th CP to make arrangements for gasoline and ammunition resupply,"[10] stated Captain Stewart to Troop A's commanding officer Carter Catlett. The route back through Weissensulz and on to Colonel Rose's command post had been pre-arranged, and patrols from both the 42nd Cavalry and 387th Infantry were posted along it at strategic points. It should be a milk run for Captain Verry, a staff officer from 42nd Squadron HQ.

Verry climbed into the front passenger seat of his jeep, which was driven by his radio operator, inevitably nicknamed "Radar," with the bulky transmitter stowed in the rear. It was still early morning and unseasonably cold, with scattered snow showers predicted for later in the day.[11]

Captains Stewart and Catlett stood on the front stoop of the castle's main entrance, battered tin mugs of steaming coffee in their hands. Behind them came the sounds of radio operators talking with distant patrols, or the clack-clack of manual typewriters as clerks filled out combat reports.

"I'll be back in a couple hours," said Verry to Stewart, as Radar started the jeep's engine, which coughed noisily to life.

"Don't do anything I wouldn't do," quipped Catlett. Verry grinned, touched a finger to his helmet brim in a casual salute and told his driver to go, the jeep swinging around and heading for Weissensulz. Captain Catlett took a sip of his coffee and looked up at the leaden sky. It was still very quiet, with no enemy activity reported around Hostau. He shivered before going back inside, Stewart following behind.

The jeep carrying Captain Verry sped out of Hostau. As he passed a couple of checkpoints he noted that Stewart's Foreign Legion appeared to have everything in hand. American soldiers covered all exits with their weapons, while Germans, Cossacks, and some former Allied POWs worked alongside of them, digging foxholes or camouflaging positions. The tanks, Howitzer Motor Carriages, and M8 armored cars added their firepower to the defenses, being dispersed around the positions. Then Verry and his driver were hurtling through open countryside, the cold wind chilling their exposed faces beneath their helmets.

Verry's jeep slowed down and passed through Weissensulz, where American troops saluted or raised their hands in greeting as he passed. Just beyond Weissensulz was another small hamlet. The jeep slowed. There were no American soldiers around, which was Verry's first intimation of trouble. The jeep turned a corner. A German soldier, a camouflaged smock over his field-gray uniform, a rifle in his hands, stood in the middle of the road. He turned at the sound of the jeep, his jaw dropping in surprise as Verry's vehicle squealed to a halt.[12]

"Back up!" yelled Verry at Radar, the enlisted man mashing the gears in panic. "*Alarm!*" yelled the German, as he raised his Mauser rifle and fired, the bullet whizzing past Verry's head. Time seemed to slow down. The German recycled the rifle bolt at the same moment as the jeep stalled. There was the sound of breaking glass as the German's second shot shattered the American vehicle's windshield. More Germans, all heavily armed, started to emerge from buildings up ahead, running to the aid of their comrade. A fusillade of shots cut the air around the jeep or smacked into the vehicle's body with metallic thuds. Verry grabbed his M1 carbine and with his right hand pulled Radar down.

"Take cover!" he shouted above the din of German fire and shouting. The two Americans exited the vehicle crouching low and took cover behind it as bullets continued to bounce off the road surface or slap into the damaged jeep.

"Get on the radio for help!" yelled Verry, "I'll cover you!" Verry popped his head up, shouldered the M1 and unleashed a fusillade of rapid shots at the advancing Germans while Radar reached into the back of the jeep and grabbed the microphone. He had to shout to be heard above the din, sending an urgent request for assistance to the 387th Infantry's command post, before dropping the radio mic and opening fire with his own carbine. Verry ducked back down and quickly reloaded. They couldn't stay here, of that he was sure. They needed to find cover and wait for relief. It had all happened so fast. Where in the hell had so many SS come from? The route was supposed to be secure. He popped back up and unleashed another fifteen-round volley that temporarily kept the Germans' heads down. Then he dropped back to his knees and reloaded again while Radar fired his weapon, his eyes staring around madly for some suitable cover.

"Get in there!" yelled Verry, pointing to a nearby two-storey house. "I'll cover you."[13] Radar needed no encouragement. As Verry opened fire again, the enlisted man jumped to his feet and sprinted the few yards to the front door of the house, forcing his way inside. Verry ceased firing and ran after him, German bullets impacting all around as he barreled through the front door, kicking it shut with his feet as he lay on his back in a panting, sweating pile in the hallway.

"Upstairs," he said breathlessly, and the two Americans quickly stumbled up a nearby staircase, reloading as they went.

*

The SS had managed to quickly throw up a roadblock at another point close to Weissensulz at the small hamlet of Rosendorf. It was encountered by a patrol from Troop A soon after Captain Verry had passed on his way. The American cavalrymen advanced on foot towards the block, unsure of enemy numbers. But suddenly, rifle and automatic fire opened up, sending the American patrol diving for cover. The sergeant commanding the patrol decided to pull back into the trees and regroup.

"You see that house over yonder?" said the breathless sergeant to Private First Class Raymond Manz, who was two weeks shy of his twentieth birthday. Manz, at 6 foot 2 inches the tallest man in the patrol, nodded seriously. "Set up a base of fire on the second floor," ordered the sergeant. "It should give you a perfect defilade of the Kraut machine gunners behind the roadblock. We'll cover you."

Manz nodded, taking in his orders. In his hands was the patrol's most powerful weapon, the Browning Automatic Rifle or BAR, a light machine gun with a bipod at the front. It used 20-round box magazines, carried in pouches on Manz's webbing and was lethally accurate in the right hands.

The sergeant readied his men. Once Manz was set and keeping the Germans' heads down, he would lead the rest of the cavalrymen and outflank and destroy the roadblock.

"Cover!" yelled the sergeant, and the Americans opened a brisk fire at the roadblock, bullets peppering the logs and clipping branches off the surrounding trees while the Germans temporarily ducked down. Manz was on his feet a second later and charging towards the house, his mind focused entirely upon reaching the building and making it up to the second floor. The Germans noticed the move, and tried to cut him down as he ran, but Manz's long legs powered him on. Suddenly, he fell, winded and shocked. It felt like someone had struck him on the shoulder with a baseball bat. He lay momentarily stunned amid the leaf litter and dirt. There was no pain as yet, but when he touched his shoulder his hand came away bloody. A flesh wound. German bullets continued to zip past. Manz got back to his feet, picked up the BAR and charged on, oblivious to his wound, focused once again on the house and safety.

Manz quickly stormed upstairs and wrenched open a window that partly overlooked the German position. He jammed the BAR's bipod onto the narrow window frame and loosed off a volley at the Germans, hitting one or two, who crumpled to the ground dead, while the rest crouched down further and tried to return fire at the window while also attempting to hit the rest of the American patrol as it began maneuvering through the trees to outflank the position.

Manz popped up every few seconds and aimed a controlled burst into the German position, the ejected cartridge cases rattling on the room's wooden floor. Then German fire would force him to drop below the window and reload, as enemy slugs chewed wood off the frame or thudded into the ceiling above Manz's head, sending down a shower of plaster and dust. Seconds later, locked and loaded once more, Manz would bravely stand up and begin the process all over again.

"Frag out," yelled a corporal moving up with the rest of the American patrol as he wrenched the pin from a fragmentation grenade and hurled it in the general direction of the SS roadblock. It detonated with a crump, smoke and debris pluming into the air, before the cacophony of American and German small-arms fire continued unabated. The Americans down below could still hear the reassuring hammer of Manz's BAR as they closed in on the SS.

*

In Hostau, all hell had broken loose about the time that Pfc. Manz was working his BAR and Captain Verry was scrambling into a house under fire. Reports had arrived from several Troop A outposts of large numbers of SS moving through the trees around the town and into the open fields. There had been no preliminary German artillery bombardment or even mortar fire, which indicated that the SS were without proper support and acting in a desperate measure. But they were advancing with their customary fearlessness and clearly intent on taking the town,[14] firing as they walked. Captains Stewart and Catlett and their officers immediately assessed the unfolding situation. It appeared that the SS, though strong in infantry, lacked any armored vehicles or artillery in support.

Groups of SS, dressed in dirty camouflaged smocks and helmets, advanced across the fields towards the US positions where they were brought under intense small-arms fire from not only the American troopers, but also their German, Cossack, Polish, British, and French allies. They were all fighting to protect both themselves and the horses, and it was vital that the SS did not achieve a breakthrough into the town just as other parties of Germans were trying to isolate Hostau with roadblocks and incursions into the surrounding hamlets.

The SS attacks were being broken up by American mortar fire, the 60mm tubes being worked furiously by the cavalry troopers, the 3-pound bombs impacting into the heavy soil, white-hot shrapnel cutting down the SS, while machine-gun and rifle fire stitched across their ranks. The American and Allied positions were peppered by German bullets, but the Americans had the advantage of prepared positions and armored vehicles while the SS repeatedly attempted to advance on the town over open fields or through scattered nearby woods. The SS fire was heavy though inaccurate.[15] The deciding factor for Captain Catlett and his multinational force were the two Chaffee tanks and pair of Howitzer Motor Carriages, whose fire was lethally accurate, with the SS held beyond the range at which their Panzerfaust rocket launchers could have proven decisive.[16]

At the Hostau Stud and the two satellite farms the horses were terrified by the explosions and the constant rattle of small arms, whinnying and crashing around their stalls as the grooms, themselves now armed with rifles, did what they could for them. Fortunately, the skirmishes around the American perimeter were far enough from the horse stables that the animals were out of range of the flying lead.

The SS continued to probe the Hostau defense ring, attempting to find a weak spot which they could immediately exploit, but Captains Stewart and Catlett had planned the defense carefully, and though short of troops, the deciding factor was the high level of firepower that the defenders could deploy, particularly the vehicles, which were driven from point to point as each new crisis unfolded. The SS suffered hundreds killed and wounded, with the fields and woods around Hostau littered with bloodied corpses, blackened, smoking mortar craters and burning trees.

*

Captain Verry and his radio operator had none of the advantages in firepower and weaponry of their comrades at Hostau. They crouched, breathless and sweaty inside an upstairs room of a shot-up house waiting for rescue. The firing had quieted down outside as the SS moved in on their position.

At the 387th Infantry's command post, the frantic radio message had been received and help was on its way. The 387th's CO, Colonel Long, immediately dispatched a platoon from 1st Battalion who piled into jeeps and, led by the mechanized troop commander, blasted up the road towards the small hamlet where Verry was trapped.[17]

Inside the house Verry and Radar crouched on the floor, their weapons at the ready. Downstairs there were sounds of movement, followed by hushed talking.[18]

"They're inside the property," whispered Verry to his companion. They exchanged looks and raised their weapons towards the door of the room.

*

At Rosendorf, the sergeant commanding the Troop A patrol led the charge on the SS roadblock with several of his men close behind. A barrage of grenades thrown by the attackers landed in front of or behind the makeshift barricade, the detonations mixed with the horrible screams of the dying and wounded. Then the troopers were among the SS, shooting and clubbing them down until the position was overrun.

With the SS eliminated, thoughts turned to Pfc. Manz. Some of his comrades hurried over to the house from which Manz had been firing and climbed upstairs calling his name.

They found Manz lying on the floor of the room surrounded by brass cartridge casings and empty magazines, his blood mingling with the dust, the BAR still gripped in his hands. A neat hole had been drilled through his forehead, killing him instantly. He had been killed raising his head to give his comrades covering fire. For his gallantry that day, Raymond Manz would receive a posthumous award of the Distinguished Service Cross.

Other casualties had been sustained during the firefight at Rosendorf. Sergeant Owen W. Sutton from North Carolina was mortally wounded and later died in hospital. Staff Sergeant Fred R. Foyles was seriously wounded but managed to pull through, while Technician Fifth Class Malcolm E. Rhodes and Corporal Samuel Fletcher were also wounded, though less seriously.[19]

*

The German voices and footfalls that Verry and his companion could hear were coming closer to the room in which they crouched, weapons at the ready for their last stand. Their eyes were on the back of the closed door and its brass handle. Both men expected a stick grenade to be flung into the room at any minute. But then other sounds cut in—firing from the other end of the hamlet. Verry listened—it was unmistakable. Mixed in with the thump of German weapons were the familiar sounds of American M1 Garands and BARs. It was the relief, and just in the nick of time.

The platoon from 1st Battalion, 387th Infantry, went straight into the assault, catching the SS patrol by surprise. They worked their way through the hamlet, house by house, street by street, beating back the SS who took a hammering before breaking and fleeing back into the forest, leaving several of their comrades behind dead or wounded. The hamlet was taken. Verry and his radio operator gingerly emerged from the house where they had taken cover, shaken but unharmed after their harrowing experience. Order was soon restored.[20]

*

The SS attempts to take Hostau were shot to pieces. After five hours of determined assaults the fight drew to a close in the late afternoon of April 30. The surviving SS simply melted into the countryside, while American patrols moved out to collect prisoners and deal with the many enemy wounded.

About the same time that American soldiers at Hostau were checking the dead bodies of SS men or carefully searching the more than one hundred prisoners they had taken, hundreds of miles to the north one of the final dramas of the Second World War had already played out.

At around 3.30pm Adolf Hitler, palsied and broken and sitting beside his wife of less than twenty-four hours in the sitting room of his Berlin bunker, had crushed a vial of cyanide between his teeth and simultaneously pulled the trigger of the Walther automatic that was pressed to his right temple. As Hitler's SS lay in bloody and smoldering heaps across the fields before Hostau, so in Berlin the Führer's body was consigned to a shell hole in the Reich Chancellery garden, doused with gasoline and unceremoniously burned. But Hitler's death did not end the fighting in Berlin or the wider war. A new Nazi government was even then forming in the north of Germany under Grand Admiral Karl Dönitz, and the German forces in Czechoslovakia and Austria would continue to resist fiercely. The horses that the Americans had bravely rescued were still in as much danger as before, perhaps more so as the situation in the region continued to deteriorate.

"Stewart's Foreign Legion" had beaten off the SS on this occasion, but Hostau still remained a tiny and isolated American island in a sea of shifting German military power. And the horses were going nowhere, with foaling season under way. For now, the Americans had simply to sit tight and protect that which they had endeavored so hard to obtain.

CHAPTER 14

All Quiet on the Western Front

"Maintain order and discipline in town and country.
Let everybody do his duty at his own post."

Reich President Karl Dönitz

Snow was falling when Tom Stewart left his command post in company with Captain Catlett to make his rounds of the Troop A positions.[1] Since the battle with the SS the day before, everyone had remained on full alert lest the enemy reappeared. The weather didn't help allay those fears, with visibility limited across the fields and woods that surrounded Hostau and its environs. Spring stubbornly refused to break in this part of Europe and though not heavy, the white dusting nonetheless reminded the American veterans of the Ardennes. More than one thanked the Almighty that unlike at the Battle of the Bulge, the Germans they faced here seemed to lack those dreaded 88mm anti-aircraft guns that they had used to such effect in Belgium, firing air bursts among the tall fir trees that looked eerily similar to the stands of timber around Hostau.

Stewart climbed behind the wheel of a jeep, with Catlett jumping in the passenger seat. They drove by way of the Hostau Stud, where Colonel Rudofsky and the veterinarians Lessing and Kroll came out to greet them and reported that all was well with the horses—in fact, some more of the mares had foaled, adding more little black bodies to the growing collection. Then Stewart set off to make his rounds of the outpost positions, talking to the platoon and squad commanders and checking that the positions were properly sited, weapons and men secure and that they were well supplied with ammunition and water. Hot food made an occasional appearance, though many of the men were living off K rations or the larger multi-man ration packs from their vehicles.

Using his field glasses, Stewart scanned the fields over which the SS had attacked the day before. The German bodies lay where they had fallen, grotesque lumps covered in a thin layer of snow, only recognizable as corpses by the occasional frozen hand or boot that poked into the air. Stewart was pleased with the performance of the "tame" Germans, those of the Hostau garrison and stud who had chosen to fight for the Americans. The former prisoners-of-war and Cossacks had also done well, and many continued to help run the stud and the two outlying farms, tending to the horses and carrying out the multitude of tasks that had to be completed with such a reduced staff.

When Stewart and Catlett returned to their command post at the castle, they reviewed their large situation map tacked to the wall in Stewart's rudimentary office. From the messages that they had received from the rest of the 42nd Squadron, they knew that their comrades were in constant action against the Germans further south, securing the Eisenstein Pass for whatever General Patton might decide to do next. But for the time being at Hostau, all was quiet—too quiet. Neither Stewart nor Catlett thought that the stillness could last long.

*

Twenty-five miles to the northeast at Kladrau Castle another pair of officers examined a situation map. German Lieutenant General Karl Weisenberger and his chief of staff, Colonel Bennicke, were going over the deployments of their few units. Since their voluntary ceding of Hostau to the enemy, the German line had reformed to take the American bulge into consideration. Ominously for the Americans, the Germans continued to reinforce the area.

"The overall situation is relatively quiet, General," said Bennicke. "Apart from the American fighter-bombers, of course." He was referring to the P-47 Thunderbolts that during good flying weather continued to harry German forces, attacking any vehicles or groups of soldiers that were spotted moving on the country roads. Such was their level of activity that Captain Stewart had had one of his own jeeps shot up by an American plane in a case of mistaken identity. Fortunately, the occupants had managed to get out before the vehicle had been hit and destroyed.

"Our front line remains thinly garrisoned," continued Bennicke, "but the situation of the troops has improved somewhat with the arrival of fresh reinforcements."

Weisenberger raised one eyebrow quizzically.

"Newly activated units?" asked Weisenberger with a long sigh.

"Yes, General, mostly from unwanted Luftwaffe ground crews. But we have received a handful of artillery from Pilsen, which has been deployed here,"[2] said Bennicke, pointing to the positions on the map.

"The 2nd and 11th Panzer Divisions remain to the rear of our line, General."

"What state are they currently in?" asked Weisenberger. Bennicke consulted his papers.

"The 2nd has about twenty operational Panzers and approximately two thousand men. They are deployed at Plan, Mies, and the Nürschau-Staab area. But they have no fuel."[3]

Weisenberger grunted dismissively.

"And the 11th?"

"In much better shape, General. Most of the division has concentrated southeast of Taus. They have some fuel for their Panzers, with most of the men acting as infantry. They have established security points behind our units. A portion of the division has departed for Austria to protect Linz."

"But neither unit has been placed under my command, despite my urgings at Army headquarters, Bennicke,"[4] said Weisenberger bitterly.

Instead, he had been told to make do with the ragtag assortment of odds and ends that were occupying strongpoints and roadblocks in front of the Americans.

"General Schulz at Mirikau and the other commanding officers report that their men's training is inadequate, they have insufficient artillery, unit cohesion is fragmented and desertion rates remain intolerably high,"[5] said Bennicke, riffling through the reports in his hands as he spoke.

Weisenberger shook his head mournfully and sat down behind his desk.

"So what do we think?" he asked, changing the subject. "Is the great Patton coming?"

"I don't know, sir," replied Bennicke honestly.

"Well, I'm inclined to think that the Americans have stopped for political reasons. Take this situation at the Hostau horse depot, for example. Patton has *not* exploited this bulge in our line. It supports my impression that the Americans do *not* intend to move into Czechoslovakia."

"I hope that you are right, General, for one real attack by the enemy will smash our defenses with little effort,"[6] replied Bennicke gloomily. Weisenberger stared back at him before nodding slowly, despair etched on his face.

Weisenberger was right in his assumption that politics had prevented Patton from exploiting a wonderful opportunity to smash the Germans in western Czechoslovakia. But the halt would only be a temporary one, if "Old Blood and Guts" had anything to do with it. Patton still pushed General Eisenhower for permission to strike for Prague, his dream of pissing in the Danube still at the forefront of his mind. But if it was to happen, it had better happen fast. Moving into position to assault Prague and western Czechoslovakia from the east were 1.7 million Red Army soldiers.

Patton had a strong ally in the British Prime Minister Winston Churchill, who believed Prince von Bismarck's old adage that stated,

"He who holds Prague, holds Central Europe." Churchill did not want to see the Soviets take Czechoslovakia, and the Czechoslovak government-in-exile in London was pushing him hard. He was also concerned by the influence of a Soviet-occupied Czechoslovakia on neighboring Balkan nations.[7] Though promises had been made to Stalin at Yalta, there was everything still to play for. The problem for Patton and Churchill was the new American president, Harry S. Truman. He seemed loath to go back on the agreement made at Yalta by Roosevelt.

Patton did order Third Army units to push into western Czechoslovakia on May 1, 1945, but they only moved a few miles inside the border, some through the Eisenstein Pass secured by 2nd Cavalry Group, before Eisenhower ordered Patton to halt. For the time being, Patton champed at the bit but didn't dare risk defying Eisenhower and his president.[8] On the same day Stalin issued orders that the assault on Prague was to commence in six days' time.

Task Force Stewart remained horribly exposed at Hostau. Stewart knew that he wasn't going anywhere for the time being. Rudofsky and the veterinarians were adamant that the mares and foals couldn't yet be moved, certainly not under their own steam. The previous day's fighting with the SS had demonstrated that American-occupied Hostau was a juicy target, and with only a handful of men with which to defend the place, Stewart knew that they could only withstand a few such attacks before the worst happened. Would a general like Weisenberger tolerate a bulge into his front line forever? After all, the agreement that Stewart and Lessing had struck with the local German command was that the horses would be evacuated to the American lines. That hadn't occurred. Weisenberger could view American inaction as a ploy to build a bridgehead. Patton could reinforce Hostau and totally undermine the rest of the German line by attacking it from behind. And what of the Soviets? If the German front in the east collapsed and the Red Army came steamrolling across the open terrain past Hostau to the American front line in the Bohemian Forest, what about his little command and the horses? Would the Red Army just stand by and allow the Americans to evacuate the horses? That seemed unlikely. Most probably Stewart and his men would be politely asked to leave while the horses and the German staff and their families were turned over to the tender mercies of the Soviets. One thing was abundantly clear to Captain Stewart—the situation needed to be resolved as rapidly as possible, for every passing day brought the likelihood of an extremely undesirable outcome to the whole mission.

At the stud, Captains Lessing and Kroll remained busy with not only the horses under their jurisdiction, but also with a constant flow of refugees. Though the town was under temporary American jurisdiction, the human wave that was fleeing the advancing Red Army had not been staunched—in fact, as the Soviets grew closer, more and more Sudeten Germans were abandoning their homes and trying to move into Germany proper and the protection of the Western Allies.[9] Mixed in among the refugees were other Germans from the eastern provinces, Russians who had fought for the Nazis, forced laborers and Allied POWs who had escaped from relocation marches or camps as confusion reigned in the countryside. With this tide of human misery came more horses, and more work for the veterinarians. The Americans tried to keep the refugees moving on to the US lines, rather than using up precious resources in the town.

It must have been a shock for some of the displaced persons to have arrived in Hostau. Finding it occupied by the Americans, they would have thought they had made it to safety, only to discover that the town was an isolated outpost and vulnerable. Colonel Rudofsky worked hard for his new masters, ensuring that the stud was properly run and the horses well cared for, even with a more limited staff than before. He also complied with Colonel Reed's orders, and began to create lists of the horses, equipment and supplies that would need to be taken out by the Americans when the time came for the evacuation of the stud and its precious animals.

One of the immediate problems that faced Rudofsky was maintaining discipline. The arrival of the Americans had signaled to many of the former Allied POWs working at the three stable sites that they had been liberated. But many remained working, often reluctantly, as they could not be returned to the Allied lines for political or logistical reasons. And some, like the Soviets, were causing trouble. A few had turned aggressive, and looked to confront Germans, while others behaved in a truculent or mutinous fashion. Colonel Reed had left Rudofsky in command at the stud and its two satellite stations, but though Rudofsky was still in German uniform, he was now technically a civilian. Some of the workers resented taking orders from a German, though Rudofsky looked to First Lieutenant Bill Quinlivan's platoon to protect him and his men from any unpleasantness. Quinlivan managed, through some rough but extremely effective measures, to prevent unruly behavior from taking root. His no-nonsense demeanor and tough Irish attitude carried the day, and allowed some semblance of normality to continue even though the surrounding countryside was in uproar as the old order collapsed and anarchy gradually took over.

*

"General, Radio Hamburg has just warned the German people to stand by for a grave and important announcement," said Colonel Bennicke to Weisenberger after knocking and quietly entering his office at 9.35pm. Weisenberger looked up from his paperwork, removed his glasses and rubbed the bridge of his nose.

"Switch on the wireless," he said, and Bennicke went over to a radio set that sat on a side table and warmed it up. Martial and funereal music soon wafted through the ether from besieged Hamburg far to the north, filling both men with a mournful feeling. Bennicke sat in the chair opposite Weisenberger's desk and crossed his arms, both men waiting in silence for whatever was to come.

At 10.36pm the music stopped abruptly and there followed three drum rolls. Then an announcer began to speak.

"It is reported from the Führer's headquarters that our Führer, Adolf Hitler, fighting to the last breath against Bolshevism, fell for Germany this afternoon in his operational headquarters in the Reich Chancellery." Weisenberger and Bennicke's eyes locked, both men in a state of shock. The Germans had yet to discover that Hitler had actually shot himself the day before in the bunker. "On April 30th the Führer appointed Grand Admiral Dönitz his successor," the announcer continued. "The grand admiral and successor of the Führer now speaks to the German people."

Karl Dönitz took the microphone. Far from ending the war, the new Reich President assured his listeners that the war of resistance against the Soviet invaders would continue, as would fighting against the British and Americans if they chose not to come to terms with Germany. The situation for the remaining armed forces of Germany remained unchanged. "Give me your confidence because your road is mine as well," said Dönitz plaintively. "Maintain order and discipline in town and country. Let everybody do his duty at his own post." The leadership may have changed, but the rhetoric remained the same.

*

Captain Stewart was roughly shaken awake by an orderly just after first light on May 2, 1945. He came to and sat up.

"What's up?" he asked, instantly alert and expecting trouble. When an officer was suddenly awakened it usually wasn't for ham and eggs.

"Sorry to wake you, sir, but we've had a report that Captain Verry has been attacked," replied the orderly clerk.

"Details?" asked Stewart. The orderly quickly outlined what was known. Captain Verry's jeep had been ambushed again while returning to squadron headquarters.[10] Stewart got out of bed and began issuing orders while looking at a situation map. It appeared that Verry and Radar had bumped into some SS within the "no-fire line."

"Have Sergeant Walker report to me immediately,"[11] ordered Stewart.

When Walker arrived, Stewart told him to have his platoon ready for immediate deployment. He also ordered that all outposts be placed on full alert, weapons manned and eyes skinned. His fear was that the SS was trying another attack on Hostau in a rerun of their earlier assault.

As Stewart gathered his jacket, helmet and M1 carbine and hurried downstairs to where his jeep was parked, the corporal who was to drive him piped up.

"Did you hear the good news, sir?" asked the corporal, grinning.

"What good news?" demanded Stewart, clipping on his belt with its leather holster and heavy .38 revolver.

"Hitler's dead," said the corporal, "just came over the BBC."

Stewart stopped fiddling with his equipment and gave his companion a strong look.

"That's swell, Corporal. But it looks like someone forgot to tell the Krauts, don't you think?"

Stewart's jeep thundered along towards the edge of the forest with Sergeant Walker's platoon strung out behind in their M8s and jeeps. Fortunately no Americans had been injured in the initial ambush. The column halted and Stewart gave orders for the platoon to debark and take up positions, establishing a base of fire. Stewart and his men didn't have long to wait before the threat materialized.

The GIs scanned the thick trees, searching for the enemy. Eventually, movement was spotted. The Americans were well down and waiting for the signal to open fire. The German soldiers moved carefully but purposefully through the trees, wearing camouflaged smocks and helmet covers, or else bundled up in thick greatcoats, their weapons held at the port across their chests ready for instant use, heads scanning from side to side as they fanned out. A twenty-strong group of "field-expedient" armed British ex-prisoners-of-war joined the American soldiers, each man carrying a German rifle. They had been ordered to remain in reserve but could not resist jumping into the fight.[12]

Stewart judged the enemy group to be a lightly armed patrol of indeterminate numbers—obviously the reconnaissance element for a bigger force that was as yet unseen. Stewart waited until the distance dropped before giving the order to fire.

A fusillade of American lead raked the trees, taking down several of the Germans, the rest hitting the dirt and returning fire with their rifles and machine pistols. Grenades were flung in both directions and the fire was rapid, chipping bark off tree trunks and cutting down branches. Stewart was in the thick of the action, but reports arrived that more SS were arriving on the scene, outnumbering the small American force. As the GIs slowly eliminated the SS patrol, "I became conscious that a force of about company strength, using marching fire, was coming through the forest in a skirmish line,"[13] recalled Stewart. The SS, numbering perhaps a hundred men, moved forward deliberately, firing as they came. Stewart immediately recognized the danger his command was in, outnumbered and outgunned. But he still had the M8s and their 37mm cannons and heavy machine guns and help was but a radio call away.

"Get on the horn and tell the two Chaffees to join us," said Stewart to his radio operator. Then he ordered Sergeant Walker to take his M8 armored car up on to high ground to the right and enfilade the exposed German line while the dismounted troopers kept the enemy pinned in the trees. But then another sound broke in over the firing, a deeper thumping of heavy weapons. And it sounded familiar. Stewart could see Walker frantically pointing from his M8's turret and following his signals he started to make out olive-drab uniforms moving in the trees.

"Cease fire, repeat, cease fire," Stewart ordered urgently to all squads and vehicles.[14] The German fire had stopped and instead SS started to emerge from the trees with their hands above their heads, prodded on by US infantrymen armed with Garand rifles and Thompsons. At their head were Captain Verry and Radar, who sought out Stewart.[15]

The other GIs were from the 387th Infantry, and their officer turned to his radio operator and ordered him to send an immediate message. "From White Three, report for Easy Six. Patrol has entered six-five and met friendlies."[16] "65" was the 387th's codename for Hostau. Colonel Long had ordered his battalions forward to push slightly ahead of Stewart's "no-fire line" and to maintain patrol contact with the 42nd's Troop A at Hostau. The town and the stud were no longer sticking out like an appendix into hostile territory, but were now forming part of the American front line.[17]

CHAPTER 15

The Green Light

"There is no time to lose and the American Army has got to act."

Colonel Alois Podhajsky

Colonel Rudofsky was a worried man. He sat at his desk inside Hostau Castle slowly smoking a cigarette. His desk was littered with reports on the horses under his care, but at this moment his eyes had a glazed and reflective look and he was staring into space while smoke from his cigarette curled upwards in the still air. Though he attended to his duties assiduously and ingratiated himself with his new American masters through his in-depth knowledge of the precious horses and his excellent administrative skills, he was torn by worry about his family.

Ever since April 29, when Colonel Reed had peremptorily ordered him to accompany the horses to Bavaria and perhaps onwards to the United States, Hubert Rudofsky had been in a state of fair agitation. He was worried about his elderly mother who lived near Hostau and was not in the best of health. He was worried about his young nephew Ulli and sister-in-law in Bischofteinitz,* twenty-five miles southwest of Pilsen. The Soviets could capture his family while he remained in the custody of the Americans. He also worried about his property.

Rudofsky stubbed out his cigarette and walked over to the window. He smoothed his uniform tunic and stared out, the stud's stable block roofs visible beyond the wall that enclosed the castle's

---

* Now Horšovský Týn.

formal gardens. A bored-looking American soldier stood beside the gate, his carbine slung over his right shoulder.

Rudofsky turned away from the window, his mind racing. He had been perfectly truthful when he had told Reed that he wanted to stay because he was a Sudeten German. He had been born and raised in the old Kingdom of Bohemia, in that narrow strip of Germanic territory the Nazis called the Sudetenland. He had served the Czechoslovak state honorably before the war, and from 1938 until now had merely done his duty in the German Army. He was no Nazi. He wished only to remain in the land of his birth alongside his kith and kin. With Reed's intractability obvious and unchallengeable, how could Rudofsky continue to help the Americans but also resolve his internal conflict?

Rudofsky had had no news of his family since the arrival of the Americans. Even more alarmingly, the American advance appeared to have stopped for the time being, and Rudofsky was beginning to believe that the Soviets would sweep up his family while Patton sat and watched. Rudofsky had come to at least one firm decision— when the Americans evacuated the horses and the stud's staff to Germany, he would not go with them. He was determined to remain in Czechoslovakia, come what may. For now, there was nothing that he could do but bide his time. He settled himself back behind his desk and sighed, before opening a buff folder in front of him and starting work once again.

*

For General Weisenberger, who on May 4, 1945, was still clinging to the increasingly impossible defense of the German line before Hostau, events were changing rapidly and from within. During the whole time of his command of Wehrkreis XIII, Weisenberger, though his threadbare units had managed to hold the line against minor American incursions, had known that standing at his back was the powerful 11th Panzer Division.[1]

The day before, two momentous events had occurred that

had further eroded the German will to resist. In Italy, all German forces had surrendered, while in Berlin the Red Army had proven victorious, with the remaining German defense units emerging from bunkers into the ruined city to lay down their arms and go into Soviet captivity. Each day brought news of fresh German surrenders, begging the question: how much longer until the final capitulation?

While Colonel Rudofsky at the recently captured stud was determined to remain on Czechoslovak soil, a large part of the German forces were as equally determined to get back into Germany and save themselves from Soviet captivity by going into American or British captivity instead.

Unknown to Weisenberger, the 11th Panzer's previous commander, Major General Wend von Wietersheim, had made his decision. Von Wietersheim had remained with the bulk of the division at Taus while the new commander, General von Buttlar-Brandenfels, using the last remaining stocks of gasoline, had taken a combat group sixty miles south to try to prevent an American advance on Linz. On May 2, von Wietersheim had first proposed surrendering the division to the Americans, and his officers had mostly backed him. But the first attempt to parley with the Americans had been rebuffed. A second attempt was made at 0715 hours on May 4 when a German officer arrived at an outpost of the US 359th Infantry Regiment. He was taken to the 90th Infantry Division's HQ at Cham, Germany, and the surrender worked out. Needless to say, Colonel Hank Reed was heavily involved in working out how such a surrender could be accomplished as fighting continued between his own 2nd Cavalry Group and other XII Corps units against scattered SS opposition. An agreement was reached whereby the thousands of 11th Panzer troops around Taus, along with over 1,000 vehicles, would come into the American lines under white flags on the late afternoon of May 4, after being sent sufficient supplies of US Army gasoline, the same day that all remaining German forces in Bavaria surrendered.[2]

*

At Hostau, Captain Tom Stewart received an urgent radio message from Colonel Reed on May 4. He was informed that the bulk of a German Panzer division would be passing by the town that afternoon. Reed warned him against any displays of hostility, regardless of what happened. "Don't engage them," was Reed's emphatic order. Stewart knew what could happen to his little command and the horses if a misunderstanding led to fighting—the 11th Panzer would squash any resistance like a bug in its haste to get to the safety of the US lines.

"A lot of Krauts are going to pass by this town over the next few hours," said Stewart to his assembled officers. "On no account are we to open fire, regardless of any provocations. I want all NCOs and men made aware of this order from Colonel Reed. Make sure that all checkpoints are manned and alert, but do not, repeat, not engage the German column."

Inducing an entire German armored division to surrender was a major coup for the Americans and a complete disaster for the German defense. General Weisenberger had first got wind that something was awry at 1700 hours, when it was reported to him that 11th Panzer security detachments had been withdrawn from the exits out of the Bohemian Forest.[3] More alarming had been the sudden arrival at his headquarters of an SS captain attached to the 11th. The SS captain, in a voice that betrayed his disgust with the whole affair, informed Weisenberger that von Wietersheim had unofficially reassumed command of the division and was going to surrender it to the Americans.[4]

"Sir, the commanding general is on the line," said Colonel Bennicke to Weisenberger at 2300 hours. Weisenberger nodded and picked up the telephone receiver. The voice at the other end was cold and curt. No contact had been made with von Wietersheim, despite repeated attempts.

"Effective immediately, *you* are to assume command of the 11th Panzer Division," ordered Weisenberger's superior. "At all costs, you are to prevent its surrender."[5]

"At your command, *Herr General*," barked Weisenberger, his mind racing as to what *he* could do to stop the surrender.

Weisenberger replaced the receiver and started to issue orders. Some staff cars were quickly assembled in the courtyard beneath his office and a gaggle of officers stood ready to depart. Weisenberger pulled on his greatcoat and cap and quickly joined them. The cars raced off into the darkness, heading towards the 11th's last reported positions.

Into the early hours of the next morning Weisenberger's little convoy of staff vehicles drove from place to place, trying to locate the rearguard of the 11th Panzer, but all they found were local defense troops who informed him that the mighty armored division was long gone. Its desertion to the Americans had just torn a huge hole in the German defense line. "The unexpectedly hurried departure of the 11th Panzer Division meant exposure of our southern flank and clearance of the Taus–Pilsen road for the Americans,"[6] wrote Weisenberger in his official report. The question was: would Patton exploit that hole and roll up the German line?

The one person who was praying for such an outcome was Colonel Rudofsky. The forward movement of Patton's line would mean the capture of Bischofteinitz and the saving of his family from the Soviets. As General Weisenberger led his convoy of cars through darkened Czechoslovak country lanes on his mission to prevent the surrender, Rudofsky stalked impatiently around the stable blocks at Hostau, which were dimly lit by oil lamps. The Lipizzaners and Arabians slept in their stalls, or shuffled about, occasionally snorting or banging their feet on the floors. He himself couldn't sleep, and being with the horses calmed him a little. But although the knot of tension that had settled deep in his stomach ever since he had begun the process of saving the horses had loosened a little, it never really left him. The lack of news was agonizing.

*

The other colonel who shared responsibility for the living heritage of the Spanish Riding School, Alois Podhajsky, was still on the German side of the lines. Since the evacuation of the Lipizzaner stallions to Saint Martin im Mühlkreis, Podhajsky had been totally focused on their welfare, and barely keeping up with the rapidly changing fortunes of the war. His fear that the Soviets might arrive at St. Martin had been slightly offset by news that American forces were advancing into Upper Austria. But then a message had arrived for him that threatened everything that he had worked so assiduously to protect.

The envelope that an orderly handed to Podhajsky was marked "Most Secret," never a good sign. The letter was a bombshell. Podhajsky, as the ranking Wehrmacht officer in the town, was hereby appointed defense commandant and ordered to take command of the local Volkssturm forces. Further, he was ordered to prepare the town for defense. The town was not to fall to the enemy![7] In his hand Podhajsky held the seeds of the destruction of the Spanish Riding School. Should resistance be offered to the enemy, they would most assuredly destroy the town with artillery fire and with it the stallions. But to refuse a direct order would place Podhajsky's head in a noose. The SS and Nazi Party functionaries were hanging defeatists from lampposts across the remaining length and breadth of German territory for offenses far less serious. If Podhajsky were executed, who would take care of the stallions and their precious heritage? Podhajsky decided upon a clever compromise. It would be better to appear to acquiesce to command's decision, but to be careful how far he went with preparing the town for defense.

Liaising with the local mayor, Podhajsky ordered him to place his Volkssturm irregulars around the town with orders to prevent any looting that might break out. This order was easy for the mayor to acquiesce to, for he owned the largest butchery business in St. Martin.

For the time being, Podhajsky did not order anti-tank barricades to be erected across the streets as Colonel Rudofsky had done at

Hostau. This was in spite of the orders from the local Nazi Party leader, who had received an order to do this from the Kreisleiter, the regional Nazi Party leader. As a compromise, Podhajsky ordered that guards be stationed at checkpoints covering the roads into St. Martin. For the time being, it appeared to be the best solution—keep the diehards busy while leaving the town only lightly defended. However, the local leader warned Podhajsky that the Kreisleiter was on his way to St. Martin, and he was not happy.

A young army lieutenant arrived next, requesting orders for the deployment of his 78-strong signals company. Podhajsky ordered them to remain in a local school on alert until further notice.[8]

Podhajsky returned to his quarters inside Arco Castle. There, he removed his German uniform and put on civilian clothes. He had just settled himself down to rest when the phone rang. The Kreisleiter had arrived at the local Party headquarters in the town, and Podhajsky was to report at once.

Podhajsky, his heart thumping in his chest, grabbed his officer's greatcoat and put it on over his civilian suit. He was wearing riding boots, and with his cap on he appeared to be properly uniformed. He quickly took out his Luger pistol, checked it, cocked the weapon and leaving the safety off, thrust it deep inside his coat pocket. The Luger was his "ace in the hole" should things go badly for him.

*

Someone else receiving a very important phone call on the evening of May 4, 1945, was General George S. Patton. Furious at the halt imposed on Third Army by Eisenhower following his early foray into western Czechoslovakia on May 1, there had been a change of heart at Supreme Allied Headquarters. The hole in the German line caused by the sudden surrender of the 11th Panzer Division was just too good an opportunity to let slip.

"Ike has just called," said General Omar Bradley, Patton's immediate superior, down a crackly telephone line. "You have a green light for Czechoslovakia, George." Patton grinned fiercely and gripped the receiver tightly.

"When can you move?" asked Bradley. Patton didn't hesitate.

"Tomorrow morning,"[9] he replied resolutely. The Soviet offensive to take Prague and the rest of western Czechoslovakia was scheduled to commence in just three days time. With luck, Patton could beat Stalin to the capital.

*

At the town of Saint Martin im Mühlkreis, Colonel Podhajsky hastened to his meeting with the regional Kreisleiter. He was nervous and worried. He had not fulfilled his orders as security commandant, and he feared punishment. The sound of artillery fire in the distance had abruptly ended. Had the American advance stalled? Hitler may have been dead for days, but the organs of the Party continued to function with brutal efficiency and the war had still not ended.

At the Party office a nervous and ashen-faced local official, who evidently greatly feared his superior, met him. Suddenly, there came the sounds of jackboots ringing on the floor of the passage outside the office, before the door was thrown open and two hard-looking SS men entered the room, followed by the Kreisleiter, who was still dressed in his brown and gold Party uniform. He slammed his heels together and out shot his right arm. "*Heil Hitler!*" he bellowed in a rough voice.

The local group leader gave the Nazi salute, while Podhajsky executed a smart military salute, which did little to endear him to the Kreisleiter. The Kreisleiter was well fed compared with the malnourished refugees that crowded the town. His face was red with anger. His head swiveled around and his eyes blazed at the cowering group leader.

"Have the anti-tank barriers not been closed, as I expressly ordered?" yelled the Kreisleiter. His subordinate visibly cringed, but did not reply, struck dumb by terror.

"No," said Podhajsky, "or else your car would not have been able to get here."

"Why were my orders not carried out?" demanded the Kreisleiter. His two SS bodyguards glared up at the tall Podhajsky, who stared back, his face a mask. The room was very quiet. At that moment, Podhajsky genuinely feared for his life. He could feel the heavy pistol resting in his pocket. "I was resolved not to die alone,"[10] he recalled.

"When our troops brought the advance of the Americans to a halt," explained Podhajsky in a level tone, "as indicated by the fact that the sounds of firing ceased, I did not consider that any useful purpose would be served by closing the streets, since this might hinder the freedom of movement of our own soldiers."

One of the Kreisleiter's eyebrows rose quizzically. Podhajsky quickly continued.

"But I have had the barriers manned by the Volkssturm and made the necessary arrangements for them to be closed in the shortest possible time when I give the order."[11]

The Kreisleiter continued to stare at Podhajsky, like a snake inspecting a piece of prey. But suddenly he broke the spell.

"Then everything is in good order," he said gruffly, before turning on his heel and stalking from the office followed by his henchmen. He was never to return.

On his way back to the castle, Podhajsky was forced to confront a mob of locals who were attempting to pillage. Order was starting to break down in the town, and Podhajsky faced down the mob with his pistol drawn and a detachment of Volkssturm at his side until it could be dispersed. Podhajsky's greatest fear was that the locals, who were severely short on food, might yet attempt to slaughter the Lipizzaner stallions.

A few hours after his confrontation with the Party leadership, the sound of gunfire had recommenced, and louder. The Americans were almost into St. Martin. "Change out of your uniforms and then bring them to me," instructed Colonel Podhajsky to his assembled riders. The Spanish Riding School staff, hitherto wearing the same German Army field-gray as their erstwhile commander, went to the special room that contained civilian clothing and emerged carrying their uniforms in bundles. Podhajsky had them hidden in the castle. American forces had been reported close by, and the echoing of gunfire could be clearly heard from the castle and stable blocks. Podhajsky's only concern now was the horses. He had ordered all of his men's weapons gathered before he locked them up. Podhajsky would remain with his staff until the US Army had taken the town.

For a couple of hours the situation was confused as the GIs drove off a smattering of Volkssturm and Wehrmacht who attempted to resist, eventually sweeping into the town proper to round up prisoners and take over the administration. The Spanish Riding School stallions and their human guardians waited in the half-light of the securely locked stables until American infantrymen arrived to investigate the building. As there were no weapons or German soldiers in evidence, just a collection of twenty young and middle-aged Austrian men and sixty-five horses, the GIs gave the place the once over and moved on, leaving the horses' fates to follow-up troops. But Colonel Podhajsky could breathe a massive sigh of relief—the stallions and his riders had made it through unscathed. And as things would turn out, Arco Castle would soon be utilized as a headquarters for the new American administration in the region. Podhajsky was still concerned, though, about the mares and foals at Hostau. Owing to the chaotic situation and haphazard communication, he was unaware that the stud there was already in American hands, and he resolved to do all he could to save the animals that represented the future of the Spanish Riding School.

In the late afternoon some green-painted staff cars peeled off from the seemingly endless column of American vehicles and men that were passing through St. Martin towards the new front line; the cars, with big white stars painted on their doors, swung in to the castle and disgorged several senior officers. Chief among them was

Brigadier General William Collier, XX Corps chief of staff.[12] He established his headquarters in the castle.

Podhajsky quickly presented himself, in the hopes of persuading the Americans of both the importance of the Spanish Riding School stallions and staff at the castle, but also of the necessity of saving the mares and foals at Hostau. But he didn't get very far. Encountering Collier in the castle's courtyard, the general and his staff swept past almost without glancing at the tall, thin Austrian dressed in civilian riding clothes, Collier muttering, "How do you do?" in Podhajsky's direction without waiting for a reply.

But later, some of Podhajsky's riders reported to him that an American major had visited the stables and was seeking him out. By an amazing stroke of luck, the major was horse mad and remembered Podhajsky from the 1936 Berlin Olympics. "I recognized you from the dressage events," said the major, pumping Podhajsky's hand. "How are you getting on, Colonel? Is there anything I can do for your horses?"

"I don't have many of the best horses," said Podhajsky, after he had recovered from his shock at this chance encounter.

"What!" the major exclaimed, "how come?"

"The Nazis took them to Czechoslovakia," said Podhajsky. He fixed the major with a piercing look.

"May I speak to you about something important?"

"Of course," replied the major.

"There is no time to lose and the American Army has got to act," said Podhajsky urgently. "The Russians will certainly get these horses and ship them east. And once they get them, they are lost to the world."[13]

The major was shocked, but he seemed determined to help. By sheer good fortune Podhajsky had found a friend who understood the cultural value of the horses, and was a fan of the Spanish Riding School. He was also a headquarters officer, and carried some weight.

As Podhajsky and the major stood chatting inside the stables, a fresh visitor arrived at the new American headquarters, the short, thick-set Lieutenant General Walton H. "Bulldog" Walker, commander of XX Corps. Walker was one of Patton's favorites, and, accompanied by General Collier, the major introduced Podhajsky and quickly outlined the problem.

Walker and Collier listened patiently as they slowly strolled down the long line of stalls, each with a Lipizzaner head poking over the gate. After hearing Podhajsky out Walker stopped and began to stroke the long nose of one of the stallions, seeming to consider his words. After a while, he spoke.

"Maybe we should invite General Patton down here for a show, and in that way we can get more stars in back of this than I've got."[14] Walker's bulldog-like face broke into a grin. Podhajsky was astounded. The great Patton coming here to see a show! They were nowhere near ready for such an important visitor or such an important event. But Podhajsky enthusiastically embraced Walker's idea, for if anyone had the power to resolve the crisis that faced the Spanish Riding School it was America's most famous cavalryman.

*

Colonel Hank Reed's 2nd Cavalry Group successfully secured the passes through the mountains along the German–Czech border. On May 5, the 90th, 5th, and 1st Infantry Divisions attacked. General Weisenberger's small defensive units fell to pieces, as he himself had predicted, and the Americans opened routes for an armored assault on Prague. The 1st Division drove on Karlsbad while the 97th Infantry Division headed for Pilsen, hitherto protected by the powerful 11th Panzer. The Soviets protested loudly, but had yet to launch their own assault. General Eisenhower urged caution. Under no circumstances was Patton to enter Prague.

The sudden American push liberated a host of Czech towns from the Germans included Bischofteinitz. Colonel Rudofsky was soon informed that his family was safe, easing his mental anguish a little. But it had not alleviated the question of whether he should leave his homeland or try to stay on, defying Colonel Reed's order.

Rudofsky shared some of his problems with Dr. Lessing, who was busy ministering to the horses along with Dr. Kroll. When Lessing learned of Rudofsky's determination to stay after the Americans had left, he was dumbfounded.

"You must be mad," he said forcefully. "The Czechs hate us Germans. And the partisans are communists and agents of the Russians. They want us out of Czechoslovakia, including Sudeten Germans like you." Lessing was perfectly right. The countryside around Hostau was lousy with Czech partisans, hard men armed with cast-off German weapons or Soviet gifts, who followed Moscow's line and desired a postwar communist Czechoslovakia. They favored brutally ejecting the 3 million Germans who lived in their country, regardless of the fact that most families had lived in the region for generations. Ethnically cleansing the Sudetenland of Sudetens was one of their major postwar goals. Colonel Rudofsky was unmoved by Lessing's arguments, clinging to the belief that once peace had been fully restored, democracy would once again return to Czechoslovakia.

Captain Stewart had also noticed the upsurge in partisan activity in the area since the Germans had been forced back. Reports had been reaching him of illicit visits to the stud by these resistance fighters. For what purpose was as yet unclear. What was obvious to Stewart, Captain Catlett, and First Lieutenant Quinlivan was the necessity to get the horses out of Hostau and into the safety of American-occupied Germany and end the uncertainty surrounding them as soon as possible.

*

US forces took Pilsen on May 6, 1945. General Bradley called Patton.

"The halt line through Pilsen is mandatory for V and XII Corps, George," said Bradley, stopping the two main units that made up

Patton's Third Army. "Moreover," continued Bradley, "you must not—I repeat *not*—recce to a greater depth than five miles northeast of Pilsen. Ike doesn't want any international complications at this late date."[15]

"For God's sake, Brad," fumed Patton, "it seems to me that a great nation like America should let others worry about complications."[16] Bradley was unmoved by Patton's attitude. He must stop. He would never piss in the Danube in Prague after all.[17]

CHAPTER 16

Day of Days

"The people are poor peasants, and they can accommodate only
a very limited number of horses on their modest estates."

Captain Dr. Gustav Kroll

Colonel Alois Podhajsky, resplendent in his dark brown frock coat, white riding breeches, tall black boots, and bicorn hat, urged his mount Neapolitano Africa towards where General George S. Patton stood on a raised viewing dais alongside a host of American dignitaries. The metal fittings on the Lipizzaner stallion's double reins jangled in the hushed quiet of Arco Castle's small and plain riding hall, resembling more a large covered shed. The loudspeakers through which tinny music had blared during the performance of the eight Lipizzaner stallions and their riders had ceased. Beside Patton sat US Undersecretary-of-War Robert Patterson, dressed in a civilian suit and fedora hat, and four generals and four colonels from Third Army, XX Corps, and its constituent infantry and armored divisions.[1]

The performance had been a slightly surreal experience for both sides. Podhajsky and his men had worked flat out to prepare the castle for the performance. The stallions and their riders had first gathered in a courtyard outside the riding hall, a space that was usually crammed full of refugees and locals bartering and trading. Now it had been cleared and scrubbed clean, with American soldiers guarding all the entrances.[2]

Sitting astride their stallions, the horses beautifully harnessed in gold-trimmed double bridles, and the riders resplendent in their traditional uniforms, the performers made quite an impression on General Patton and his guests. They "presented an unusual picture," wrote Podhajsky, "pushing the prosaic world of everyday into the background and evoking the picture of a dream stretching hundreds of years into the past."[3]

At 11.00am, Patton and his guests had arrived at the castle from Frankfurt. Patton, tall and imperious, had stalked past the line of horses and riders, whom he saluted, and then into the hall where a raised platform had been prepared for him and his guests.

"I must admit that a certain nervousness filled us all," wrote Podhajsky. "We had to present a type of art bound up with tradition, and, like the ballet, built not on sensation but triumphing in the harmony of movement and music, to these foreigners from distant lands who up to yesterday were our enemies …"[4]

Podhajsky and his men had seen their liberator Patton up close for the first time, and the colonel had watched Patton's face for some sign that he was interested in the spectacle and perhaps even appreciative of this most ancient and noble form of dressage. The signs initially had not been good. Patton, wearing a polished helmet liner adorned with four silver stars, had frankly looked rather bored by the whole thing, only appearing to warm to the performance during the finale, when Podhajsky had performed alone, mounted upon Africa, making a perfect display that awed the audience and drew rapturous applause from around the hall. Then Podhajsky had trotted towards Patton, removed his bicorn hat and doffed it towards the general with a flourish. Patton saluted. Colonel Podhajsky had just made the most important performance of his life—not in the great ornate marble riding hall in the Hofburg Palace in Vienna, but in a small Austrian village just liberated from tyranny, in a hall so shabby that swatches of freshly cut foliage had been used to camouflage holes in its walls. The question in Podhajsky's mind was simple enough: had he impressed Patton into believing that the Spanish Riding School was worth saving?

General Patton's day had got off to a rather disappointing start, which perhaps contributed to his somewhat depressed mood on his arrival at Arco Castle for the performance. He had received a telephone call just after 0400 hours on May 7 from his superior, General Omar Bradley, just as he was preparing to fly south to St. Martin.

"Ike just called me, George," said Bradley, without fanfare. "The Germans have surrendered." It did not come as a shock to Patton, for the news had been expected. German forces had been progressively surrendering in separate agreements with the Western Allies for several days. On May 4, German troops in North West Germany, Denmark, and the Netherlands had surrendered to the British 21st Army Group under Field Marshal Montgomery. That same day, the Americans had taken the surrender of all remaining German forces in Bavaria. On May 5, Czechoslovak nationalists had triggered a general uprising in German-occupied Prague, and Marshal Stalin had brought forward to May 6 his operation to invest the city, launching a massive offensive that would sweep through western Czechoslovakia up to Patton's front lines.

General Alfred Jodl, second-in-command of the German Army, had signed the unconditional German surrender at Eisenhower's Reims headquarters at 0241 hours on the morning of May 7, and a ceasefire was due to come into effect at 2301 Central European Time on May 8, 1945, to be celebrated as "Victory in Europe Day."

Patton was not flavor of the month at SHAEF anyway, with Eisenhower believing that the Third Army commander, through some earlier mistakes—particularly the Hammelburg Raid to rescue American prisoners of war and his handling of the American press over the raid's failure, as well as the discovery of the German gold reserves stashed in a salt mine at Merkers—had become something of a liability. Eisenhower had political ambitions, and close association with Patton was damaging.[5] Many, including Eisenhower, considered Patton to have become increasingly reckless and arrogant as the war neared its conclusion.[6] As for Patton, he had his sights set on a high command position in the Pacific, where the war continued against the Japanese.

For now, these worries and ambitions were of another world as Colonel Podhajsky, still mounted stiff-backed astride Africa, prepared to plead his case before the commanding presence of the most famous American general of World War II. The real show was now about to begin.

*

Dr. Gustav Kroll had arrived back at Hostau Stud on May 7 after a difficult two days away. Colonel Reed, who had returned to check on the horses and Captain Stewart's command from his new headquarters in the Skoda Castle at Zinkovy, had finally been able to begin to make preparations to move the horses to safety in Germany.

Reed faced several very difficult problems, and it would take all the ingenuity and skill of Stewart's little task force as well as Colonel Rudofsky and his staff to help resolve them.

"The main problem is the mares," said Reed to Rudofsky during a meeting he called to try to decide on some options for the move. "We need to work out how we can move them without inducing labor." Many of the Lipizzaner brood mares were heavily with foal, and were incapable of walking far. Any disturbances could result in them foaling, and if this was on the move the dangers to the mares and the newborns were massive. Reed had decided that the best way to move these delicate animals was on the back of trucks, but the 2nd Cavalry did not have sufficient spare and they were not designed for carrying horses.

"Quin," said Reed, turning to First Lieutenant Bill Quinlivan, who since April 28 had been responsible for security at the stud with his single platoon of men from the 42nd Squadron's Troop A. "I'm putting you in charge of moving the mares that are with foal," continued Reed. "I want ideas as to how we can increase our transport capacity, and most importantly, how the trucks can be outfitted as horse transports."

Quinlivan nodded seriously—it was a problem that would require all of his ingenuity to solve.

"The rest of the horses will have to march out," said Reed. "Obviously, we'll need to break them down into manageable groups." He delegated responsibilities to various other officers at the meeting, along with the German veterinarians Lessing and Kroll.

"As well as vehicles protecting the horses on the march, we are going to need riders with the herds," continued Reed. "I want a list of every man in your command who can ride," said Reed to Captain Stewart. It was not going to be easy. Most of the officers were fair horsemen, but among the enlisted men there were only a handful of cowboys or men used to riding.

"The shortfall in experienced riders from our own outfit will have to be made up with enemy personnel," said Reed. The Cossacks under Prince Amassov immediately volunteered. They had proven to be excellent workers since the stud had been liberated, keen to ingratiate themselves with the Americans and keener still to leave with them when the time came to evacuate Hostau. They were highly skilled horsemen and a valuable addition to the operation, and would provide between fourteen and sixteen riders to aid the short-handed Americans. Rudofsky's German staff would also ride out on some of the stallions as well as a few of the Polish workers who had been sent to Hostau from the great stud at Debica and some German infantry officers from the Hostau garrison. But even with help, the number of riders would be pitifully small to help control hundreds of highly strung horses moving across a land full of partisans, mines, displaced refugees and former concentration camp prisoners, not to mention desperate and heavily armed SS trying to avoid capture. The stallions and mares would also have to be widely separated during the march to prevent trouble. Colonel Rudofsky had noted that many of his staff had disappeared since the German surrender, and though he had a few former Volkssturm and Hitler Youth representatives assisting his remaining men in running the stud, they "were not to be made over night into trained nurses."[7]

In return for helping the Americans, Reed agreed to allow the Germans and Cossacks to bring their families and personal belongings out with the horse caravan, adding more problems to an already overburdened operation. The Cossacks were ecstatic.

The big question facing Reed and the others was where to take the horses to? The whole country was in an uproar, and Germany was no better, with its cities and towns heavily damaged by aerial bombing and street fighting, the food situation precarious and millions of civilians and German soldiers wandering around or being processed into massive open-air prison camps.

After consultations with both higher command and Colonel Rudofsky, a decision had been reached. The horses would initially be sent to Kötzting and Furth im Wald, small and picturesque Bavarian towns forty miles away, almost directly south of Hostau and just over the German border.

Reed had sent Dr. Kroll to Kötzting and Furth im Wald to inspect the available horse facilities, their condition, forage and pasture. Kroll had returned with mixed news after a very complex two-day mission.

"The stables and cowsheds that I viewed are inadequate for the animals that we have here," said Kroll, still dressed in German Army uniform, but unarmed and wearing a white armband. He had carried a signed pass from Reed to show to American patrols and had been driven to the towns in a jeep with a GI driver and an armed escort.

The facilities at Kötzting consisted of small stables widely distributed around farms outside the town, as well as some dirty and ramshackle cowsheds that could also be pressed into service.

"The region is very poor, Colonel," reported Kroll. "The people are poor peasants, and they can accommodate only a very limited number of horses on their modest estates."[8] But notwithstanding his insistence that the stabling was "inadequate," through patient and often very tedious work Kroll had managed to find hosts for all of the horses at Hostau. He had driven from village to village and town to town over the two days, viewing facilities and negotiating with their owners. Compiling a huge list of locales, it was worked out that two mares could go to one place, three to another, five to another and so on until the hundreds of horses at Hostau were allocated shelter. But the facilities were a far cry from those of a military stud farm like Hostau or Piber. Colonel Rudofsky looked positively alarmed as he listened to Kroll deliver his report. Purebred horses like the Lipizzaners and Arabians would be unused to such deprived conditions, and the threat to their health and wellbeing was obvious. It would also mean that the two German veterinarians would have to shuttle constantly by jeep around dozens of properties to care for their charges, a completely unsatisfactory system.

"What about the available pasture?" asked Reed.

"In my opinion, it could only support more than five hundred horses for a few weeks at most, Colonel," replied Kroll gloomily. The young veterinarian ran through several other drawbacks to the sites.

"It will have to do," said Reed, bringing the meeting to a close. He would seek a more long-term solution for the horses later, but for now getting them out of Czechoslovakia alive was his only priority. The news that the Soviets had launched their Prague offensive the day before had invigorated Reed and the Americans—they fully expected the Red Army to smash its way through the remaining German divisions and start advancing on the Bavarian border very soon.

*

Alois Podhajsky held his reins in one hand and his cap in the other as he spoke in good English to General Patton and his high-ranking guests in the shabby riding hall at Arco Castle. Behind him, his seven riders were drawn up in a line, their Lipizzaner stallions occasionally snuffling at their bits or tossing their heads.

"Honorable Mr. Secretary and General," Podhajsky began, nodding in turn to Under-Secretary-of-War Patterson and to Patton. "I thank you for the honor you have done the Spanish Riding School. This ancient Austrian institution is now the oldest riding school in the world, and has managed to survive wars and revolutions throughout the centuries, and by good fortune, has lived also through the recent years of upheaval."[9] Podhajsky paused for effect, feeling Patton's steady blue eyes watching him intently from beneath the brim of his helmet.

"The great American nation which has been singled out to save European culture from destruction, will certainly interest itself also in this ancient academy, which with its riders and horses presents, as it were, a piece of living baroque, so I'm sure I shall not plead in vain in asking you, General, for your special protection for the Spanish Riding School."[10] He had said it—Podhajsky had asked for Patton's formal help in saving the school from destruction. He sat still in the saddle and watched as Patton bent and spoke to Patterson in hushed tones before he straightened up again and faced Podhajsky. Patton prepared to reply. The moment of truth had arrived. Three hundred and eighty seven years of history hung precariously in the balance.

*

"We've been receiving reports of unauthorized visits to the stud by Czechs and Russians," announced Colonel Reed to his gathered officers. The Germans were excluded from this particular meeting.

"I think that we have to face the fact that we've a rat in the house," continued Reed, his face serious. Somebody had been secretly negotiating with Soviet agents, who had crossed into the American lines in company with communist partisans. The visits to the stud were becoming more frequent. Reed was concerned the Czechoslovaks might try to seize the horses themselves, perhaps with Russian help.

Colonel Rudofsky later denied that he was the officer who negotiated behind Reed's back with the communists, writing in 1981:

"When and if any Russian spies visited Hostau, I know nothing of it."[11] Reed didn't believe him and named "a certain Czech-born Lieutenant Colonel" as the culprit.[12] Regardless of Russian and Czechoslovak overtures, Reed saw the illicit activities as a further warning to move the horses to Germany and out of the reach of the communists. As for Colonel Rudofsky, though he was not particularly popular with the Americans, they still needed him, in spite of his suspected extra-curricular activities.

*

"I hereby place the Spanish Riding School under the official protection of the American Army in order to restore it to a newly risen Austria,"[13] declared General Patton proudly in the riding hall at Arco Castle. For a few seconds Colonel Podhajsky had trouble taking in Patton's words—it was so much more than he had expected. The Americans had offered a solid guarantee.

As for Patton, he had mixed feelings about the Spanish Riding School. As he watched the performance it had struck him "as rather strange that, in the midst of a world war, some twenty young and middle-aged men in great physical condition ... had spent their entire time teaching a group of horses to wiggle their butts and raise their feet in consonance with certain signals from the heels and reins." But, he conceded, who was he to judge? "It is probably wrong to permit any highly developed art, no matter how fatuous, to perish from the earth—and which arts are fatuous depends on the point of view. To me the high-schooling of horses is certainly more interesting than either painting or music."[14]

Colonel Podhajsky urged that Patton take immediate steps to secure the brood mares at Hostau, about which he had heard nothing for weeks.

"You see, General, the Russians are going to claim those horses as war booty," said Podhajsky, his face dour. "They'll say they are German property."

"Just let 'em try it!" roared Patton. "Colonel, from now on you and *all* of your horses are under the protection of the American Army. And the American Army *is* going into Czechoslovakia and get those horses!"[15]

Patton knew full well that Colonel Reed's 2nd Cavalry Group had already taken the stud at Hostau and had matters in hand a week earlier. The arrival of Reed's own assessment of the dangers then facing the stud and the value of the horses caused Patton to issue the necessary authorization for the colonel to begin the evacuation when ready.[16] Reed set a provisional departure date—May 12, 1945.

*

A jeep containing First Lieutenant Quinlivan and three men pulled up outside the main gate to a German Army artillery training school a few miles from Hostau. The chain-link gates stood open, the sentries long since departed. Paper from buildings blew across the abandoned parade square while the odd open window swung in the breeze. A few German steel helmets and bits of equipment lay scattered on the ground. Behind Quinlivan was a big six-by-six truck piled up with jerrycans of gasoline and more of his men, including a couple of vehicle mechanics.

Quinlivan's mission was to find more transport to help with the movement of the horses from Hostau. He had been informed that the artillery school had vehicles, but no fuel. The Americans drove around until they found what they were looking for. Parked in a neat row behind the abandoned barrack blocks was a collection of gray-painted German Army trucks—they were open-topped flatbeds with low wooden sides and a tailgate at the rear. The Americans stopped and piled out of their vehicles to inspect the trucks. Within minutes Quinlivan had selected the best runners, and his men set about refueling their tanks with the jerrycans that they had brought along, while the mechanics checked under the hoods.

A few hours later and Quinlivan's convoy, now considerably

bigger, and led by the American vehicles, started to make its way back to Hostau, each German truck driven by a GI, his carbine or M3 sub-machine gun (known as the "Grease Gun") on the bench seat beside him. Now it was just the matter of converting the trucks, American and German, into ersatz horse carriers.

At Hostau a new aroma started to overtake the odors of horses, hay, and dung. The pleasant smell of freshly sawn timber was everywhere during the few frantic days Quinlivan had to convert almost thirty trucks. All day long there came the sounds of sawing and hammering, as lengths of timber were hastily knocked up into sides for German and American trucks, and, most importantly, ramps up which the horses could be led on to the vehicles. The construction of ramps was the most time-consuming task of all, and as Colonel Reed's May 12 departure date rapidly approached, Quinlivan realized that he would not be finished in time. Reed would have to delay by a few days—something that he did not even want to contemplate.

As Quinlivan's truck conversion team worked day and night, the other Americans and Germans had other tasks to attend to. The horses still required their usual exercise and daily care, but Rudofsky, Lessing, and Kroll also oversaw the organization of the horses into their evacuation groups, which would number between thirty and eighty horses each. Prince Amassov and his Cossacks continued to prove their worth, while Captain Stewart's men assisted the stud's staff in sorting out a small mountain of food, supplies and harness that would also be coming with them. Pretty much everything that was not nailed down at the stud was to be loaded on to trucks and taken to Germany. Nothing was to be left for the Russians or Czechoslovaks. The great detailed inventory that Colonel Reed had ordered Rudofsky to prepare on April 29 listed every single article. Soon the courtyard in front of the stud resembled one gigantic yard sale.

"Sir, we got reports of tanks moving towards our position from the east," said the signals clerk to Captain Stewart. It was May 11,

1945, and feverish preparations were still ongoing for moving the stud and its precious horses, but it was looking increasingly unlikely that things would be ready by tomorrow, when they were supposed to leave.

Stewart radioed around his security points for any further information. Tanks had been heard in the distance. No information had been received from headquarters concerning American armor moving through his position, so Stewart ordered his command to action stations. Colonel Reed was immediately informed and drove out with Stewart to where the reports had originated.[17]

As soon as the American officers debarked from their jeep on the edge of Hostau they could hear the heavy engines of tanks in the distance. Both men considered whether they could be German. Though it had been four days since the German capitulation, fighting had continued beyond that date against the Soviets. The SS was still in evidence here and there. They couldn't be British—Field Marshal Montgomery was operating far in the north of Germany. Reed and Stewart knew that the American front line ran ten miles southeast of Pilsen, then through Horsice, Zinkovy and to the 42nd's command post at Nepomuk. The closest front-line location to Hostau was Horsice, roughly forty road miles east.[18] But the front line was not a solid barrier—instead it was porous and full of gaps that American units had yet to fill or properly watch.

The tank engine sounds grew louder, accompanied by the strange clanking and grinding sounds made by their caterpillar tracks. Whatever they were, they were bigger vehicles than the two M24 Chaffee tanks that Stewart still retained to help protect the town. And they were definitely not Shermans, whose engine note was familiar to all American soldiers.

The road was overlooked by machine guns nestled inside hastily erected sandbagged positions, with an M8 armored car sitting further back in cover, its puny 37mm gun pointing towards the approaching threat.

Reed and Stewart took cover behind one of the positions and waited. A bazooka team crouched, their long green tube pointing east. Whatever was coming, it would shortly appear from around a bend on the tree-lined road a few hundred yards away. Stewart cocked the M1 carbine in his hands and glanced at Reed. His commander looked cool and unruffled as ever, but his right hand had fallen to his pistol holster and was slowly unclipping the flap.

CHAPTER 17

Operation Cowboy

*"Generals discussing our outfit say we are the best
Cavalry unit in the Third Army."*

Colonel Charles Reed,
Nepomuk, Czechoslovakia, May 12, 1945

The sounds of accelerating tank engines grew louder and louder, mingled with the clatter of metal tracks on the road surface. Then the first armored beast appeared around the forested corner a few hundred yards in front of Colonel Reed's position. Blue smoke belched from the tank's two rear exhausts as its big diesel engine powered it forward. Then another tank appeared behind the leader, followed by yet another.

"T-34s!" exclaimed Captain Stewart as the green-painted tanks, their tall turrets placed forward on their chassis, ground on down the road towards the American position, hardly slowing.[1]

"What in the hell are Russians doing this far behind our lines?" exclaimed an astonished Reed. He had hardly finished speaking when the column of T-34s clattered to a halt. Standing in the open hatch of the first tank was a young Soviet lieutenant, wearing a padded cloth helmet. He started to wave his right arm in a sideways direction, and to shout.

"*Raschishchat' dorogu!*" yelled the Soviet officer several times.

"Tell the men not to open fire without my express order, Captain. I'll investigate," said Colonel Reed, standing up and walking out into the roadway. Stewart passed Reed's order around his men before joining the colonel.

"*Raschishchat' dorogu!*" shouted the Soviet officer, still waving his arm furiously.

"We got anyone who speaks Russian?" demanded Reed, standing with his hands on his hips in the middle of the road a few yards from the first halted tank. Fortunately, a trooper of Russian heritage was found and ordered up to assist the colonel a few minutes later. In the meantime, several Soviet soldiers had clambered out on to the turrets of their tanks and were watching the unfolding drama with interest.

"Ask him what he wants," said Reed, jerking his thumb towards the Soviet officer, still standing high up in his turret.

"He says you must clear the road, Colonel," replied the trooper. Reed raised his eyebrows.

"Ask him on whose authority," said Reed.

"*Raschistit' put' dyla Krasnoy Armii,*" shouted the Soviet officer.

"He says you must clear the way for the Red Army, sir," translated the trooper.

"Tell him to get his CO up here," demanded Reed. The Soviet officer disappeared back into his turret, presumably to radio someone in higher authority. Ominously, the tank engines remained switched on and idling noisily.

Reed could see exactly what the Soviets were up to. They intended to push straight through into Hostau, probably to snatch the horses before the Americans could send them out to Germany. All those illicit visits by Czechoslovak partisans and Soviet spies had led to some kind of flying column from the 1st Ukrainian Front, which was then pushing out into the countryside beyond Prague, being sent to try to intimidate the Americans into leaving. With the front line so porous, this small column of tanks and vehicles had been able to slip through unnoticed and race west.

Reed had first been made aware of Soviet incursions into the American line on the evening of May 9, when patrols from the 42nd Squadron had reported Red Army columns moving at speed through Nepomuk towards Pilsen.[2] It had required half of the 42nd Squadron to induce the Soviets to stop. The 42nd's executive officer and an interpreter had eventually chased them down two miles northeast of Nepomuk. The Americans had halted four SU-76 self-propelled guns from the 25th Tank Corps, some with female crews.[3] It had appeared from reports that the 42nd had the situation in hand and that no further Soviet penetrations into US territory had succeeded.

The impasse outside Hostau continued for some time, and worsened with the arrival of a senior officer and his staff to try to force the issue.

"You must clear way for Red Army," said a young Soviet captain who was translating in halting English for the column's commander, Brigadier General Fomenich. The Soviet general had been driven up to the head of the column in an armored car, with a couple of jeeploads of officers and NCOs following, and launched immediately into a heated argument with Colonel Reed.

Though ostensibly Allies, the Soviets didn't look all that friendly, and there were none of the staged photocalls of GIs shaking hands with smiling Red Army soldiers on busted bridges that had already started appearing in *Stars and Stripes* and the newspapers as the Eastern and Western Fronts finally merged into one in Germany. These particular Soviets looked hard-bitten and tough, their uniforms dirty and oil-stained, many in possession of PPsH machine guns, with drum magazines slung across their chests.

General Fomenich, wearing a heavy gray greatcoat with tsarist-style shoulder boards and a Sam Browne belt and revolver, didn't appear to be in the mood to negotiate, his ice-blue eyes and wind-burnt face giving the impression of a seasoned campaigner.

"You have no jurisdiction here, General," said Reed, locking eyes with the Russian officer. "You are behind the American lines."

Fomenich shook his head and reeled off a barrage of Russian at his aide, who translated again.

"My general, he say that you *Amerikantsy* are behind *our* lines. You must move your men aside. This all belong Union of Soviet Socialist Republics."

Reed knew that he was on shaky ground diplomatically, for it was true that at the Yalta Conference it had been agreed with Stalin to turn over *all* of Czechoslovakia to Soviet control once the Germans were defeated. Though General Patton had managed to push forward some forty to fifty miles to just beyond the city of Pilsen, American forces would probably be ordered to return to Germany in the near future to avoid an escalation with the USSR.[4] But for the time being, Reed knew that he had to bluff it out in front of the Soviets in order to buy some time to get the horses out. They were almost finished constructing the horse loading ramps and modifying the American and German trucks.

"Tell him I am not moving from this place as I have received no orders to that effect."

The captain relayed Reed's words to Fomenich, but it only brought on another tirade of Russian.

The argument flowed back and forth for some minutes as Fomenich continued to demand the road, while Reed refused to budge. Reed was able to quote an order that he had received on May 9 from XII Corps delineating the forward American line in Czechoslovakia as running Budejovice–Pilsen–Karlsbad–Chemnitz. XII Corps had stated explicitly: "In order to avoid any possible incidents with Soviet forces U.S. forces will not advance beyond the line …"[5] It was clear to Reed that Hostau was well within the authorized boundary and the Soviets had no jurisdiction or rights in regards to the town of Hostau.

But regardless of his strong position based upon XII Corps' instructions, Reed was growing increasingly nervous. If General Fomenich decided to force the issue and order his tanks forward into Hostau, how should the Americans respond? They were outnumbered and outgunned. If shots were exchanged between American and Soviet troops only days after the German capitulation heads would roll on both sides, particularly as Patton had made it clear that Reed was on his own in Czechoslovakia should anything go wrong with the mission to save the horses. But Reed also knew that if he allowed the Red Army to occupy Hostau, he could forget about saving the horses. The Soviets would never allow the Americans to take them out. He would also be sealing the fates of Colonel Rudofsky, Captains Lessing and Kroll, and the other German staff at the stud, who along with their families might not be permitted to leave. And Reed was using Prince Amassov's Cossacks to help look after the horses—Soviet citizens who had, in the eyes of the USSR, betrayed the Motherland. Such men and their families, including Amassov's fourteen-year-old daughter and their other women and children, could expect no mercy from the Red Army. All of this flashed through Reed's mind in seconds as he stood facing the Soviet general. Then his face took on a harder look and he pointed at Fomenich's chest with his index finger.

"If you go forward," said Reed in a low but menacing tone, "remember, our guns are still loaded."[6] After receiving the translation, Fomenich visibly blanched. His bluff was being called. He looked into Reed's eyes and knew that the American was not faking.

For several minutes the Soviet officers discussed the situation out of earshot of the Americans before Fomenich abruptly left. Then, almost in unison, the Soviet tank engines were all shut off, a deep and unsettling silence falling over the scene. Hatches were opened and tankers jumped down into the road and lit up cigarettes or stood staring at the Americans. The Red Army was clearly not going forward, at least for the time being, but equally perturbing for the Americans, it was also not withdrawing. Instead, like a large and hungry cat staring into a small bird's cage, the Soviets would wait patiently until fresh orders arrived. The unseasonable chill in the air seemed to presage a much colder war to come.

The sudden and unexpected arrival of the Russians galvanized the Americans into moving the horses out as fast as possible. The operations to prepare the transport vehicles swung into high gear. A strong barrier of US armored vehicles and men was placed across the roads leading into Hostau from the east to hopefully forestall any sudden forward movement by General Fomenich's men. The plan was for the American perimeter to collapse like a bag as the horses and vehicles left under escort from the western side of the town, a rearguard from Troop A being the last American forces to leave, covering the tail of the convoy back to Germany.

"We leave tomorrow morning, at dawn," said Captain Stewart to the assembled task force officers and senior NCOs on the night of May 14. At 11pm, Colonel Reed had received the final order to move the horses and personnel the forty miles to a safe area in Germany the following day, and immediately transmitted the thrilling news to Stewart. The codename for the operation: "Cowboy."

First Lieutenant Quinlivan's team had completed the vehicle conversions and built sufficient ramps for the loading of the pregnant mares and those with new foals in tow. All equipment and supplies had been mustered and inventoried, and all personnel made ready for the move. Those GIs who had been detailed to ride with the herds had selected their mounts from among the stallions at the stables.

Captain Stewart would lead the first group, riding not a Lipizzaner but a jeep. Behind would come the trucks containing the very young horses with their mothers and the mares heavy in foal.[7] More jeeps and armored cars would provide flank protection during the drive to the German frontier. Military police or Colonel Long's infantrymen of the 387th Regiment would be in position at each crossroads to keep them clear for the evacuation convoy, some using scout cars to cover them. The other groups of horses would be on foot, with armed jeeps with each herd, along with outriders and guides.

In total, there would be four distinct groups. First, the thirty-truck convoy, then three horse herds with vehicles and outriders, moving along at intervals of twenty to thirty minutes to prevent bunching and snarl-ups. Resting points had also been marked on the officers' maps, where a midday break could be taken and the horses and men fed and watered.

The loading continued all night. German, Polish and Cossack women and children, together with their scanty possessions and as much food as they could carry, piled onto overloaded German trucks. Horse-drawn wagons were also utilized to bring out yet more equipment and supplies, pulled by animals already broken to harness by Colonel Rudofsky.[8] The German stud commander was everywhere during the night of May 14/15, overseeing the loading, checking items and horses off his lists held on a clipboard while the veterinarians Lessing and Kroll supervised the animals.

The movement of so many people, animals, and possessions was impressive, and the caravans resembled the refugee columns that had been passing by the stud for weeks. Was there any real difference between them? Both the refugees, and now the American soldiers with their ragtag collection of "willing helpers," the former enemies and former POWs, were all intent on placing as much space as possible between themselves and the Red Army. The horses, both a great prize and a thorny political hot potato, were the focus of this multinational collection of men, women, and children who all sought freedom in the West.

Though now technically civilians, but still in German uniform, Rudofsky's officers and men continued with their jobs with discipline and dedication, not knowing what might happen to them once they arrived in their occupied homeland.

Rudofsky, however, would be the only one not to go to Germany. He had confronted Colonel Reed on this subject again during one of his frequent visits to the stud, and this time Reed had not pressed the matter.

"Well, if you do not want to go," said Reed, without apparent rancor, "stay here. Dr. Lessing will take over in the convoy." Reed's opinion of Rudofsky was fairly low. "Because of Rudofsky's 'treachery,'" wrote Captain Stewart, "Col. Reed considered making him a prisoner, but we decided that justice could be served by leaving him to the Russians. When you are predisposed to dislike someone, it is easy to fuel your antipathy."[9]

Refugees continued to be a problem at Hostau. When word got out that the Americans were going to take the horses and German staff and their families to their own lines, many refugees approached Dr. Lessing asking to come along as well. The refugees' carts and carriages mixed in with the official transport that was going to leave the stud, and many tried to get seats on the vehicles that were transporting out food and other supplies. They pleaded with Lessing. "For God's sake, take us with you," one of the refugee leaders said, "It's our only chance to get out of this hell." Colonel Reed had already made clear to Lessing that this was not a problem.

"You know I can't organize a general escape here," said Reed when Lessing first informed him of the refugees' demands. "But if you and your people manage to get a corresponding number of horses and wagons, these people are simply counted as stud staff, and in this way they *can* be taken away." Lessing was taken aback by Reed's humanity. "I have nothing against them,"[10] said Reed, before changing the subject back to the horses and trucks.

Colonel Rudofsky looked up at the dawn sky and smiled. It was a beautiful spring morning, with hardly a cloud in sight. The sun shone down upon Hostau, warming the backs of the men who were still laboring to load the last horses and equipment for the move. After so many weeks of cold, wet and snowy weather, the morning of May 15, 1945, was glorious. Rudofsky walked into one of the empty stable blocks at the stud. It was dead quiet. "No neighing, no stamping, no snorting," he wrote. "The thrushes are singing, the turtle doves calling, buzzards wheeling."[11]

After carefully inspecting each of the empty stables and storerooms, Rudofsky walked out into the yard, where preparations were still under way, and down the line of German and American trucks. In the backs of the trucks the mares and their young stood quietly, their big eyes staring out over the hastily constructed wooden sides, tails flicking and feet shuffling. The engines started up, and all along the convoy truck doors were slammed and drivers' elbows poked out of open windows. The escort vehicles waited to protect the convoy, with American soldiers carrying small arms or standing in the rear of jeeps holding on to the machines guns mounted on metal posts set into the floor.

Captain Stewart nodded to Rudofsky as he walked down the line of trucks, casting a final eye over the vehicles and horses. Then Stewart climbed into his jeep at the head of the convoy. Also in the jeep was Major Rollin Steinmetz, the regimental S-4, with a copy of the order of march in his lap.[12] Stewart glanced at his watch, then stood up and raised his arm above his head.

"Lets move out!" bellowed Stewart, his arm shooting forward towards the west, before he resumed his seat, the jeep pulling ahead as the trucks gunned their engines and took the strain of their precious loads. Blue exhaust smoke billowed in the clear air as the line of trucks, engines revving and gears mashing, lurched forward, the horses in the rear swaying and shuffling to maintain their balance. Here and there an M8 armored car tagged alongside the flanks of the convoy, the commanders standing in their turrets talking to each other on the radio net, while more jeeps hummed along behind. Hubert Rudofsky stood and watched until the last vehicle and last horse had passed out of sight before turning sadly away and walking back into the stud.

The convoy made good time, though the vehicles kept their speeds down so that the horse groups that were walking could stay close behind. As the convoy lumbered up and down the rolling countryside it grew warmer. At each crossroads smiling military policemen waved them on, Stewart saluting at each checkpoint. The young captain scanned his maps and maintained an eye on his watch as his jeep drove slowly ahead of the convoy, having regular brief conversations on the radio with other officers protecting the flanks and rear.

The horse parties were organized in at least three distinct groups. Prince Amassov's Cossacks and their group, who numbered in total twenty-six riders, were proving their worth, with over a dozen acting as flank riders on their tough Panje horses, with their families also mounted and following on behind. Only seven GIs rode stallions, including First Lieutenant Bill Quinlivan, who was mounted on the famous Polish racehorse Lotnik. Contrary to stories that circulated after the war, there were no mounted Texans among the Americans. Sergeant Bill Boyer from Idaho rode the stallion Tristan, while the other six GI riders were all from North Carolina. Captain Stewart rode part of the way, occasionally swapping his jeep for a stallion and checking on the different groups.[13]

Some Polish grooms, some Austrians, and a few released German prisoners made up the numbers of European riders to about fifty, but there was by no means enough men to properly control the hundreds of horses moving in loose roundups towards Germany.

Some German officer prisoners were determined to ride some of the two- and three-year-old stallions, with disastrous results. Ignoring the advice of the stud's staff, within minutes of leaving Hostau thirteen riders were unhorsed in an almost comical scene of chaos, "and there was an appalling confusion of uncontrolled, riderless stallions and mares defending themselves." The whole sorry episode was recounted to Colonel Podhajsky a few days later by stud staff, and he recounted that: "In this whirling mass of biting, kicking horses, the attendants, some of whom were totally inexperienced, had the greatest difficulty in halting the excited animals and avoiding being trampled under the hoofs of the now frenzied herd."[14] The baker's dozen of riderless stallions bolted back to the stables at Hostau and were abandoned by the Americans for the time being. Eventually, order was restored to this part of the column, which proceeded without further incident towards Germany.

Though the distance to Kötzting and Furth im Wald was only around forty miles from Hostau, Stewart did not push the animals too hard. The journey, including the trucks that kept their speeds low, was made over two days. When night fell at the end of the first day, the horses were placed in fields that had already been selected in advance, and the accompanying riders and drivers accommodated in requisitioned barns. Many of the horses that were walking were not accustomed to such distances, and were very footsore. Captains Lessing and Kroll were kept busy attending to these animals.

The following day dawned bright and clear—perfect weather. The horses were loaded back aboard the trucks or mustered into their marching groups. It appeared a straightforward run down to the Czechoslovak–German frontier.

Dr. Lessing, mounted on Indigo, was at the head of the column accompanied by several other German riders. They were close now to the Bavarian border. Up ahead lay the small town of Furth im Wald, its collection of solid three-storey red roofed houses clustered up against the Chamb River, an arched stone bridge connecting the Czechoslovak side of the border with Germany.

Lessing's group of horsemen rode in advance of Captain Stewart's jeep and the convoy of heavily laden trucks, with the rest of the horses moving along in their usual three groups strung out over several miles behind. Passing through a ravine, the road snaked up towards a crest, bright sunshine dappling through the trees. Beyond that lay the river and Furth im Wald. Lessing could see the black, onion-shaped dome of the Baroque parish church in Furth, but he also saw that the entrance to the bridge was blocked. A customs house left over from when Czechoslovakia had been an independent nation had been manned, and its red and white painted barrier was down and locked in place, firmly blocking the road. But more ominously, three men stood in the middle of the road, their leader raising his hand to stop the column. Lessing could see that the men were Czechoslovak partisans, for each was dressed in an odd assortment of civilian and cast-off military clothing, with a red communist armband, and they were carrying German rifles or Soviet machine guns.

Lessing reined in his horse, raising his right hand to halt the column.

"You can't take these horses out of Czechoslovakia!"[15] bellowed the partisan leader, pointing his machine gun at Lessing. A Ukrainian horseman who spoke some Czech was quickly brought up to translate for Lessing, who demanded that the partisans immediately clear the road. But though this was an American operation, Lessing was still in German uniform, as were his men, though all of them were unarmed and helpless. The Czechoslovak leader's hatred for their recent occupiers was clear and undisguised. The partisan repeated his demand, adding that the horses "must remain here until we decide with the Russians as to just how they should be disposed of."[16] Dr. Lessing tried to explain that the United States Army was moving the horses into Germany, but this had little effect. As they spoke, the next group of horses on foot had started to arrive, bunching up behind the convoy of trucks. Lessing turned in his saddle as someone shouted out from behind, just in time to see three or four stallions bolt into the trees. The group was degenerating into a tangle of tired, highly strung and footsore horses jammed into an expanding bottleneck at the border.

The other two partisans suddenly stepped forward and dragged one of Lessing's German riders from his horse, evidently preparing to beat him with their rifle butts. But a shout stopped them in their tracks and all eyes turned as an American officer galloped to the head of the caravan, his horse kicking up dust as he thundered along, reining in beside Lessing.

"What's going on here?" shouted First Lieutenant Quinlivan, his right hand unclipping his pistol holster. Captain Stewart, who was standing in the front of his jeep some way back in the column, watching the situation carefully, had called Quinlivan forward.

Lessing quickly explained to Quinlivan about the refusal of the partisans to remove the barrier. Quinlivan stared down at the leader of the partisans and then at the obstacle. He ordered an American private who had followed him on horseback to ride back down the line and get help. Quinlivan's eyes took in the chaos that was starting to manifest itself as a large group of horses with inadequate escorts milled about in the roadway and among the trees as riders struggled to corral them, and the convoy of trucks sat immobile with their precious loads overheating under the sun. He knew that the next group of walking horses would not be far behind, and when they arrived the crush and confusion would be complete.

"Tell him to open the goddamn barrier, right now!" growled Quinlivan at the Ukrainian interpreter. The Americans were not going to take any nonsense from the Czechoslovaks, as the US refused to countenance that they had *any* rights to the horses.

When the Czechoslovak partisan leader refused to remove the barrier, Lieutenant Quinlivan knew that he had to act, and act fast before the situation went totally beyond his control. There were only three partisans guarding the crossing, but there could well be many more in concealed positions close by, waiting to intervene. But Quinlivan had an ace up his sleeve. The rider that he had detached would by now have passed on the message and help would be on its way. Sure enough, within a few minutes an M8 armored car came rumbling through the trees. Quinlivan rode over and spoke briefly to its commander before returning to Captain Lessing's side. The M8's turret swung round and the muzzle of its 37mm gun depressed until it was pointing straight at the partisans and the tollhouse.

Quinlivan turned to the Ukrainian interpreter, his saddle creaking as he rested his hands on his reins.

"You tell him," he said slowly and clearly, jerking a thumb at the partisan leader, "that I'm going to count to three." The partisan leader listened, the color draining from his face as his eyes flicked backwards and forwards between Quinlivan's angry face and the muzzle of the M8's 37mm cannon. His bluff was being called.

"One! ..." shouted Quinlivan, raising an index finger in the air.

CHAPTER 18

The Grand Drive

"Only Bill Quinlivan stood there like a rock in the surf."

German Captain Dr. Rudolf Lessing

First Lieutenant Quinlivan, mounted on Lotnik, turned in his saddle and glanced briefly at the sergeant whose head and shoulders were sticking out of the M8 armored car's turret. The sergeant's eyes were locked on the officer, waiting for a signal. Then Quinlivan turned back to the trio of Czechoslovak partisans who were blocking the route into Germany, raised his right hand again and extended another finger.

"Two!" he bellowed, his horse restless. Behind him were sounds of confusion, as now two groups of horses and riders had become entangled with the truck convoy loaded with mares and foals in a growing bottleneck on the road in front of the border crossing. More horses would be lost if this unplanned delay continued for much longer.

The partisan leader still held his PPsH machine gun in his hands, but his eyes and face had lost their previously defiant expression—this American officer clearly meant business. The partisan licked his lips nervously and glanced at the M8, and at the muzzle of the gun that was trained perfectly on the barrier and his men, then back at Quinlivan astride Lotnik. Inside the M8 the sergeant in command, who also acted as gun loader, had rammed a high explosive shell into the breech. Suddenly, his mind made up, the partisan leader barked an order to his men and the barrier was hauled up, the partisans

237

standing with surly expressions on their faces, giving the Americans and their "friends" the road.

Quinlivan didn't hesitate, but ordered the parties to begin crossing into Germany immediately. The trucks started up, and spewing plumes of blue exhaust smoke they lurched on to the bridge, the horses in back moving with the motions of the trucks as they drove. Next came the two groups of horses that were walking. A barely controlled mass of Lipizzaner stallions, mixed up with the black or bay Arabians and Thoroughbreds plunged across the bridge, hooves thundering on the stone roadway. American, German, Polish, Cossack, and Ukrainian outriders struggled to prevent more runaways, sometimes turning out quickly to fetch back loose horses. Unlikely American cowboys in olive-drab uniforms and M1 helmets kicked their mounts along, their carbines slung across their backs, while field-gray-clad Germans in peaked field caps worked to separate the herds into orderly groups, helped by Polish grooms in riding breeches, roll-neck sweaters and driving caps. Adding a certain rustic romance to the scene were the Cossacks on their tough ponies, which contrasted strongly with the aristocratic lines of the Lipizzaners and Arabians, working hard in kaftans and fur caps, weaving their mounts between the American vehicles that guarded the caravan's long flanks. It was, by any account, one of the strangest spectacles of the war.

And then suddenly they were all inside Germany. Dr. Lessing, riding at the head of the great caravan, spoke for all of them, regardless of nationality, when he later described how it felt: "We really felt in our hearts that we were saved. Actually saved. Now we knew that nothing could happen to us."

It was perhaps appropriate that the person who had kick-started the rescue of the horses at Hostau should have been there when the horses drove or walked into Germany and freedom. Unfortunately Captain Ferdinand Sperl, the intelligence officer whose polite discussion with Colonel Holters had led to so many adventures, had little chance to welcome Stewart's great procession into Kötzting.

Sperl was running a massive prisoner-of-war discharge center, processing nearly 10,000 members of the recently surrendered 11th Panzer Division.[1]

For days and days, columns of German soldiers, most loaded down with rucksacks, bedrolls and mess tins, shuffled along the roads around Kötzting, or sat under guard in fields. Each morning, another five hundred would be processed through large wooden cowsheds that had been hastily converted to document, medically examine, and discharge the German soldiers. It was already clear to Dr. Lessing and other officers that trying to keep the horses in an area that was completely overcrowded with former German soldiers and refugees from the east was not going to be a long-term solution. Although Dr. Kroll's plan had swung into action, and the horses were distributed in penny packets to farms and estates, the level of disorder and crime in the area meant that the priceless horses were not out of danger quite yet. The Lipizzaner mares and foals were mostly kept together, in the largest spaces that Kroll had commandeered.

In the meantime, Colonel Podhajsky had been flown from St. Martin in Upper Austria on May 15 to Colonel Reed's new headquarters at the huge Skoda Estate at Zinkovy, Czechoslovakia.[2] He had been invited to accompany Reed into Germany the next day to help select which of the Lipizzaners belonged to the Spanish Riding School and assist with their transfer to St. Martin.

Colonel Reed received Podhajsky with great warmth and invited him to dine with him and some of his officers at the Skoda Castle. The two colonels discussed the Olympics and the US Army's cavalry school, and how Podhajsky's name had been familiar to Reed before the war. Reed also explained to Podhajsky how his regiment had taken measures to secure the safety of the horses at Hostau on Patton's orders, and that he had had the horses evacuated to Bavaria. It was an enormous relief to Podhajsky. Reed now invited Podhajsky to inspect the horses and sort out which animals should be returned to Austria.[3]

It was a long drive from Zinkovy to Kötzting, and Podhajsky made it seated in the back of Colonel Reed's jeep.[4] Reed sat in the front passenger seat beside his regular driver Sergeant O'Leary. Both Americans were well armed: the war may have been over, but the region was still alive with partisans, bandits, ex-Russian and Polish prisoners-of-war, concentration camp and slave labor camp survivors, refugees and tens of thousands of German troops, including disgruntled SS.

As Reed's jeep roared through Czechoslovak towns and villages at high speed, the occupants could see which way the political winds were blowing in this part of Europe. Large homemade banners adorned many public buildings or were festively hung from buildings across roads. But the words written upon them were anything but festive. "*We Greet the Red Army*" was the commonest declaration. Podhajsky stared and was reminded of his trips through this country in the preceding years to visit Hostau, when he had gauged the barely concealed hostility of the Czechoslovak people to their German occupiers. Now civilians turned in the streets as the American jeep trundled through and stared at Reed and O'Leary, dressed in their steel helmets and olive-drab uniforms. It was not a friendly look. Colonel Reed emitted a short and humorless laugh and turned to speak to Podhajsky in the back of the jeep after seeing yet another pro-Soviet banner.

"The inhabitants of this country don't love us much, and can hardly wait for the Russians to arrive," shouted Reed over the sound of the engine and the wind. "Now you will understand why I had the horses brought to Bavaria as quickly as possible."[5]

When Colonel Podhajsky alighted from Reed's jeep at Kötzting, Captain Lessing was on hand to greet the two men. Lessing, now that Colonel Rudofsky had deserted the horses, had been appointed commandant of the stud. Perhaps it was the new responsibility, or exhaustion, or a combination of both, but Dr. Lessing was far from pleased to see Podhajsky. Only a year before, during one of Podhajsky's visits to Hostau, he had been entertained in Lessing's quarters, and the two men had got on well. Now, though, Dr. Lessing's demeanor was considerably chillier.

"I intend to leave Europe and accompany the horses to America," stated Lessing. Podhajsky was privately somewhat shocked and appalled by what he saw as Lessing's personal ambition intertwining itself with the fate of the horses. But Lessing's next suggestion truly horrified Podhajsky.

"In my opinion, Colonel" said Lessing to Reed, "the horses should be transferred from here to the Army Remount sections at Bergstetten and Mansbach. The pasture hereabouts will not last a fortnight."[6] Gestütsweg Mansbach was a famous horse-raising stud that had been taken over by the Wehrmacht in 1933. It had a capacity to stable eight hundred horses and was located near Munich.

Podhajsky strongly objected to Lessing's plan, arguing that the Austrian horses in the collection should be taken to St. Martin and thence back to the Piber Stud where Lipizzaner mares had been originally stabled before Gustav Rau's interference. Moving them further into Germany was, in his opinion, unnecessary. It would become increasingly difficult to extract them from American control, dooming the Spanish Riding School to oblivion. But Dr. Lessing was not persuaded.

"Austria is much too small to retain the Lipizzaner stud," he said to Reed and Podhajsky. "The entire stud should be sent to America where these noble horses can be preserved for posterity." Podhajsky's face flushed at Lessing's suggestion.

"I must object *most* strongly," protested Podhajsky to Colonel Reed. "The Austrian Republic appreciates the cultural importance of the Spanish Riding School, as well as the generous help of General Patton, sufficiently to look after the Lipizzaner stud herself."[7]

What Lessing and Podhajsky did not realize was that Patton had already decided to return the Spanish Riding School's mares to Austria. Colonel Reed explained this to Lessing and Podhajsky, much to the latter's evident relief, though Podhajsky was also worried. He had almost seventy stallions at Arco Castle, and absolutely no room for hundreds of mares and foals.

"The Lipizzaners will be taken in trucks to Upper Austria," declared Reed. "And *you* get to make the arrangements," he added, tapping Dr. Lessing on the chest with one index finger.

Not all of the Lipizzaners belonged to the Spanish Riding School. Mixed up with the horses at Kötzting were Italian and Yugoslavian Lipizzaners. Podhajsky undertook a careful inspection, with Colonel Reed joining him, picking out horses that had been branded with a crown with a capital "P" above, indicating Piber-born animals.[8]

For some of Reed's men, though they were technically cavalrymen, flesh-and-blood horses remained a complete mystery to them. One such was Sergeant Vito Spadafino, a Technician Fourth Grade and usually the radio operator in an M8 armored car. His 3rd Squad from 3rd Platoon, Troop A, had been detached to guard the Lipizzaners and other horses.[9] As Colonel Reed walked through one of the stables with Podhajsky and Lessing, Sergeant Spadafino followed behind, a Thompson sub-machine gun slung over one shoulder. While the German and American officers chatted, Spadafino glanced into the stalls. He knew nothing about horses, but one thing about the mares did strike him.

"Gosh, they look like they're pregnant, sir," muttered Spadafino to Reed. Reed stopped and turned.

"Sergeant, where do you come from?" he inquired.

"The Bronx, sir," said Spadafino.

A broad smile creased Reed's face. "Well," he said, "where I come from we say they are *in foal*."[10]

*

In all, there were 219 Lipizzaner mares, including several still in foal. Some had already foaled at Hostau, but because of Gustav Rau's Nazi breeding program, their bloodlines and purity were in doubt. Podhajsky appeared pleased with the condition of the horses, and he could not fault the diligent work of Colonel Rudofsky and Captains Lessing and Kroll.[11] Of one thing Colonel Podhajsky was sure—the future of the Spanish Riding School was assured, just as long as the horses could be returned to Austria safely. How he was going to find room for so many horses weighed heavily upon his mind as he drove back to the Skoda Castle and prepared to fly back to St. Martin.

At the airfield, as Podhajsky was about to board the large green-painted C-47 Skytrain that would take him back to Austria, he grasped Colonel Reed's hand and shook it vigorously. He thanked the American for all that he had done for the Spanish Riding School. Reed shook his head and raised his other hand to cut Podhajsky off mid-sentence.

"I have only acted as a fellow rider should," said Reed, "and I am convinced that you would have done the same if the positions had been reversed."[12] Podhajsky nodded solemnly at Reed's generous statement before he took his seat inside the plane. The American colonel was quite right—the love of horses transcended even love of nation. He settled his body back against the C-47's fuselage, feeling the metal vibrate as the two engines started up with a deafening roar. Without Reed and the other Americans, the Spanish Riding School would have been scattered to the wind.

*

Lieutenant Colonel Hubert Rudofsky was not quite done with the horses. He had returned to the largely deserted Hostau Stud only to find that the few remaining staff had managed to find and stable some of the stallions that had unhorsed their riders and bolted during the movement towards the German border. On the morning of May 16 the sounds of truck engines was heard driving through the village towards the stud.

Thinking that the Red Army was finally moving into Hostau, Rudofsky was surprised when three American six-by-sixes roared up the hill to the stud and ground to a halt at the gates. A young officer and a handful of GIs in steel helmets and web equipment jumped down from the trucks.

"There are still various things that we could not take yesterday," explained the officer to Rudofsky. Some boxes and bales of equipment and supplies were still neatly stacked in one of the stable blocks, and these were now loaded in quick time aboard the trucks. The Americans were certainly being thorough, leaving behind nothing for the new owners.

"Have any horses returned?" asked the officer. Rudofsky showed him the few stallions that had been gathered up, and the Americans loaded them aboard the trucks, led by a proud and haughty Polish Anglo-Arab. Then, the young officer strode over to where Rudofsky stood watching the horses standing in their ersatz horse transporters, their heads hooked over the high wooden sides.

"Colonel," he said, saluting respectfully. Then the young officer turned and boarded the leading truck. Within a few minutes all was quiet again, as the sound of the convoy faded into the distance. The Americans had done with Hostau. Rudofsky gazed about him one last time, then headed for his quarters inside the castle. He would pack and go home. His job at Hostau was over too. He was also the only one left who could explain what had happened to the horses.

As Rudofsky walked over to the castle two Czechoslovak policemen appeared. They were dressed in long dark-blue greatcoats and service caps and wore armbands in the old Czechoslovak national colors as a sign that they were no longer serving their German conquerors, but rather the new regime that was gradually establishing its authority over the region.

"Lieutenant Colonel Hubert Rudofsky?" demanded one of the policemen, his tone cold.

"Yes," replied Rudofsky, his voice level. "What can I do for you?"

"You are the commandant of the Hostoun stud?" asked the policeman, using the Czechoslovak name for Hostau.

"I *was*," replied Rudofsky proudly.

The policeman unclipped his brown leather holster and took out his pistol, pointing it at Rudofsky's stomach.

"By order of the Republic of Czechoslovakia, you are under arrest."

*

The dilemma that faced Colonel Podhajsky was a serious one. Finding suitable stabling for hundreds more horses at St. Martin appeared to be impossible. All available accommodations at Arco Castle were full of refugees, and every stall not housing Spanish Riding School stallions was filled with surviving horses from the Hungarian stud. But Podhajsky refused to be defeated. He toured the local area, determined to find some space. At the Stallion Depot at Stadl-Paura, near Lambach, he managed to free up six boxes for stallions. That wasn't enough. But then he heard about Reichersberg Airfield, just two-and-a-half-miles from Arco Castle and almost twenty miles from Passau on the German border.

Reichersberg had been a Luftwaffe base, but had been put out of action permanently by a low-level bombing and strafing attack by American P-51 Mustangs on April 16, 1945. The grass runways and dispersal areas were littered with shot-up and abandoned German fighters and bombers. Due to aviation fuel shortages towards the end of the war, with most aircraft grounded, the Luftwaffe had used part of the airfield to instead stable draft horses employed to haul military supply wagons. Podhajsky approached Brigadier General Collier at XX Corps with a proposal to move on to the airfield, and Collier gave his permission.[13]

Podhajsky wasted no time. He managed to procure a Kübelwagen field car and with one of his grooms acting as driver, motored out to the airfield. The premises appeared ideal—small hangars that could be easily converted to hold the horses, a barracks block where Podhajsky's staff could live, and abundant green fields for exercising the horses or putting them out to pasture. But there was one major problem. Former Polish POWs and displaced persons who, in Podhajsky's words, "terrorized the local neighborhood" had taken over the old German base. The moment the Poles spotted the German Army vehicle and its German-speaking occupants, they became extremely hostile, swearing at Podhajsky and threatening to do unspeakable things to his person should he not quit the airfield immediately. Unarmed and dressed in civilian clothing, Podhajsky was in no position to argue, and ordered his driver to take him back to the castle. He went straight to General Collier and explained his predicament.

The next day Colonel Podhajsky returned to the airfield, only this time with an escort. Following behind Podhajsky's field car was a jeep containing an American lieutenant colonel from Collier's staff and a couple of military policemen. The Poles came out and resumed arguing and threatening, but the American officer quickly got on the radio and half an hour later a truck full of military police drove through the airfield's gates, followed by a couple of empty trucks, the heavily armed policemen quickly forming a cordon around the barracks area where the Poles lived. In no uncertain terms, the Poles were ordered to leave. Faced with so many armed Americans, the Poles did as they were told and boarded the trucks that the Americans had brought with them, and they were driven away for repatriation to their homeland.[14]

The American colonel strolled over to Podhajsky and smiled as the last truck left.

"All yours, Colonel," he said, saluted and then boarded his jeep. Podhajsky now had an airfield to convert into a horse center.

Immediate steps were taken to change the layout of the hangar interiors, Podhajsky's men constructing wooden stalls for the horses. These were lined with fresh straw from Podhajsky's limited supply. Fresh water was available from a stream nearby, and the barracks were cleaned and tidied up for use by the grooms and riders.[15] Podhajsky had been told that he would be informed when the first shipment of horses from Kötzting was expected to arrive, so he could have everything ready. But as with so much to do with the Spanish Riding

School during this turbulent time, expecting the unexpected had become the norm.

*

"The distance to Reichersberg Airfield is about sixty miles," First Lieutenant Quinlivan told Lessing and Kroll, as they decided how to move the Spanish Riding School's horses from Kötzting. "The question is how to get them there intact."

It was a serious problem, for while some horses had been driven from Hostau to Kötzting in trucks, those that had walked were exhausted and needed plenty of time to recover.

"They will have to go in the trucks," said Dr. Lessing. The trucks that Quinlivan had "liberated" from the German artillery training school and converted into rudimentary horse carriers would be pressed into service once more. A few more Opel Blitzes were gathered from the surrendered 11th Panzer Division and quickly converted with timber, enabling each to carry several horses. Others would be used to convey the grooms and their kit. In total, Quinlivan and Lessing gathered together forty trucks. The question of drivers and grooms was a problem. Quinlivan visited the POW transit camp and recruited dozens of German prisoners for the task. Still in uniform, these Germans were distributed as drivers while others, mostly unwillingly, would act as grooms. A small escort of jeeps from 3rd Platoon, Troop A, would protect and guide the convoy on its final journey.

For the Thoroughbreds and Arabians at Kötzting and Furth im Wald, their destiny lay at an old German Army stud at Mansbach, 200 miles northwest of Kötzting. The Spanish Riding School horses were finally separated from the mass of animals that Gustav Rau had forced together at Hostau, and were following their own fresh path to their homeland.

*

Darkness had long since fallen at Reichersberg Airfield on May 22,

1945. All was quiet after another hectic day for Colonel Podhajsky and his men. Preparations for the arrival of the mares and foals from Kötzting continued from dawn to dusk, as buildings were carefully converted and stores put in place. There was much to do, and little time, though General Collier had assured Podhajsky that he would receive plenty of notice of the arrival of the convoy.

Podhajsky was exhausted. He glanced at his watch. It was a little before midnight. He yawned and stretched. He was for his bed. But as he strode across the grass before one of the aircraft hangers towards his simple quarters inside the old barrack block a sound cut the stillness of the night. Podhajsky stopped and listened. It sounded like engines. As he stared into the inky black of the night, he suddenly made out lights twinkling in the distance on the far side of the airfield. They were unmistakable—headlights! And then another pair and another pair joined the first until the whole horizon became an ever-lengthening string of headlights, accompanied by a deep rumbling from dozens of engines growing louder by the minute. Others of his staff joined Podhajsky to witness the amazing spectacle. They stood silent and spellbound as the line of twinkling, flickering, moving lights snaked their way towards the airfield's entrance.[16] As the long line of vehicles drew closer, Podhajsky could make out white blobs standing in the rear of the trucks, long white heads bobbing up and down with the motion, or hooking over the sides, ears twitching all around in excited confusion. Podhajsky's heartbeat increased and he took a few tentative steps forward without even realizing. They were coming ... at long last, they were coming! The Spanish Riding School was coming home. The bright headlights seemed to herald hope, cutting through the darkness of the previous years of uncertainty, conflict and suffering.

At that moment, standing on an airfield in Upper Austria, Alois Podhajsky knew that the Spanish Riding School was finally safe and reunited. The horses' white coats, like white doves, seemed almost symbolic of a new dawn ... of peace, and hope for a better future.

Epilogue

"The 2nd Armored Cavalry Group performed admirably many more difficult and dangerous operations in the European Campaigns. However, all of our members recall with especial pride their contribution to Austrian culture and happiness."

Colonel Hank Reed

Two hundred and nineteen Lipizzaner horses were returned to Colonel Podhajsky and the Spanish Riding School. Colonel Reed and the 2nd Cavalry Group were left with around a hundred Thoroughbreds, Arabians, and a few non-Austrian Lipizzaners that were considered important enough to continue under American protection. With these horses moved to an old German Army stud farm at Mansbach, two hundred miles northwest of Kötzting, it was only a matter of time before Reed's men would be reassigned. Reed was worried that the horses that they had expended so much time, effort and blood to save might yet end up being sold off piecemeal, and their important bloodlines lost in the mess that was postwar Germany.

The 2nd Cavalry Group was reduced in size, with drafts of men being sent home to the States, and it was renamed the 2nd Constabulary Regiment and assigned guard and patrol duties along the German–Czechoslovak frontier, which had become very tense following the return of the Beneš government from exile in Britain. Over 2 million German and Hungarian citizens were dispossessed and violently expelled from Czechoslovakia. The Communist Party was extremely popular in the Czech area of the country, which included the border region with Bavaria. Reed organized a mounted unit to patrol the forests, trying to demonstrate to the US Army that horses still had a role to play in modern warfare.

First Lieutenant Bill Quinlivan remained in command of the very small number of 2nd Cavalry soldiers who continued to watch over the liberated horses at Mansbach. The horses continued to be guarded by 3rd Squad, 3rd Platoon, Troop A. Running the squad was Sergeant Vito Spadafino.

In June 1945, Colonel Reed, Captain Stewart, and former Colonel Rudofsky were called to testify before Third Army headquarters staff concerning the ownership of the horses. Hungary and Czechoslovakia had lodged formal complaints. The three officers all gave clear-cut evidence that the horses moved from Hostau were lawful war prizes. This became the official position of the US Government.

General Patton, on leave in the States, met with the incoming head of the US Army's Remount Service, Colonel Fred Hamilton, to discuss what to do with them. Hamilton headed for Europe with a small staff and inspected all captured German Army horse depots and studs, beginning with Mansbach. He was so impressed by the fine collection of Thoroughbreds, Lipizzaners, and Arabians at Mansbach that he arranged to have them shipped to the States to join the Army's remount program.

The summer months of 1945 at Mansbach were something of an idyll for Quinlivan and his men. They rode almost every day, and were joined by Dr. Lessing, who had become a close friend of Quinlivan's. They hacked through the quiet countryside or practiced in the stud's arena. The American soldiers made some friends among the local farmers, and Colonel Reed visited often to ride. Prince Amassov and his Cossacks stayed at Mansbach too, helping to care for the rescued horses as well as their own Panje horses, and they put on riding shows for visiting American troops.[1]

Mansbach received a steady stream of important and curious visitors, including Gustav Rau, now a civilian. Colonel Reed tried to find useful employment for the horses, even having a pair of

Lipizzaner coach horses shuttle him around in an old carriage. But the discharges of men continued, and some familiar faces left Europe for home. On September 1, Captain Stewart—after Reed, the man most responsible for saving and protecting the precious Hostau horses— took his final leave and returned home. Eventually, only Quinlivan, now promoted to captain, remained as the sole representative of the 2nd Cavalry still involved with the horses.

Later in September, Colonel Hamilton and his group of "horse detectives" made a selection of the best horses across the four main German studs for shipment to America. In total, 150 horses were selected, including the Arabian stallion Lotnik, ridden by Quinlivan during Operation Cowboy, and Witez II, the most famous Polish racehorse. Veterinarians would be required during the transit across the Atlantic, and Colonel Reed offered berths to Lessing and Dr. Kroll. Kroll, who wasn't married, accepted the opportunity of beginning a new life in America without hesitation, but Lessing declined when he realized that because of space considerations aboard ship, his wife and children would not be permitted to travel with him. Though Reed tried to assure Lessing that his family could follow a few months later, Lessing declined and decided to remain in Germany.

On October 12, 1945, the horses set sail aboard the Liberty ship *Stephen F. Austin* from Bremerhaven. Quinlivan and Kroll accompanied them, alongside Colonel Hamilton's team. The crossing was stormy and extremely rough, and it was only through Quinlivan's resourcefulness and Kroll's veterinary skills that none of the horses died. In fact, a foal was born while at sea. They all arrived, exhausted but intact, at Newport News, Virginia, on October 28 after sixteen days at sea.

The horses were transferred to the Aleshire Depot at Front Royal, Virginia but then dispersed to five different horse-breeding centers. The Thoroughbreds remained at Aleshire; Witez II was moved to Pomona, California. Bill Quinlivan, meanwhile, was transferred to Fort Robinson, Nebraska.

For Colonel Podhajsky and the Spanish Riding School, the great period of uncertainty came to an end in April 1946, when the mares and their young were transferred from Reichersberg Airfield to an old dragoon barracks at Wels, Austria. Though run-down and damaged, the stabling and facilities were excellent, and Podhajsky and his men worked hard to put the barracks back into good order. The horses were happy and content. Podhajsky's only sorrow was that he could not return to the Spanish Riding School's home inside the Hofburg Palace in Vienna, for the city was in the Soviet Zone of occupation in Austria. The Soviets tried on many occasions to lure both Podhajsky and his stallions back to the Hofburg, but he knew deep down that any such move, after so much effort had been expended to keep the Lipizzaners out of Russian hands, would have doomed the School once again.

A second shipment of horses was made from Germany to the States, bringing the total number of animals to 231. But US Army interest in horses in the age of atomic warfare was, despite Reed and Hamilton's best efforts, lukewarm at best. Hamilton was forced to auction off the sixty-four Thoroughbreds at Front Royal in late 1946. Most ended up in the hands of ordinary horse owners, and remained unregistered by the American Jockey Club. In July 1948 President Truman ordered the Department of Defense to transfer all remount depots to the Department of Agriculture, ending the military's link with horses. Most horses were promptly sold off. An attempt was made in October 1948 to auction off the most valuable horses brought back from Europe, including Witez II, but public sentiment stopped this from occurring and they were kept together. But the Agriculture Department moved them to Fort Reno, Nevada, where they were declared surplus government property. In spring 1949, the remaining horses were auctioned off. In the strange circular way of history, Colonel Podhajsky and his Spanish Riding School arrived in New York City less than a year later, in 1950, to begin a tour of the United States. His performances introduced Americans to the wonders of haute école, and the Baroque splendor of the Spanish Riding School and its incredible white horses. In sell-out performances, the Lipizzaners thrilled and impressed wherever they went, gaining legions of new fans and wide media coverage. The United States could take pride that it was their men who had risked life and limb to save this ancient but fragile jewel of European culture from the fires of war, and Podhajsky never forgot the debt of gratitude that he and Austria owed to General Patton's "ghost riders."

Finally, in 1955, the stallions went home to Vienna following the Soviet withdrawal from the city, and they have remained there ever since.

*

Each of the men involved with the saving of the Spanish Riding School horses survived the war and had different experiences in the peace that followed. Here are a few of their stories (in alphabetical order):

Carter Catlett

Captain Catlett finished World War II with the Silver and Bronze Stars, but due to wartime injuries he was unable to return to competitive sport. After he returned from the war he was a successful baseball coach for his two sons' many teams, and supported his daughter's horse-riding competitions.

Catlett worked as an engineer for NASA at Langley, Virginia, for thirty-eight years. After retiring, he lived in Poquoson, Virginia, and loved to crab, enjoy his boat and play ball with his children and grandchildren. He was inducted into the VMI Sports Hall of Fame and the Virginia Sports Hall of Fame. Carter Catlett died in 1998 at the age of 81. In 2017, the 2nd Squadron, 2nd Cavalry Regiment, based at Vilseck, Germany, dedicated their conference room to Catlett's memory.

Gustav Kroll

Dr. Kroll didn't remain in the United States for long after accompanying Captain Quinlivan and the horses to Virginia. He went back to Germany, where he worked as a vet in a traveling circus. After obtaining a letter of commendation from General Patton, Kroll returned to the States and found a job as a veterinarian at San Diego Zoo. He later worked for the Department of Agriculture in Chicago as an inspector in a meat-packing plant.

Rudolf Lessing

The war was not kind to Lessing. His family estate ended up on the wrong side of the Iron Curtain, the land and house being seized by the East German authorities. Lessing worked hard trying to find homes for the horses that the Americans left behind in Bavaria, particularly the Cossack ponies. Afterwards, he worked in the German horse-breeding industry. In 1985 he was, along with Colonel Rudofsky, a guest of honor at a special performance at the Spanish Riding School and also received a medal from the Austrian authorities. Lessing did eventually travel to America to attend a 2nd Cavalry reunion. Dr. Lessing featured in Arnold Dietbest's book *Talks With a Horse Husband* (1995).

Robert McCaleb

After successfully commanding Troop C during the horse rescue operation, McCaleb served on in Germany until 1947 with the 2nd Constabulary Regiment. A keen horseman, he bought a horse in Germany that he named "Aces High" and managed to ship him back to the States. Awarded a Purple Heart for wounds received in France in 1944, McCaleb stayed in the army, serving in Korea, where he was wounded twice more, the last time by Chinese mortar shrapnel during operations on the Pusan Perimeter, which led to his medical evacuation. After Korea, McCaleb served in Alaska, Utah, and Texas, retiring a lieutenant colonel from the 2nd Armored Division in 1961.

Robert McCaleb died in June 2012, age 95.

George S. Patton

Patton went back to the States for a rest in June 1945, and was mobbed by huge crowds wherever he appeared. Denied a command in the Pacific, and with his behavior increasingly erratic, he returned to Germany in July as Military Governor of Bavaria. General Eisenhower removed Patton from his post in September 1945 after unfavorable press concerning his running of the province, and he was removed from command of the Third Army in October. Patton was given a new command, Fifteenth Army, headquartered at Bad Nauheim, but its only job was to write the official history of the European campaign. Bored, Patton traveled around Europe and tried to find ways to entertain himself. On December 8, 1945, he accepted an invitation to hunt pheasant near Speyer. While traveling on roads still littered with wartime debris, his staff car collided with a US Army truck. Patton suffered a broken neck and was left paralyzed.

General George S. Patton died in a hospital in Luxembourg on December 21, 1945, of pulmonary edema and congestive heart failure at the age of sixty. As per his request, he was buried alongside casualties of the Third Army.

Alois Podhajsky

Colonel Podhajsky would remain as director of the Spanish Riding School until his retirement in 1965, touring all over the world to huge audiences. He oversaw the transfer of the School and its stallions back to the Hofburg Palace in Vienna in 1955. After retirement, Podhajsky continued to teach classical horsemanship and wrote a series of successful books, including *The White Stallions of Vienna* (1963), *My Dancing White Horses* (1964), and *The Complete Training of Horse and Rider* (1967). The story of Podhajsky and Operation Cowboy were fictionalized in the 1963 Walt Disney movie *Miracle of the White Stallions*, with Robert Taylor playing Podhajsky. He was honored several times, including receiving Order of Isabel la Católica from General Franco in 1954, and the Grand Service Order of the Federal Republic of Germany.

Alois Podhajsky died in Vienna in May 1973, age 75.

William Quinlivan

Bill Quinlivan stayed with the Hostau horses the longest of any of the 2nd Cavalry Group soldiers, only being transferred from Front Royal, Virginia to Fort Robinson, Nebraska in 1946. Quinlivan returned to Germany in 1947, meeting his future wife on the voyage over. He was discharged a major in 1949 and settled in Los Angeles. In 1964 he was part of a delegation of 2nd Cavalry veterans of the Hostau rescue who, led by Colonel Reed, visited Philadelphia to meet Colonel Podhajsky and watch the white stallions perform. It was an emotional event for all concerned.

William Quinlivan died in 1985. As a mark of the high regard in which his wartime activities were held, the Austrian Military Attaché to the United States attended his funeral.

Charles Reed

Hank Reed ended World War II with a Distinguished Service Cross, Purple Heart, two Silver Stars and a Bronze Star. France honored him with the Légion d'Honneur and the Croix de Guerre. Even though Reed was responsible for keeping the Red Army out of Hostau until the horses had been evacuated, the USSR decorated him with the Order of the Patriotic War 2nd Class on June 12, 1945, presented to him by Lieutenant General Tihonov of the 39th Guards Rifle Corps.

Reed's command of the 2nd Constabulary Regiment came to a close in 1947, and he transferred to Fort Monroe, Virginia, bringing home an Arabian mare from Germany. In February 1949, though nominated for promotion to brigadier general, Reed left the army to help his ailing father run the family business. He and his wife Janice built "Foundry Place" on Reed family land, where he rode his Arabian each morning.

Reed was heavily involved in state life, serving as Rector of Radford College, was on the board of the Virginia Polytechnic Institute and State University, was a director of five Richmond-area firms, President of the National Association of Textile and Apparel Wholesalers, Vice-President of the National Association of Wholesalers, Director of the Bank of Virginia, and he was, most appropriately, President of the 2nd Cavalry Association for twenty-five years. He also appeared as a character in the 1963 Disney movie *Miracle of the White Stallions*, portrayed on screen by Philip Abbott.

Hank Reed died in April 1980 at age seventy-nine. He was carried to his final resting place by twenty 2nd Cavalry combat veterans, the chief pallbearer being former Sergeant Jim O'Leary, who had been Reed's wartime driver.

Hubert Rudofsky

Following his arrest by the Czechoslovak Police, Lieutenant Colonel Rudofsky was sent to an internment camp for Nazi collaborators established at Taus/Domažlice, where he experienced difficult times. His mother died in the camp. Released in early 1946, he was deported to Germany, his dream of remaining in the Sudetenland finally crushed. His sister-in-law and young nephew immigrated to the United States, Ulli ironically later serving in the US Army.

Rudofsky found work on a horse stud in Bavaria, where his expertise as a breeder of Arabians was much respected. In later life he lived in a small flat surrounded by paintings and photographs of horses. Eventually, his role in preserving the Spanish Riding School was finally recognized by both Austria and Germany. In 1985 Rudofsky received a special certificate from the Austrian government and was guest of honor at a performance at the Spanish Riding School in Vienna. It was his first Austrian honor since receiving the Silver Medal of Courage from the old Emperor Franz Josef during the First World War. In 1986, it was the turn of the

Federal Republic of Germany to honor Rudofsky, awarding him the Adalbert-Stifler Medal for special contribution to the cultural life of the Sudeten German national group.

Hubert Rudofsky died in 1986, age 89.

Ferdinand Sperl

Promoted major, Sperl was awarded the Silver Star for his two hazardous trips behind enemy lines to negotiate the surrender of Colonel Holters and his Dienststelle Ost intelligence outfit. He also received a Bronze Star for his other wartime heroics. He remained in the reserves after the war, but returned to the industry that had dominated the lives of four generations of his family—hotels. He was one of the men responsible for developing Aspen as a resort in 1946, and worked for the Boss Hotels Company in Des Moines and Peoria, eventually as Executive Vice-President of the Boss Hotel Chain. In 1978 Sperl became Vice-President of Shearson Lehman Bros. brokerage firm before eventually retiring in 1987. He was a member of the Reserve Officers' Association, and a major in the Honorary Squadron, 2nd Dragoons.

Ferdinand Sperl died in May 2006, age 87.

Thomas Stewart

Awarded the Bronze Star in May 1945 for his adventures rescuing and protecting the horses at Hostau, Stewart attempted to put some of his more troubling wartime experiences behind him by working his way across the American West. The senator's son toiled as a day laborer or pumped gas when he needed money. He turned up at Fort Reno, Nevada, in May 1949 to witness the auction of Witez II, the world-famous Polish racehorse that he had helped save back at Hostau in May 1945. Returning home, Stewart became an investigator for Dupont at their Savannah River plant, and there met his wife, a young widow from Georgia, Anne Evans Scott. They lived in Tennessee, where Stewart worked for the state for thirty-three years, fifteen as director of motor vehicles. He was also an administrative law judge in the Department of Revenue, and a Sunday school teacher. In 2001, Austria honored him for his part in saving the Spanish Riding School.

Tom Stewart passed away in January 2011, age 95, the father of three children, grandfather to six, and great-grandfather to five.

Karl Weisenberger

General Weisenberger remained in command of Wehrkreis XIII right up to the final end of the Third Reich on May 7, 1945, when the district was dissolved by Germany's surrender, and his surviving troops made prisoners-of-war. Weisenberger was detained by US forces for questioning. He later, in common with all senior surviving German officers in American captivity, was asked to write a detailed report of his command's activities.[2] This report survives in the National Archives in Washington, D.C., and provides invaluable insights into the collapse of the German defenses in Czechoslovakia in April–May 1945, and his part in permitting the rescue of the horses at Hostau. Karl Weisenberger died in Kempten, Germany, in March 1952, age 61.

Acknowledgments

I should like to extend my great thanks to the many individuals, organizations and institutions that gave so freely of their time and resources during the research and writing of this book.

Firstly, a great many thanks to Vito Spadafino, one of the last veterans who took part in Operation Cowboy, as a sergeant in Troop A, 42nd Cavalry Reconnaissance Squadron, Mechanized, for taking the time to answer my many questions. Thanks also to his sons Joseph and John for assisting with the interview process.

I am indebted to the relatives of the heroes who took part in the rescue of the horses at Hostau for assisting me in this project, sending me documents and precious family photographs and sharing their memories of their fathers' war, as well as providing practical assistance in tracking down living veterans and other sources. They are: Cary LaPlante, daughter of Captain Carter Catlett, commanding Troop A, and Gary McCaleb, son of First Lieutenant Robert McCaleb, commanding Troop C.

Archival assistance is vital on a project such as *Ghost Riders*, and I have received outstanding advice and practical support from a variety of kind individuals and institutions. Many thanks to Ryan Meyer, Curator and Historian of the Second Cavalry Museum in Vilseck, Germany, and his successor Lance T. Dyckman, for their outstanding efforts in providing me with archival material, contacts and photographs; Colonel Bryan Denny, Historian and President of the 2nd Cavalry Association; Mike Constandy of Westmoreland Research in Alexandria, VA, for his fantastic assistance at the National Archives; Chris Golden, 2nd Cavalry historian; Katerina Chodova,

2nd Cavalry liaison for the Hostoun area; Patrick Biddy and Dave Gettman, 2nd Armored Cavalry veterans and 2nd Cavalry Association members; Len Dyer, Director, National Armor & Cavalry Museum, Columbus, Georgia; Alexis Adkins, Archivist, University Library, California State Polytechnic University, Pomona; Jeanne Brooks Abernathy, Director, W.K. Kellogg Arabian Horse Center, California State Polytechnic University, Pomona; Carol R. Mori, Patton Family Archives, South Hamilton, MA; Robin Cookson, National Archives and Records Administration, Washington D.C.; Mary Burtzloff, Archivist, Eisenhower Presidential Library and Museum, Abilene, Kansas; and Andrea Kerssenbrock of the Spanish Riding School, Vienna.

Many thanks to Karen Jensen and Stephen Harding of *World War II* magazine; Martha Cook at Trafalgar Square Books, Vermont; Frank Westerman, author of *Brother Mendel's Perfect Horse*; and Gillian Tidmus-Whiting, widow of renowned author Charles Whiting.

Many thanks to Bob Pigeon, my superb editor at Da Capo, for recognizing that the full story of Operation Cowboy needed to be told, and to my excellent literary agent Andrew Lownie, for his sound advice and enthusiasm. Thanks also to my UK publishers, Icon Books, and in particular my editor Robert Sharman for his excellent work. As always, I cannot thank my incredible and accomplished wife Fang Fang enough for all of her generous support, from acting as a sounding board for ideas, reading rough material, and working as my unpaid research assistant during field work undertaken for this book in the United Kingdom, Germany, Austria, Slovakia and the Czech Republic. My writing takes me far and wide, but always with my soulmate by my side.

Bibliography

Correspondence with veterans and relatives
Carey LaPlante
Gary McCaleb
John Spadafino
Joseph Spadafino
Vito Spadafino

Archival sources
Library of Congress, Washington D.C.
"XII Corps: Spearhead of Patton's Third Army" by Lieutenant
    Colonel George Dyer, *Question of Ownership of Captured Horses*,
    United States Congress: Committee on Armed Services, 1947,
    Washington D.C., 1948
"Headquarters Military Area XIII from mid-April to the beginning
    of May 1945 (Naab Front to the Bohemian Forest)" by Lieutenant
    General Karl Weisenberger, *Foreign Military Studies, 1945–54*,
    Department of the Army, Washington D.C., 1954
"Headquarters Military Area XIII from early May 1945 to the
    Surrender (Bohemian Forest to the Area West of Pilsen)" by
    Lieutenant General Karl Weisenberger, *Foreign Military Studies,
    1945–54*, Department of the Army, Washington D.C., 1954

National Archives & Records Administration (NARA), College Park
"42d Recon. Sq. S-3 Journal," April–May 1945
"42d Cavalry Reconnaissance Squadron, After Action Report, April
    1945"
"42d Recon Cavalry Squadron, Unit History"
"Intelligence and Operations Summary No. 3," 26 April 1945
"S-3 Journal," 2d Cavalry Group (Mechanized), 27 April 1945
"Unit Report No. 233," 42d Cavalry Reconnaissance Squadron,
    29 April 1945

"Report of Operations, 1 March–8 May 1945," Headquarters, 2d Cavalry GP (Mecz)

"XII Corps Report of Operations 1 April 1945–30 April 1945"

"Operations Reports: XII Corps, Spearhead of Patton's Third Army"

"Operations Reports: 387-INF (387)" – 0.7, Unit Journal No. 34

"12th Army Group, 371.3, Military Objectives," Vol. VIII

OPD 336, Czechoslovakia, Section 1, Case 13, "Seizure of Food Stuffs and Livestock by American Forces in Czechoslovakia"

"Memorandum: Status of the Lipizzaner Horses in U.S. Zone Austria" by Major Richard P. Weeber, 15 May 1946, US Forces, Austria

Second Cavalry Association

"Hostau Reminiscences" by Thomas Stewart, 1990

"The Rescue of the Lipizzaner Horses: A personal account" by Colonel Charles Hancock Reed, 1970

Books/other published sources

Axelrod, Alan, *Patton: A Biography* (New York: Palgrave Macmillan, 2006)

Beevor, Antony, *Ardennes 1944: Hitler's Last Gamble* (London: Viking, 2015)

Blumenson, Martin, *The Patton Papers* (Boston: Houghton Mifflin, 1972–74)

Blumenson, Martin, *Patton: The Man Behind the Legend, 1885–1945* (London: Cape, 1986)

Brett-Smith, Richard, *The 11th Hussars (Prince Albert's Own)* (London: Leo Cooper, 1969)

Broszat, Martin, *Bayern in der NS-Zeit* (Bd. 6. Oldenbourg-Verlag, 1983)

Clarke, Dudley, *The Eleventh at War: Being the Story of the XIth Hussars (Prince Albert's Own) Through the Years 1934–1945* (London: Michael Joseph, 1952)

Committee on Armed Services, *Question of Ownership of Captured Horses* (United States Congress, Washington D.C.: Government Printing Office, 1948)

D'Este, Carlo, *A Genius for War: A Life of General George S. Patton* (London: HarperCollins, 1995)

Dolibois, John E., *Pattern of Circles: An Ambassador's Story* (Kindle: Kent State University Press, 2013)

Dorondo, David *Riders of the Apocalypse: German Cavalry & Modern Warfare, 1870–1945* (Kindle: Naval Institute Press, 2012)

Eisenhower, John S.D., *The Bitter Woods: The Battle of the Bulge* (Edinburgh: Birlinn, 2001)

Essame, Hubert, *Patton: The Commander* (London: Batsford, 1974)

Farago, Ladislas, *Patton: Ordeal and Triumph* (London: Mayflower: 1970)

Forty, George, *Patton's Third Army at War* (London: Arms and Armour, 1992)

FM 2-30, *Field Manual, Cavalry Reconnaissance Squadron Mechanized* (War Department, Washington D.C.: Government Printing Office, 1944)

Glueckstein, Fred, *Of Men, Women and Horses* (Bloomington: Xlibris, 2006)

Green, Michael, *Patton's Tank Armies: D-Day to Victory* (Osceola, Wis.: Motorbooks International, 1995)

Green, Michael & Gladys Elena Morales, *Patton: Operation Cobra and Beyond* (Osceola, Wis.: Motorbooks International, 1998)

Green, Michael & Gladys Green, *Weapon's of Patton's Armies* (Osceola, Wis.: Motorbooks International, 2000)

Handler, Hans, *The Spanish Riding School in Vienna and the Training of the Lipizzaner Horse* (London: Thames & Hudson, 1972)

Harley, Una, *The Lipizzaner* (London: J.A. Allen, 2006)

Hastings, Sir Max, *Armageddon: The Battle for Germany, 1944–1945* (New York: Vintage Books, 2005)

Hays, Robert, *Patton's Oracle: Gen. Oscar Koch, as I Knew Him* (Savoy, IL: Herndon-Sugarman Press, 2013)

Isenbart, Hans-Heinrich & Emil M. Bührer, *The Imperial Horse: The Saga of the Lipizzans* (Newton Abbott: David & Charles, 1986)

Jenkins, Ryan, *Saving Horses in WWII: The Untold Story of Operation Cowboy in World War 2* (Createspace Independent Publishers, 2014)

Katcher, Philip, *US 2nd Armored Division 1940–45* (London: Osprey, 1979)

Keane, Michael, *Patton: Blood, Guts, and Prayer* (Washington DC: Regnery Press, 2012)

Kershaw, Sir Ian, *Hitler: Nemesis 1936–1945* (London: Penguin Books, 2001)

Kurowski, Franz, *Hitler's Last Bastion: The Final Battles for the Reich 1944–1945* (Atglen, PA: Schiffer Military History, 1998)

Lambert, A.L. & G.B. Layton, *The Ghosts of Patton's Third Army: Second United States Cavalry: A History* (Historical Section, Second Cavalry Association, undated)

Lefevre, Eric, *Panzers in Normandy: Then and Now* (London: Battle of Britain Prints International Limited, 1983)

Letts, Elizabeth, *The Perfect Horse: The Daring U.S. Mission to Rescue the Priceless Stallions Kidnapped by the Nazis* (Kindle, Ballantine Books, 2016)

Martin, Frank Wayne with Nancy Martin, *Patton's Lucky Scout: The Adventures of a Forward Observer for General Patton and the Third Army in Europe* (Milwaukie: Crickhollow Books, 2009)

Mattson, Gregory L., *SS-Das Reich: The History of the Second SS Division 1939–45* (Staplehurst: Spellmount, 2002)

Menyhert, Renita, *Ernie Pyle Was My Hero* (Bloomington: Xlibris, 2012)

Mollo, Andrew, *The Armed Forces of World War II: Uniforms, Insignia and Organization* (London: Black Cat, 1987)

Osborne, Keith, *Berlin or Bust: A Wartime Life with the 11th Hussars, the First British Regiment to Enter Berlin* (Chester: Keith Osborne, 2000)

Podhajsky, Alois, *The White Stallions of Vienna* (London: Harrap, 1963)

Podhajsky, Alois, *My Dancing White Horses* (London: Harrap, 1964)

Podhajsky, Alois, *The Lipizzaners* (London: George G. Harrap, 1969)

Rottman, Gordon L., *World War II US Cavalry Groups* (Oxford: Osprey, 2012)

Stippler, Stefan, *Bezirk Hostau: Heimat zwischen Bohmerwald und Egerland* (Berlin: Herstellung und Verlag, 2011)

Talty, Stephan, *Operation Cowboy: The Secret American Mission to Save the World's Most Beautiful Horses in the Last Days of World War II* (Kindle Single, Amazon Digital Services, Inc., 2014)

Thomas, Nigel, *Hitler's Russian & Cossack Allies 1941–45* (Oxford: Osprey Publishing, 2015)

Toland, John, *The Last 100 Days* (London: Phoenix, 1996)

Wallace, Brenton G., *Patton and his Third Army* (Westport, Conn.: Greenwood Press, 1979)

Westerman, Frank, *Brother Mendel's Perfect Horse: Man and Beast in an Age of Human Warfare* (New York: Random House, 2012)

Whiting, Charles, *Patton* (London: Pan Books, 1973)
Whiting, Charles, *Patton's Last Battle* (Staplehurst: Spellmount, 2007)
Wistrich, Robert S., *Who's Who in Nazi Germany* (Routledge, 2001)

Academic papers
"Exploiting Combat Experience: The US Forces European Theater Study of Mechanized Cavalry Units," monograph by Lieutenant Colonel Christopher N. Prigge, School of Advanced Military Studies, United States Army Command and General Staff College, Fort Leavenworth, Kansas, 2011

Newspapers, magazines and periodicals
American Legion Magazine
Haute École
Los Angeles Times
Preussische Algemeine Zeitung
Shiners Newsletter
Sports Illustrated
The Telegraph (London)
United States Army Medical Department Journal
World War II
Zyklus

Online sources
"Carter Nelson Catlett," arlisherring.com
"Gen. George S. Patton Jr. and the Lipizzaners" by Fred Glueckstein, June 2006, *Horses and Dressage*, www.horsesanddressage.blogspot.co.uk
Encyklopedie valecneho zajeti a internace Czech Republic, www.evzi.estranky.cz
"Hostau 1945" by Dr. med. vet. Rudolf Lessing, http://panzerdivison.tripod.com/Hostau_1945.html
"How General Patton and Some Unlikely Allies Saved the Prized Lipizzaner Stallions" by Karen Jensen, 18 September, 2009, *World War II*, www.historynet.com
Kreis Bischofteinitz, doku.zentrum-gegen-vertreibung.de

"Luftwaffe: Oberst Walter O...," Axis History Forum, forum.
axishistory.com//viewtopic.php?t=198448

"Rescue of the White Mares" by Sadie Babits, www.sirwrangler.com

"The German 11th Panzer Division: Giving Up the Ghost" by
James Hart, 7 August 2014, www.warfarehistorynetwork.com

The Second Cavalry Association Regimental History Center,
history.dragoons.org

U.S. Army Medical Corps, history.amedd.army.mil

Notes

Prologue
1. Alois Podhajsky, *My Dancing White Horses* (London: George G. Harrap & Co. Ltd, 1964), p. 95
2. Ibid.
3. Ibid.
4. Ibid: p. 96
5. Martin Broszat, *Bayern in der NS-Zeit*, Bd. 6. Oldenbourg-Verlag 1983, p. 73
6. Alois Podhajsky, *My Dancing White Horses* (London: George G. Harrap & Co. Ltd, 1964), p. 100
7. Ibid: p. 101
8. Robert S. Wistrich, *Who's Who in Nazi Germany* (Routledge, 2001), p. 122
9. Alois Podhajsky, *My Dancing White Horses* (London: George G. Harrap & Co. Ltd, 1964), p. 102
10. Ibid.
11. Ibid.

Chapter 1: "Always Ready"
1. Charles Whiting, *Patton's Last Battle* (Staplehurst: Spellmount, 2007), p. 120
2. Ibid.
3. Ibid.
4. *Peoria Star Journal*, May 5, 2006
5. Ibid.
6. John E. Dolibois, *Pattern of Circles: An Ambassador's Story* (Kindle: Kent State University Press, 2013), p. 71
7. A.L. Lambert and G.B. Layton, *The Ghosts of Patton's Third Army: Second United States Cavalry: A History* (Historical Section, Second Cavalry Association), p. 256
8. Gordon L. Rottman, *World War II US Cavalry Groups* (Oxford: Osprey, 2012), p. 33
9. "XII Corps: Spearhead of Patton's Third Army" by Lieutenant Colonel George Dyer; "Question of Ownership of Captured Horses," United States Congress: Committee on Armed Services, 1947, Washington D.C., 1948, p. 242
10. Gordon L. Rottman, *World War II US Cavalry Groups*, (Oxford: Osprey, 2012), 33
11. "Question of Ownership of Captured Horses," United States Congress: Committee on Armed Services, 1947, Washington D.C., 1948, p. 242

12. Ibid.
13. A.L. Lambert and G.B. Layton, *The Ghosts of Patton's Third Army*: *Second United States Cavalry: A History* (Historical Section, Second Cavalry Association), p. 287
14. "XII Corps Report of Operations 1 April 1945–30 April 1945," Archives II, NARA, MMRC
15. A.L. Lambert and G.B. Layton, *The Ghosts of Patton's Third Army*: *Second United States Cavalry: A History* (Historical Section, Second Cavalry Association), p. 287
16. Ibid.
17. "XII Corps Report of Operations 1 April 1945–30 April 1945," Archives II, NARA, MMRC
18. A.L. Lambert and G.B. Layton, *The Ghosts of Patton's Third Army*: *Second United States Cavalry: A History* (Historical Section, Second Cavalry Association), p. 287

Chapter 2: Colonel "H"

1. Fred Glueckstein, *Of Men, Women and Horses* (Bloomington: Xlibris, 2006), p. 73
2. Ibid.
3. Michael Keane, *Patton: Blood, Guts, and Prayer* (Washington DC: Regnery Press, 2012), p. 137
4. *The Rescue of the Lipizzaner Horses: A personal account by Colonel Charles Hancock Reed*, Second Cavalry Association
5. Ibid.
6. "Hostau 1945: Die Rettung der Lipizzaner – Wagnis oder Wunder?" by Brigitte Peter, *Zyklus*, 1982, 2–4, *Jahrgang* II
7. Ibid.
8. Stefan Stippler, *Bezirk Hostau: Heimat zwischen Bohmerwald und Egerland* (Berlin: Herstellung und Verlag, 2011), p. 101
9. Frank Westerman, *Brother Mendel's Perfect Horse: Man and Beast in an Age of Human Warfare* (New York: Random House, 2012), p. 189
10. Ibid.
11. Alois Podhajsky, *My Dancing White Horses* (London: George G. Harrap & Co. Ltd, 1964), p. 87

Chapter 3: Action This Day

1. Alois Podhajsky, *My Dancing White Horses* (London: George G. Harrap & Co. Ltd, 1964), p. 88
2. Ibid: p. 92
3. Ibid: p. 90
4. Fred Glueckstein, *Of Men, Women and Horses* (Bloomington: Xlibris, 2006), p. 74
5. "Hostau 1945: Die Rettung der Lipizzaner – Wagnis oder Wunder?" by Brigitte Peter, *Zyklus*, 1982, 2–4, *Jahrgang* II

6. Frank Westerman, *Brother Mendel's Perfect Horse: Man and Beast in an Age of Human Warfare* (New York: Random House, 2012), p. 189

7. Alois Podhajsky, *My Dancing White Horses* (London: George G. Harrap & Co. Ltd, 1964), p. 92

8. "The Rescue of the Lipizzaner Horses: A personal account by Colonel Charles Hancock Reed," Second Cavalry Association

9. "XII Corps Report of Operations 1 April 1945–30 April 1945," Archives II, NARA, MMRC

10. "Landkreis Bischofsstein," Encyklopedie valecneho zajeti a internace Czech Republic, www.evzi.estranky.cz, accessed 1 November 2014

11. Ibid.

12. "XII Corps Report of Operations 1 April 1945–30 April 1945," Archives II, NARA, MMRC

13. Encyklopedie valecneho zajeti a internace Czech Republic, www.evzi. estranky.cz, accessed 1 November 2014

14. "Hostau Reminiscences" by Thomas Stewart, unpublished, March 1990, p. 6

15. "Report of Operations, 1 March–8 May 1945," Headquarters, 2d Cavalry GP (Mecz), Archives II, NARA, MMRC, p. 22

16. "Intelligence and Operations Summary No. 3," 26 April 1945, Archives II, NARA, MMRC

17. 42d Recon. Sq. S-3 Journal, April–May 1945, Archives II, NARA, MMRC, pp. 76–7

18. A.L. Lambert and G.B. Layton, *The Ghosts of Patton's Third Army: Second United States Cavalry: A History* (Historical Section, Second Cavalry Association), 289-290

19. "Report of Operations, 1 March–8 May 1945," Headquarters, 2D Cavalry GP (Mecz), Archives II, NARA, MMRC, p. 22

20. A.L. Lambert and G.B. Layton, *The Ghosts of Patton's Third Army: Second United States Cavalry: A History* (Historical Section, Second Cavalry Association), pp. 289–90

21. "The Forgotten Spanish Riding School: The Story of the Royal Hungarian Spanish Riding School of Budapest and its Last Commander" by Jan S. Maiburg, *Haute École*, Volume 15, Issue 4

22. "Als der rote Terror Deutschland erreichte – Vor 60 Jahren begingen Rotarmisten das Massaker von Nemmersdorf" by Father Lothar Groppe, *Preussische Algemeine Zeitung*, 16 October 2004

23. Fred Glueckstein, *Of Men, Women and Horses* (Bloomington: Xlibris, 2006), p. 74

24. "Headquarters Military Area XIII from mid-April to the beginning of May 1945 (Naab Front to the Bohemian Forest)" by Lieutenant General Karl Weisenberger, *Foreign Military Studies, 1945–54*, Department of the Army, Washington D.C., 1954, p. 114

25. "Headquarters Military Area XIII from early May 1945 to the Surrender (Bohemian Forest to the Area West of Pilsen)" by Lieutenant General Karl Weisenberger, *Foreign Military Studies, 1945–54*, Department of the Army, Washington D.C., 1954, p. 128

Chapter 4: White Gold

1. "Hostau Reminiscences" by Thomas Stewart, unpublished, March 1990, p. 6
2. "The Rescue of the Lipizzaner Horses: A personal account by Colonel Charles Hancock Reed," 4 November 1970, *Haute École*, Second Cavalry Association
3. "Headquarters Military Area XIII from early May 1945 to the Surrender (Bohemian Forest to the Area West of Pilsen)" by *General der Infanterie* Karl Weisenberger, *Foreign Military Studies, 1945–54*, Department of the Army, Washington D.C., 1954, p. 128
4. "Headquarters Military Area XIII from mid-April to the beginning of May 1945 (Naab Front to the Bohemian Forest)" by Lieutenant General Karl Weisenberger, *Foreign Military Studies, 1945–54*, Department of the Army, Washington D.C., 1954, p. 115
5. "42nd Cavalry Reconnaissance Squadron, After Action Report, April 1945," Archives II, NARA, MMRC
6. Nigel Thomas, *Hitler's Russian & Cossack Allies 1941–45* (Oxford: Osprey Publishing, 2015), pp. 24–8
7. "Hostau 1945: Die Rettung der Lipizzaner – Wagnis oder Wunder?" by Brigitte Peter, *Zyklus*, 1982, 2–4, *Jahrgang* II
8. Interview with Sergeant Vito Spadafino, lately Troop A, 42nd Cavalry Squadron, 6 June 2017
9. "Hostau 1945: Die Rettung der Lipizzaner – Wagnis oder Wunder?" by Brigitte Peter, *Zyklus*, 1982, 2–4, *Jahrgang* II
10. "Headquarters Military Area XIII from mid-April to the beginning of May 1945 (Naab Front to the Bohemian Forest)" by Lieutenant General Karl Weisenberger, *Foreign Military Studies, 1945–54*, Department of the Army, Washington D.C., 1954, p. 114

Chapter 5: Operation Sauerkraut

1. "Headquarters Military Area XIII from early May 1945 to the Surrender (Bohemian Forest to the Area West of Pilsen)" by Lieutenant General Karl Weisenberger, *Foreign Military Studies, 1945–54*, Department of the Army, Washington D.C., 1954, p. 128
2. "XII Corps Report of Operations 1 April 1945–30 April 1945," Archives II, NARA, MMRC
3. "Hostau Reminiscences" by Thomas Stewart, unpublished, March 1990, p. 2
4. "42nd Cavalry Reconnaissance Squadron, After Action Report, April 1945," Archives II, NARA, MMRC
5. "The Rescue of the Lipizzaner Horses: A personal account by Colonel Charles Hancock Reed," Second Cavalry Association
6. Whiting, Charles, *Patton's Last Battle* (Staplehurst: Spellmount, 2007), p. 170
7. Ibid: p. 171
8. "Hostau Reminiscences" by Thomas Stewart, unpublished, March 1990, p. 3
9. "How General Patton and Some Unlikely Allies Saved the Prized Lipizzaner Stallions" by Karen Jensen, *World War II*, 18 September 2009

10. "Hostau 1945: Die Rettung der Lipizzaner – Wagnis oder Wunder?" by Brigitte Peter, *Zyklus*, 1982, 2–4, *Jahrgang* II
11. Elizabeth Letts, *The Perfect Horse: The Daring U.S. Mission to Rescue the Priceless Stallions Kidnapped by the Nazis* (Kindle, Ballantine Books, 2016), unpaginated
12. Ibid.
13. David Dorondo, *Riders of the Apocalypse: German Cavalry & Modern Warfare, 1870–1945*, (Kindle: Naval Institute Press, 2012), unpaginated
14. "Hostau 1945: Die Rettung der Lipizzaner – Wagnis oder Wunder?" by Brigitte Peter, *Zyklus*, 1982, 2–4, *Jahrgang* II

Chapter 6: Plenipotentiary

1. "Hostau 1945: Die Rettung der Lipizzaner – Wagnis oder Wunder?" by Brigitte Peter, *Zyklus*, 1982, 2–4, *Jahrgang* II
2. Stephan Talty, *Operation Cowboy: The Secret Mission to Save the World's Most Beautiful Horses in the Last Days of World War II* (Kindle; Amazon Digital Services, 2014), unpaginated
3. Michael Keane, *George S. Patton: Blood, Guts, and Prayer* (Washington DC: Regnery Press), p. 137
4. Elizabeth Kaye McCall, *The Tao of Horses: Exploring How Horses Guide Us on Our Spiritual Path* (Kindle Unlimited: Adams Media, 2004), unpaginated
5. "Headquarters Military Area XIII from early May 1945 to the Surrender (Bohemian Forest to the Area West of Pilsen)" by Lieutenant General Karl Weisenberger, *Foreign Military Studies*, 1945–54, Department of the Army, Washington D.C., 1954, p. 133
6. "How General Patton and Some Unlikely Allies Saved the Prized Lipizzaner Stallions" by Karen Jensen, *World War II*, 18 September 2009
7. "Hostau 1945: Die Rettung der Lipizzaner – Wagnis oder Wunder?" by Brigitte Peter, *Zyklus*, 1982, 2–4, *Jahrgang* II
8. First Lieutenant William D. Quinlivan, Memorandum, 12 July 1946, Kellog Arabian Ranch, California State Polytechnic University, Pomona
9. "Headquarters Military Area XIII from early May 1945 to the Surrender (Bohemian Forest to the Area West of Pilsen)" by Lieutenant General Karl Weisenberger, *Foreign Military Studies*, 1945–54, Department of the Army, Washington D.C., 1954, p. 133
10. Ibid.
11. Ibid.
12. "An Account of the 2nd US Cavalry taking the Remount Depot in Hostau, Czechoslovakia, and the return of a breeding band of Lipizzaner horses held there to Austria" by Thomas M. Stewart, unpublished, 11 November 2007, p. 2
13. Stephan Talty, *Operation Cowboy: The Secret Mission to Save the World's Most Beautiful Horses in the Last Days of World War II* (Kindle; Amazon Digital Services, 2014), unpaginated
14. "Hostau 1945: Die Rettung der Lipizzaner – Wagnis oder Wunder?" by Brigitte Peter, *Zyklus*, 1982, 2–4, *Jahrgang* II

15. "Hostau Reminiscences" by Thomas Stewart, unpublished, March 1990, p. 3
16. "Headquarters Military Area XIII from mid-April to the beginning of May 1945 (Naab Front to the Bohemian Forest)" by Lieutenant General Karl Weisenberger, *Foreign Military Studies, 1945–54*, Department of the Army, Washington D.C., 1954, p. 117
17. Ibid: pp. 119–20
18. "Headquarters Military Area XIII from early May 1945 to the Surrender (Bohemian Forest to the Area West of Pilsen)" by Lieutenant General Karl Weisenberger, *Foreign Military Studies, 1945–54*, Department of the Army, Washington D.C., 1954, p. 130
19. "An Account of the 2nd US Cavalry taking the Remount Depot in Hostau, Czechoslovakia, and the return of a breeding band of Lipizzaner horses held there to Austria" by Thomas M. Stewart, unpublished, 11 November 2007, p. 3
20. Wolf Schmoekel, *The Dragoon's Story: A History of the 2d Armored Cavalry Regiment* (Randall Print Company, 1958), p. 74
21. "Hostau Reminiscences" by Thomas Stewart, unpublished, March 1990, p. 3
22. "Question of Ownership of Captured Horses," United States Congress: Committee on Armed Services, 1947, Washington D.C., 1948, p. 242
23. "Hostau Reminiscences" by Thomas Stewart, unpublished, March 1990, p. 3
24. Ibid.
25. "Hostau 1945: Die Rettung der Lipizzaner – Wagnis oder Wunder?" by Brigitte Peter, *Zyklus*, 1982, 2–4, *Jahrgang* II
26. "Hostau Reminiscences" by Thomas Stewart, unpublished, March 1990, p. 4
27. Ibid.

Chapter 7: Duty

1. "Question of Ownership of Captured Horses," United States Congress: Committee on Armed Services, 1947, Washington D.C., 1948, p. 242
2. "Hostau Reminiscences" by Thomas Stewart, unpublished, March 1990, p. 5
3. Ibid: p. 12
4. "Question of Ownership of Captured Horses," United States Congress: Committee on Armed Services, 1947, Washington D.C., 1948, p. 242
5. "Hostau Reminiscences" by Thomas Stewart, unpublished, March 1990, p. 4
6. Ibid.
7. Michael Keane, *George S. Patton: Blood, Guts, and Prayer* (Washington DC: Regnery Press, 2012), p. 138
8. "Hostau Reminiscences" by Thomas Stewart, unpublished, March 1990, p. 5
9. Ibid.
10. "Question of Ownership of Captured Horses," United States Congress: Committee on Armed Services, 1947, Washington D.C., 1948, p. 242
11. Michael Keane, *George S. Patton: Blood, Guts, and Prayer* (Washington DC: Regnery Press, 2012), p. 138
12. "Hostau Reminiscences" by Thomas Stewart, unpublished, March 1990, p. 5
13. Ibid.

14. Ibid.
15. Ibid.
16. "Question of Ownership of Captured Horses," United States Congress: Committee on Armed Services, 1947, Washington D.C., 1948, p. 242
17. "US Remount Service and its Stallions & Rescue of WWII Hostau POWs and of the Lipizzans, Part 1" by Earl Parker, *Haute École*, Volume 20, Issue 4, Spring/Summer 2012, p. 5
18. "Hostau Reminiscences" by Thomas Stewart, unpublished, March 1990, p. 6
19. Ibid.
20. Elizabeth Letts, *The Perfect Horse: The Daring U.S. Mission to Rescue the Priceless Stallions Kidnapped by the Nazis* (Kindle, Ballantine Books, 2016), unpaginated
21. Stephan Talty, *Operation Cowboy: The Secret Mission to Save the World's Most Beautiful Horses in the Last Days of World War II* (Kindle, Amazon Digital Services, 2014), unpaginated
22. Ibid.
23. "Headquarters Military Area XIII from mid-April to the beginning of May 1945 (Naab Front to the Bohemian Forest)" by Lieutenant General Karl Weisenberger, *Foreign Military Studies, 1945–54*, Department of the Army, Washington D.C., 1954, pp. 123–4

Chapter 8: *"Adolf ist Kaput!"*

1. "Headquarters Military Area XIII from mid-April to the beginning of May 1945 (Naab Front to the Bohemian Forest)" by *General der Infanterie* Karl Weisenberger, *Foreign Military Studies, 1945–54*, Department of the Army, Washington D.C., 1954, p. 114
2. Ibid: p. 129
3. Ibid: p. 130
4. Ibid: p. 130
5. Ibid: p. 134
6. Ibid: p. 134
7. Ibid: p. 133
8. "Hostau 1945: Die Rettung der Lipizzaner – Wagnis oder Wunder?" by Brigitte Peter, *Zyklus*, 1982, 2–4, *Jahrgang* II
9. Ibid.
10. Ibid.
11. "Headquarters Military Area XIII from mid-April to the beginning of May 1945 (Naab Front to the Bohemian Forest)" by Lieutenant General Karl Weisenberger, *Foreign Military Studies, 1945–54*, Department of the Army, Washington D.C., 1954, p. 133
12. "Hostau Reminiscences" by Thomas Stewart, unpublished, March 1990, p. 7
13. Ibid: p. 6
14. Ibid: p. 7
15. "The Rescue of the Lipizzaner Horses: A personal account by Colonel Charles Hancock Reed," Second Cavalry Association

16. "Hostau 1945: Die Rettung der Lipizzaner – Wagnis oder Wunder?" by Brigitte Peter, *Zyklus*, 1982, 2–4, *Jahrgang* II
17. "Hostau Reminiscences" by Thomas Stewart, unpublished, March 1990, p. 8
18. Michael Keane, *George S. Patton: Blood, Guts, and Prayer* (Washington DC: Regnery Press, 2012), p. 139
19. "Hostau Reminiscences" by Thomas Stewart, unpublished, March 1990, p. 8
20. Ibid.
21. Fred Glueckstein, *Of Men, Women and Horses*, (Bloomington: Xlibris, 2006), p. 76
22. "Report of Operations, 1 March–8 May 1945," Headquarters 2D Cavalry GP (Mecz), Archives II, NARA, MMRC

Chapter 9: The Road Less Traveled

1. "Hostau 1945: Die Rettung der Lipizzaner – Wagnis oder Wunder?" by Brigitte Peter, *Zyklus*, 1982, 2–, *Jahrgang* II
2. "An Account of the 2nd US Cavalry taking the Remount Depot in Hostau, Czechoslovakia, and the return of a breeding band of Lipizzaner horses held there to Austria" by Thomas M. Stewart, unpublished, 11 November 2007, p. 8
3. "Hostau Reminiscences" by Thomas Stewart, unpublished, March 1990, pp. 8–9
4. "S-3 Journal," 2nd Cavalry Group (Mechanized), 27 April 1945, Archives II, NARA, MMRC, p. 86
5. Ibid.
6. "The Rescue of the Lipizzaner Horses: A personal account by Colonel Charles Hancock Reed," Second Cavalry Association
7. Ibid.
8. FM 2-30, *Field Manual, Cavalry Reconnaissance Squadron Mechanized*, War Department, 28 August 1944, p. 41
9. "Office of Medical History, Chapter XIII: Animal Procurement," U.S. Army Medical Department, 511, history.amedd.army.mil, accessed 15 January 2017
10. Ibid: 512
11. FM 2-30, *Field Manual, Cavalry Reconnaissance Squadron Mechanized*, War Department, 28 August 1944, p. 25
12. Ibid: p. 30
13. "Exploiting Combat Experience: The US Forces European Theater Study of Mechanized Cavalry Units," monograph by Lieutenant Colonel Christopher N. Prigge, School of Advanced Military Studies, United States Army Command and General Staff College, Fort Leavenworth, Kansas, 2011, p. 41
14. Ibid: p. 49
15. "Question of Ownership of Captured Horses," United States Congress: Committee on Armed Services, 1947, Washington D.C., 1948, p. 242
16. Charles Whiting, *Patton's Last Battle* (Staplehurst: Spellmount, 2007), p. 123
17. Ibid: p. 128
18. "Question of Ownership of Captured Horses," United States Congress: Committee on Armed Services, 1947, Washington D.C., 1948, p. 242

19. Ibid.
20. Ibid.
21. Charles Whiting, *Patton's Last Battle* (Staplehurst: Spellmount, 2007), pp. 139–40
22. S-3 Journal, 2nd Cavalry Group (Mechanized), 27 April 1945, Archives II, NARA, MMRC

Chapter 10: Enemy Situation Unknown

 1. "Unit Report No. 233," 42d Cavalry Reconnaissance Squadron, 29 April 1945, Archives II, NARA, MMRC
 2. A.L. Lambert and G.B. Layton, *The Ghosts of Patton's Third Army: Second United States Cavalry: A History* (Historical Section, Second Cavalry Association), p. 292
 3. "S-3 Journal," 2nd Cavalry Group (Mechanized), 27 April 1945, Archives II, NARA, MMRC, p. 86
 4. Gordon L. Rottman, *World War II US Cavalry Groups: European Theater* (Oxford: Osprey, 2012), p. 31
 5. "No. 21: Use of the Volkssturm in the battles in the Bohemian Forest; The events in Waier during the invasion of the Americans and the arrival of the Czechs, Report of the FJ from Waier," Kreis Bischofteinitz, 1955, www.doku.zentrum-gegen-vertreibung.de, accessed 2 January 2017
 6. FM 2-30, *Field Manual, Cavalry Reconnaissance Squadron Mechanized*, War Department, 28 August 1944, p. 39
 7. "S-3 Journal," 2nd Cavalry Group (Mechanized), 27 April 1945, Archives II, NARA, MMRC, p. 42
 8. "Unit Report No. 233," 42d Cavalry Reconnaissance Squadron, 29 April 1945, Archives II, NARA, MMRC
 9. "S-3 Journal," 2nd Cavalry Group (Mechanized), 27 April 1945, Archives II, NARA, MMRC, p. 86
10. "No. 21: Use of the Volkssturm in the battles in the Bohemian Forest; The events in Waier during the invasion of the Americans and the arrival of the Czechs, Report of the FJ from Waier," Kreis Bischofteinitz, 1955, doku.zentrum-gegen-vertreibung.de, accessed 2 January 2017
11. Ibid.
12. A.L. Lambert and G.B. Layton, *The Ghosts of Patton's Third Army: Second United States Cavalry: A History* (Historical Section, Second Cavalry Association), p. 292
13. FM 2-30, *Field Manual, Cavalry Reconnaissance Squadron Mechanized*, War Department, 28 August 1944, p. 41
14. "Question of Ownership of Captured Horses," United States Congress: Committee on Armed Services, 1947, Washington D.C., 1948, p. 242
15. A.L. Lambert and G.B. Layton, *The Ghosts of Patton's Third Army: Second United States Cavalry: A History* (Historical Section, Second Cavalry Association), p. 292
16. Gordon L. Rottman, *World War II US Cavalry Groups: European Theater* (Oxford: Osprey, 2012), p. 24

17. A.L. Lambert and G.B. Layton, *The Ghosts of Patton's Third Army*: *Second United States Cavalry: A History* (Historical Section, Second Cavalry Association), p. 292
18. Ibid.
19. Ibid.
20. "S-3 Journal," 2nd Cavalry Group (Mechanized), 27 April 1945, Archives II, NARA, MMRC, p. 86
21. Ibid.
22. "An Account of the 2nd US Cavalry taking the Remount Depot in Hostau, Czechoslovakia, and the return of a breeding band of Lipizzaner horses held there to Austria" by Thomas M. Stewart, unpublished, 11 November 2007, p. 8
23. "Hostau Reminiscences" by Thomas Stewart, unpublished, March 1990, p. 9
24. "S-3 Journal," 2nd Cavalry Group (Mechanized), 27 April 1945, Archives II, NARA, MMRC, p. 87
25. Ibid.
26. "Hostau Reminiscences" by Thomas Stewart, unpublished, March 1990, p. 9
27. A.L. Lambert and G.B. Layton, *The Ghosts of Patton's Third Army*: *Second United States Cavalry: A History* (Historical Section, Second Cavalry Association), p. 292
28. Gordon L. Rottman, *World War II US Cavalry Groups: European Theater* (Oxford: Osprey, 2012), p. 23

Chapter 11: Liberators and Saviors

1. "Headquarters Military Area XIII from mid-April to the beginning of May 1945 (Naab Front to the Bohemian Forest)" by Lieutenant General Karl Weisenberger, *Foreign Military Studies, 1945–54*, Department of the Army, Washington D.C., 1954, p. 133
2. "Hostau 1945: Die Rettung der Lipizzaner – Wagnis oder Wunder?" by Brigitte Peter, *Zyklus*, 1982, 2–4, *Jahrgang* II
3. "The Rescue of the Lipizzaner Horses: A personal account by Colonel Charles Hancock Reed," Second Cavalry Association
4. "S-3 Journal," 2nd Cavalry Group (Mechanized), 27 April 1945, Archives II, NARA, MMRC, p. 87
5. Ibid.
6. "The Rescue of the Lipizzaner Horses: A personal account by Colonel Charles Hancock Reed," Second Cavalry Association
7. "Question of Ownership of Captured Horses," United States Congress: Committee on Armed Services, 1947, Washington D.C., 1948, p. 242
8. Ibid.
9. "The Rescue of the Lipizzaner Horses: A personal account by Colonel Charles Hancock Reed," Second Cavalry Association
10. Ibid.
11. Ibid.

12. Ibid.
13. Renita Menyhert, *Ernie Pyle Was My Hero* (Bloomington: Xlibris, 2012), p. 142
14. "The Rescue of the Lipizzaner Horses: A personal account by Colonel Charles Hancock Reed," Second Cavalry Association
15. Ibid.
16. FM 2-30, *Field Manual, Cavalry Reconnaissance Squadron Mechanized*, War Department, 28 August 1944, p. 42
17. OPD 336, Czechoslovakia, Section 1, Case 13, "Seizure of Food Stuffs and Livestock by American Forces in Czechoslovakia," Archives II, NARA, MMRC

Chapter 12: No Way Out
1. "S-3 Journal," 2nd Cavalry Group (Mechanized), 27 April 1945, Archives II, NARA, MMRC, p. 88
2. Elizabeth Letts, *The Perfect Horse: The Daring U.S. Mission to Rescue the Priceless Stallions Kidnapped by the Nazis* (Kindle, Ballantine Books, 2016), unpaginated
3. "S-3 Journal," 2nd Cavalry Group (Mechanized), 27 April 1945, Archives II, NARA, MMRC, p. 88
4. Ibid.
5. Ibid.
6. A.L. Lambert and G.B. Layton, *The Ghosts of Patton's Third Army: Second United States Cavalry: A History* (Historical Section, Second Cavalry Association), pp. 292–3
7. Alois Podhajsky, *My Dancing White Horses*, (London: Harrap, 1964), 107–8
8. Ibid: 108
9. Ibid: 110
10. "Hostau Reminiscences" by Thomas Stewart, unpublished, March 1990, p. 10
11. Ibid.
12. "*Verzerichnis des Pferdebestandes des Heeresremonteamts Hostau, Stichtag: 29.4.45*," found in "S-3 Journal," 2nd Cavalry Group (Mechanized), April–May 1945, Archives II, NARA, MMRC
13. Ibid.
14. Ibid.
15. Ibid.
16. "Hostau 1945: Die Rettung der Lipizzaner – Wagnis oder Wunder?" by Brigitte Peter, *Zyklus*, 1982, 2–4, *Jahrgang* II
17. Alois Podhajsky, *My Dancing White Horses* (London: Harrap, 1964), p. 111
18. Ibid.
19. "Hostau 1945: Die Rettung der Lipizzaner – Wagnis oder Wunder?" by Brigitte Peter, *Zyklus*, 1982, 2–4, *Jahrgang* II
20. "The Rescue of the Lipizzaner Horses: A personal account by Colonel Charles Hancock Reed," Second Cavalry Association

21. "Hostau 1945: Die Rettung der Lipizzaner – Wagnis oder Wunder?" by Brigitte Peter, *Zyklus*, 1982, 2–4, *Jahrgang* II
22. Ibid.
23. "The Rescue of the Lipizzaner Horses: A personal account by Colonel Charles Hancock Reed," Second Cavalry Association
24. "Operations Reports: XII Corps, Spearhead of Patton's Third Army," Archives II, NARA, MMRC, p. 426
25. "The Rescue of the Lipizzaner Horses: A personal account by Colonel Charles Hancock Reed," Second Cavalry Association
26. "Hostau Reminiscences" by Thomas Stewart, unpublished, March 1990, p. 9

Chapter 13: The Alamo

1. "Hostau Reminiscences" by Thomas Stewart, unpublished, March 1990, p. 9
2. Ibid: pp. 9–10
3. "Unit Report No. 233," 42d Cavalry Reconnaissance Squadron, 29 April 1945, Archives II, NARA, MMRC
4. "S-3 Journal," 2nd Cavalry Group (Mechanized), 30 April 1945, Archives II, NARA, MMRC
5. Ibid.
6. Gregory L. Mattson, *SS-Das Reich: The History of the Second SS Division 1939–45* (Staplehurst: Spellmount, 2002), p. 170
7. "Operations Reports: XII Corps, Spearhead of Patton's Third Army," 387-INF (387) -0.6, Narrated by Col. W.D. Long, 17 Apr.–30 May 1945, Archives II, NARA, MMRC, p. 426
8. "S-3 Journal," 2nd Cavalry Group (Mechanized), 29 April 1945, Archives II, NARA, MMRC
9. A.L. Lambert and G.B. Layton, *The Ghosts of Patton's Third Army: Second United States Cavalry: A History* (Historical Section, Second Cavalry Association), p. 292
10. "Operations Reports: 387-INF (387) – 0.6," Narrative by Colonel W.D. Long, 17 Apr–30 May 45, Archives II, NARA, MMRC, p. 7
11. Interview with former Sergeant Vito Spadafino, Troop A, 42d Cavalry, 6 June 2017
12. "Operations Reports: 387-INF (387) – 0.6," Narrative by Colonel W.D. Long, 17 Apr–30 May 45, Archives II, NARA, MMRC, p. 7
13. Ibid: p. 7
14. Why this SS unit, several hundred men strong, decided to attack Hostau remains a mystery. Possibly they were after the horses—whose value was well known to the Germans—perhaps to use as their own bargaining chip when it came to surrender. Maybe they were simply doing their job, which was to kill the enemy, and what better target than an isolated American unit miles behind the German lines?
15. *The Rescue of the Lipizzaner Horses: A personal account by Colonel Charles Hancock Reed*, Second Cavalry Association
16. Ibid: p. 9

17. "Operations Reports: 387-INF (387)" – 0.6, Narrative by Colonel W.D. Long, 17 Apr–30 May 45, Archives II, NARA, MMRC, p. 7
18. Ibid: p. 7
19. "42nd Recon Cavalry Squadron, Unit History," Archives II, NARA, MMRC
20. "Operations Reports: 387-INF (387)" – 0.6, Narrative by Colonel W.D. Long, 17 Apr–30 May 45, Archives II, NARA, MMRC, 7

Chapter 14: All Quiet on the Western Front

1. "S-3 Journal," 2nd Cavalry Group (Mechanized), 30 April 1945, Archives II, NARA, MMRC
2. "Headquarters Military Area XIII from mid-April to the beginning of May 1945 (Naab Front to the Bohemian Forest)" by Lieutenant General Karl Weisenberger, *Foreign Military Studies, 1945–54*, Department of the Army, Washington D.C., 1954, p. 131
3. Ibid.
4. Ibid.
5. Ibid: p. 134
6. Ibid.
7. Charles Whiting, *Patton's Last Battle* (Staplehurst: Spellmount, 2007), p. 171
8. Ibid: p. 172
9. Frank Westerman, *Brother Mendel's Perfect Horse: Man and Beast in an Age of Human Warfare* (New York: Random House, 2012), p. 123
10. "Hostau Reminiscences" by Thomas Stewart, unpublished, March 1990, p. 11
11. Ibid.
12. "An Account of the 2nd US Cavalry taking the Remount Depot in Hostau, Czechoslovakia, and the return of a breeding band of Lipizzaner horses held there to Austria" by Thomas M. Stewart, unpublished, 11 November 2007, p. 9
13. "Hostau Reminiscences" by Thomas Stewart, unpublished, March 1990, p. 11
14. The 42nd only suffered a single casualty during the firefight—Private First Class Lloyd E. Tunnell was lightly wounded by German fire. ("42nd Recon Cavalry Squadron, Unit History," Archives II, NARA, MMRC, p. 13)
15. "Hostau Reminiscences" by Thomas Stewart, unpublished, March 1990, p. 11
16. "Operations Reports: 387-INF (387)" – 0.7, Unit Journal No. 34, Archives II, NARA, MMRC
17. "Operations Reports: 387-INF (387)" – 0.7, Unit Journal No. 34, Archives II, NARA, MMRC

Chapter 15: The Green Light

1. "Headquarters Military Area XIII from mid-April to the beginning of May 1945 (Naab Front to the Bohemian Forest)" by Lieutenant General Karl Weisenberger, *Foreign Military Studies, 1945–54*, Department of the Army, Washington D.C., 1954, p. 135
2. Ibid.
3. Ibid.

4. Ibid.
5. Ibid: p. 136
6. Ibid: p. 137
7. Alois Podhajsky, *My Dancing White Horses* (London: Harrap, 1964), p. 112
8. Ibid: p. 113
9. Charles Whiting, *Patton's Last Battle* (Staplehurst: Spellmount, 2007), p. 172
10. Alois Podhajsky, *My Dancing White Horses* (London: Harrap, 1964), p. 113
11. Ibid: p. 114
12. Ibid: p. 116
13. "The General and the Horses" by J.J. Han Lin, *American Legion Magazine*, February 1963, p. 23
14. Ibid: p. 23
15. Charles Whiting, *Patton's Last Battle* (Staplehurst: Spellmount, 2007), p. 175
16. Ibid.
17. Ibid: p. 174

Chapter 16: Day of Days

1. "Memorandum: Status of the Lipizzaner Horses in U.S. Zone Austria" by Major Richard P. Weeber, 15 May 1946, US Forces, Austria, Archives II, NARA, MMRC
2. Alois Podhajsky, *My Dancing White Horses*, (London: Harrap, 1964), p. 118
3. Ibid.
4. Ibid.
5. Charles Whiting, *Patton's Last Battle* (Staplehurst: Spellmount, 2007), p. 149
6. Ibid.
7. "Hostau 1945: Die Rettung der Lipizzaner – Wagnis oder Wunder?" by Brigitte Peter, *Zyklus*, 1982, 2–4, *Jahrgang* II
8. Ibid.
9. Alois Podhajsky, *My Dancing White Horses* (London: Harrap, 1964), p. 119
10. Ibid.
11. "Hostau 1945: Die Rettung der Lipizzaner – Wagnis oder Wunder?" by Brigitte Peter, *Zyklus*, 1982, 2–4, *Jahrgang* II
12. "The Rescue of the Lipizzaner Horses: A personal account by Colonel Charles Hancock Reed," Second Cavalry Association
13. "Memorandum: Status of the Lipizzaner Horses in U.S. Zone Austria" by Major Richard P. Weeber, 15 May 1946, US Forces, Austria, Archives II, NARA, MMRC
14. Stanley P. Hirshson, *Patton: A Soldier's Life* (New York: HarperCollins, 2002), p. 743
15. "The General and the Horses" by J.J. Han Lin, *American Legion Magazine*, February 1963, p. 23
16. "The Rescue of the Lipizzaner Horses: A personal account by Colonel Charles Hancock Reed," Second Cavalry Association
17. Ibid.
18. Ibid.

Chapter 17: Operation Cowboy

1. "The Rescue of the Lipizzaner Horses: A personal account by Colonel Charles Hancock Reed," Second Cavalry Association
2. A.L. Lambert and G.B. Layton, *The Ghosts of Patton's Third Army: Second United States Cavalry: A History* (Historical Section, Second Cavalry Association), p. 303
3. Ibid: p. 304
4. 12th Army Group, 371.3, Military Objectives, Vol. VIII, Archives II, NARA, MMRC
5. Ibid.
6. "The Rescue of the Lipizzaner Horses: A personal account by Colonel Charles Hancock Reed," Second Cavalry Association
7. Ibid.
8. Ibid.
9. "Hostau Reminiscences" by Thomas Stewart, unpublished, March 1990, p. 12
10. "Hostau 1945: Die Rettung der Lipizzaner – Wagnis oder Wunder?" by Brigitte Peter, *Zyklus*, 1982, 2–4, *Jahrgang* II
11. Hans-Heinrich Isenbart and Emil M. Bührer, *The Imperial Horse: The Saga of the Lipizzans* (Newton Abbott: David & Charles, 1986), p. 40
12. "Hostau Reminiscences" by Thomas Stewart, unpublished, March 1990, p. 13
13. Ibid.
14. Alois Podhajsky, *My Dancing White Horses* (London: Harrap, 1964), p. 129
15. "The General and the Horses" by J.J. Han Lin, *American Legion Magazine*, February 1963, p. 42
16. Ibid.

Chapter 18: The Grand Drive

1. A.L. Lambert and G.B. Layton, *The Ghosts of Patton's Third Army: Second United States Cavalry: A History* (Historical Section, Second Cavalry Association), p. 313
2. Secretary of War Patterson to Acting Secretary of State Grew, 28 July 1945, OPD 336 Czechoslovakia, Section 1, case 13, "Seizure of Food Stuffs and Livestock by American Forces in Czechoslovakia," Archives II, NARA, MMRC
3. Ibid.
4. Ibid.
5. Alois Podhajsky, *My Dancing White Horses* (London: Harrap, 1964), p. 129
6. Ibid: p. 130
7. Ibid: p. 130
8. Secretary of War Patterson to Acting Secretary of State Grew, 28 July 1945, OPD 336 Czechoslovakia, Section 1, case 13, "Seizure of Food Stuffs and Livestock by American Forces in Czechoslovakia," Archives II, NARA, MMRC
9. Interview with Sergeant Vito Spadafino, ex-Troop A, 42d Cavalry Squadron, 6 June 2017

10. Ibid.
11. Secretary of War Patterson to Acting Secretary of State Grew, 28 July 1945, OPD 336 Czechoslovakia, Section 1, case 13, "Seizure of Food Stuffs and Livestock by American Forces in Czechoslovakia," Archives II, NARA, MMRC
12. Alois Podhajsky, *My Dancing White Horses* (London: Harrap, 1964), p. 130
13. A.L. Lambert and G.B. Layton, *The Ghosts of Patton's Third Army: Second United States Cavalry: A History* (Historical Section, Second Cavalry Association), p. 314
14. Alois Podhajsky, *My Dancing White Horses* (London: Harrap, 1964), p. 130
15. Ibid: p. 131
16. Ibid: p. 132

Epilogue
1. Interview with Sergeant Vito Spadafino, late Troop A, 42d Cavalry Squadron, 6 June 2017
2. "Headquarters Military Area XIII from mid-April to the beginning of May 1945 (Naab Front to the Bohemian Forest)" by Lieutenant General Karl Weisenberger, *Foreign Military Studies, 1945–54*, Department of the Army, Washington D.C., 1954

Index